POLICE in Hackney
1945-1984

**A Report
Commissioned by
The Roach Family
Support Committee**

**Produced by
an Independent Committee
of Inquiry**

Foreword by Professor Stuart Hall

Karia Press/RFSC

Policing in Hackney 1945—1984
A Report produced by an Independent Committee of Inquiry

First published by Karia Press and RSFC in 1989

Copyright Roach Family Support Committee, 1988

Typesetting and design by Karia
Printed and bound in Great Britain by
Biddles Ltd, Guildford and King's Lynn

ISBN 0 946918 74 0

Karia Press
41 Rheola Close
London N.17 9TP
United Kingdom

Contents

Background Notes to the Inquiry   7
Acknowledgements   11
Foreword   12
Chronology of the Campaign following the death of Colin Roach   19
Introduction   23

PART I. THE COLIN ROACH STORY

Chapter 1. The Death of Colin Roach   31
Colin: The last few months   31
What really happened to Colin in prison?   33
The events of Wednesday 12 January   38
The police treatment of Mr and Mrs Roach   47
The next morning   53
Notes to Chapter 1.   56

Chapter 2. The Campaign for a Public Inquiry   57
The venue of the inquest   79
The police precept   80
After the inquest   83

Chapter 3. The Inquest   85
Inquests — An overview Part 1.   87
Some discrepancies in police evidence   88
When did Colin die?   91
Where did Colin die?   94
How did Colin die?   100
Could Colin's death have been witnessed?   105

The police reaction to Colin's death	110
Was there something in the police station that the police didn't want Mr. Roach to know?	119
Colin Roach's 'state of mind'	120
What did the inquest reveal about Colin's 'medical condition'	121
The summing-up and verdict	124
Conclusion	128
Inquests — an overview Part 2.	131
Bibliographical notes to Chapter 3	134

Chapter 4. Colin Roach and the Press — 135

The death of Colin Roach	136
The campaign for a Public Inquiry	140
Background to the Campaign	142
The Inquest	146

Chapter 5. The Wider Political Context — 157

The Police Complaints Board Investigation	157
The reasons why a Public Inquiry was refused in 1983	162
Basis and previous use of Public Inquiries	165
The response of the police	167
Other responses to the Campaign for a Public Inquiry	170

Recommendations to Part I. of the Report — 174

Public Inquiries	174
The Coroner's Inquest	175
Arrests, charges and sentencing arising from demonstrations	176
Idendification evidence	178

PART II. POLICING IN HACKNEY

Chapter 6. The Metropolitan Police: A Contextual Introduction   183
Some background   184
Police Officers and police pay   187
Changes in policing strategy in the 1970s   189
The PSI Report   193
Police powers   194

Chapter 7. Policing History in Hackney   195
Policing and Fascism   195
The 'battle of Cable Street' 1936   197
From Fascism to racism   206

Chapter 8. Police and the Community: The Black Experience in Hackney   213
Wrongful arrest   213
Unlawful use of force   216
Racial abuse   217
Stop and search   218
Police raids   220
Police over-responding to incidents   222
Conclusion   223
Police and young people   224
Policing immigration controls   228
Racial violence and the police response   234
Stoke Newington police station   239
Deaths in Stoke Newington police station   240
Other incidents   243
The White and Knight cases   248
Changing image   250
Conclusions   251

**Chapter 9. Community Relations,
Community Policing,
Consultation and Accountability**   **255**

Community relations   255
Community policing   259
Consultation   261
Accountability   264
Conclusion   270

**Conclusions and Recommendations to Part II
of the Report**   **272**
The way ahead   273

APPENDICES

Appendix 1. The Independent Committee of Inquiry —
Members.   280
Appendix 2. Individuals and Organisations
who submitted oral or written evidence   281
Appendix 3. Lord Gifford's advice   283
Appendix 4a Correspondence   288
Appendix 4b Correspondence   289
Appendix 5. The trials of those arrested during
the campaign for a Public Inquiry   290
Appendix 6. Black people, misdiagnosis
and mental health   304

Background Notes To The Inquiry

Colin Roach died in 1983; the campaign around him did not. It is a shame that "campaigning" is a word which slips too quickly from some people's tongues, yet falls so easily from their hands. We tried to avoid this in the Roach Family Support Committee ("RFSC"). Certainly, our campaign was not something we sustained unthinkingly. We became increasingly aware of how campaigns like ours, which implicate the police, often accomplish little *beyond* initial demonstrations of outrage or even the more explosive protests. As a consequence, we believe further developments in Black people's thinking and actions in campaigning are imperative. We hope the choice of reflections we provide here will contribute a little way towards that end.

Recent history informs us that Black people's campaigns against the malpractices of State agencies contain within them (consciously or otherwise) two basic objectives from which everything else that is to be demanded, must flow. The first concerns the *public establishment* of the true circumstances in which the malpractice (usually some form of atrocity) occurred. The second concerns *official acknowledgment* or acceptance of that truth. We have lost count of the number of times campaigns have struggled even to achieve the first of these twin objectives. Nevertheless, it is often with a sense of both these objectives that campaigns for "truth and rights" have been strongly motivated to demand public inquiries. And this despite the fact that our demands are never responded to positively. In addition, we confront the apparent paradox of making these demands: to what extent are government inquiries into sensitive State agencies invariably "loaded" against the citizen, against the people? Yet even if we cease to call for public inquiries, the nature of our campaigning response is such that we insist the "truth will out" — but how?

Underlying these twin objectives (and perhaps the most practical in the long term) should be a demand we make on ourselves and by extension, our community. The demand we must carry in our hearts and minds is quite simple: the atrocity, the tragedy — the results of State malpractices must be remembered. Notice, we did not say "must not be forgotten"; we said *must be remembered*. There is a difference between commemoration and simple recollection. Through commemoration we insist that what happened must not be wiped from the popular 'memory slate'; we do not allow the opportunity to forget. We attempt to 'institutionalize' the 'event' within the community, as a poem perhaps, maybe a song, some form of regular protest, a documentary or . . . even a local inquiry.

The background to the Inquiry clearly has a register in what we have been discussing so far. The idea of the Inquiry was first raised and discussed from May 1983 onwards. During 1984, RFSC conducted its own research into the Inquiry's feasibility, produced a background paper on its establishment, drew up terms of reference, applied to the GLC for financial assistance after costing the project, and began a lengthy process of identifying and interviewing potential members for the Inquiry. Recruitment of members to the Inquiry carried on into 1985. After RFSC had advertised for and appointed two researchers in March 1985, the complete Inquiry team met for the first time on 13 April 1985. The administrator was appointed in June 1985.

It was important to us to retain the idea of an *independent* Inquiry, since we wanted the project to carry credibility with a wide range of audiences. It is worth noting that none of the eventual members was personally known to us before we approached them. Indeed, perhaps it ought to be said that we were hampered by the fact that none of us had the sort of 'contacts' which could have made this stage of the process straightforward. We relied on what little knowledge we had, spoke to friends, looked through newspapers and periodicals in an effort to find out about people who could exercise independent judgement and do a job of work. As far as 'independence' goes, the other major criterion was that members of the Inquiry should not be involved in policing or community issues in Hackney.

However, it would be a mistake to think that the efforts of our own campaign suddenly collapsed themselves into the organization of the Inquiry. From late 1983 – 1985, RFSC launched what came to be known as the 'Break Links Strategy', which was based on a resolution articulated by us to the local community. The resolution stated:

> There shall be no links or co-operation with the police unless and until there has been an independent public inquiry into the death of Colin Roach and the surrounding circumstances.

This was our response, after Colin Roach's inquest, to the continued lack of government action. It was a response easily misunderstood and even more easily misrepresented. But it was not simply 'anti-police', as is the vulgar phrase used by those who seek to denigrate the views and actions of powerless people with genuine grievances against the redoubtable police bureaucracy. Rather, it was a sincere effort to raise the profile of our protest through encouraging community disengagement from the public-relations initiatives of a police force and government which had ignored the need to resolve the issues surrounding Colin Roach's death. The absence of 'official' acknowledgement is often an attempt by the government to insist that the community's 'memory slate' is wiped clean. However, there is a limit to how long we can keep up the pretence of thinking that so called 'by-gones' really can be 'by-gones'. That is why Colin Roach's death was actively commemorated by RFSC. We held community events on 12 January of the years 1984 (a late night vigil outside Stoke Newington police station); 1985 (a half-day conference: "Colin Roach — Two Years On"); 1986 (a half-day conference: "Black people, the police and campaigning").

It is a long hard slog, mostly unrewarding, campaigning against injustices associated with the State, particularly where the police are concerned. Many people, especially in the Black community, do not enter these struggles lightly. It is not with enthusiasm that we are drawn to such encounters, but with grim determination. What sense does it make to disrupt your life by campaigning unless some sense of comfort in that life has been interrupted by a serious injustice, whether against you, someone close to you someone like you or simply someone you identify with? In the Roach family there is a premature gap where once was someone who was as passionately involved in his own life as anyone else. What really happened to him? Surely they/we have a right to know? After four years the memory lingers painfully and necessarily on.

Barnor Hesse
Pauline Roach
James Roach
Maurice Hesse
Sharon Liburd
Venise Bond
Clive Palmer
Chas Holmes

ROACH FAMILY SUPPORT COMMITTEE (1987)

Acknowledgements

On a number of occasions RFSC received advice and assistance from various sources with regard to the preparation and organization of the Inquiry. We especially acknowledge the contributions of our friends: Merville Bishop, Beverly Clarke, Cathy Louis, Marsha Prescod, Elaine Smith and Fay Wiltshire. In addition, thanks are due to Michael Dummett, Patricia Hewitt, Wilfred Wood and Geoff Coggan. Finally, we acknowledge the financial assistance from the former Greater London Council and the provision of office space for the researchers and administrator by the London Borough of Hackney.

Foreword

The terms of reference of this Independent Committee of Inquiry into the death of Colin Roach are clearly set out in the Introduction. Broadly speaking, the purpose of the exercise was to clarify the circumstances in which Colin Roach died in Stoke Newington police station on the night of the 12 January 1983. The nature of the events leading up to this event and its possible causes were the subject of an inquest.

In effect what the police in Stoke Newington station appeared to have assumed, without adequate evidence, from the outset; what the Coroner recommended to his jury as the most 'plausible' account; and what the Home Secretary has since invited the Roach family and the community to accept is the following account of the events of that night: that a young Black man, who was not wanted in any way by the police, late one night, walked into a police station unknown to him, entered the foyer, took from a shoulder bag (which was not large enough to hold a weapon), an old shot-gun, put it into his mouth and, without a word to anyone, blew his head off — "You may think on the facts you heard that this is the only possible verdict..." the Coroner told his jury. You may think so. On the other hand, you may not. You may assume, as a very large number of unprejudiced people have assumed that there is something extremely unlikely, not to say 'fishy', about such a story. It is open to doubt, for example, whether any Home Secretary in his right mind would calmly and quietly acquiesce in such an implausible story as an adequate explanation of the death of his own son in similar circumstances.

That event in itself was sufficient ground for calling an independent inquiry into being. However, the death of Colin Roach did not take place in a vacuum. It happened in a place, in a community, in a context which has its own history. This history is part and parcel of 'the Colin Roach story'. Stoke Newington police station has a notoriously poor reputation in relation to the policing of the Black community and the handling of legitimate grievances and protests in the Hackney area. It is not a reputation which engenders confidence amongst the great majority of the local community who have been concerned about the suspicious circumstances in which Colin Roach died. The Report has carefully examined this background history and presented the evidence which substantiate these public perceptions.

It is worth reminding ourselves as the Report does, that this was by no means the first time in which Black people had died or been injured, in suspicious circumstances, in police stations. It is not the first time in which the subsequent accounts of deaths and injuries in custody, offered by the police, were in direct contradiction with those offered by the families and friends of the deceased or injured people. Anyone concerned to improve relations between the local police and the Black community or anxious to restore the trust on which we are told 'policing with consent' depends would have thought it their plain duty to *go out of their way to clear up in the public mind the last shred of doubt or ambiguity concerning the behaviour of the police on an occasion like this.* No such view was taken then, or since, by the powers that be. Against that background, the Roach Family Support Committee quite rightly decided that Colin Roach's death had to be examined and analysed in the context of the general problems of policing the Black community in Hackney and against the background of the long-standing and unresolved series of complaints which have arisen over the years about how Black people are treated by Stoke Newington police station in particular. That evidence, which has been the subject of a good deal of speculation on previous occasions, is now systematically set out and documented here. The Report is well aware that this is not an isolated story. It could be repeated in any inner-city area with a significant Black population in Britain today.

This, then, was the thinking behind the decision to set up an independent Inquiry and explains why the terms of reference drawn up as they were. The way the Inquiry set about its task and the evidence it saw and heard are set out fully in the Report. No attempt has been made to cover over or 'resolve' contradictions which arise from that evidence. They are, of course, pointed to and underlined, since they effectively undermine the confidence and certainty which, in subsequent years, has accreted around the quite unplausible definition of what occurred advanced by the inquest and the press.

Can definitive answers be given, on the basis of this Report, to the questions which led to its being written in the first place? The Inquiry does not commit itself to an alternative explanation of how Colin Roach died. What it clearly and incontrovertibly shows is that *he could not have died in the way the police and the inquest say he did.* The Report does not say or suggest, for example, that Colin Roach was shot by the police in their own station. But it does show convincingly *that he did not shoot himself with a gun which he carried into the station:* which is what the police and the inquest asked us to believe.

Was Colin Roach shot by *someone else,* in or outside the foyer of the station? The Report does not say definitively that he was because it does not know. However, it *does* remind us — as the inquest did not — that this is not quite so implausible a story as it appears at first. For weeks preceding the event, Colin Roach did both *talk* and *act* as if in fear of being 'got at' by *someone.* Indeed, he gave this as his reason for entering Stoke Newington police station at all, at 11 o'clock one evening, when there was — and still is — no apparent other reason for his doing so, "Someone's going to get me and I want to get in there to be safe..." Colin told his friend, moments before entering the station. Who was going to 'get him' and why, the Report is not in a position to say. But the incontrovertible fact is, *that someone did 'get to him'.* The Report brings to light the reason why *this was a plausible explanation for Colin to offer, given what had happened to him earlier in prison.* The police are not in a position to challenge this argument, says the Report, *because they never investigated it.* From the first to last, the police behaved as if the 'fact' that Colin Roach's death was a suicide was *a foregone conclusion.* The police certainly advanced an account of what they said or thought happened. But *they conducted no investigation.*

If Colin Roach shot himself, why did his body fall in the way in which it did? And why did it and the objects in contact with it appear to move around and change position, *when no one is supposed to have touched the body?* The Report cannot answer these disturbing questions either, but at least *it is prepared to ask them.* No one else was prepared to do so then, or at the inquest and no one has been willing to do so since. Indeed, far from the burden of proof lying with the police and the inquest, *the very legitimate desire of the Roach family to find out what really happened and to have answers to these awkward and unresolved questions has been consistently treated by the police, the court, the Home Office and the press as nothing more than an unjustified and illegitimate slur on the good name of the local police.*

In our view, any unbiased and objective person reading what is written here must conclude that contrary to everything which has been officially put about, nobody has the slightest idea why and how a young Black man lost his life in the foyer of one of the most controversial police stations in London. Further, that steps have been consistently blocked which might have led to these matters being systematically and satisfactorily inquired into. Why this should have been so is not for the Committee to say. But *that it is so* is clear. And the fact that it is so is a *prima facie* case for extreme public disquiet, not simply in Hackney or in the Black community but in the society at large.

The reader may also conclude that the current form and conduct of inquests leaves a great deal to be desired. The criticisms of current practice in inquest courts, which has been mounting in recent years, are now very convincing. Coroner's inquests were never designed or intended to be, and cannot function as a substitute for an independent public inquiry into matters of this kind which affect public confidence in the expectation of justice under the rule of law from the courts and the police. Nor in such circumstances can the police continue to investigate and 'clear' themselves when it is their own practices and procedures which are in question. The practice of a succession of Home Secretaries to refuse public inquiries on the grounds that the inquest was, in effect, such an inquiry is, to put it frankly, a dodge and a deceit which convinces no one, least of all the families and individuals involved.

I believe that an unbiased reader will also conclude that relations between the police and the local Black community in Hackney have deteriorated to such an abysmal level that *anyone* in office with responsibility for the policing of London *under the rule of law* (and that *is* the responsibility of the Home Secretary) must immediately institute a public inquiry, irrespective of the circumstances surrounding Colin Roach's death. Whether the Government of the day will take that view is another matter. The present Government seems to believe that the 'rule of law' (which obliges *the state itself* to be bound and constrained by the law) is the same as 'law and order' (which is nothing but a convenient political catchphrase meaning that the police and the courts should support the state, whatever it does, and protect it against any inconvenience). The ordinary people who demonstrated outside of Stoke Newington police station were exercising their civil rights under the 'rule of law'. The brutal treatment they received at the hands of the police, who appear to regard civil rights as a matter of legitimate amusement was 'law and order' in action. Far from being the same, the two are diametrically opposed, as the underlying argument in the second half of this Report clearly demonstrates.

The fact is that inner-city boroughs like Hackney, where large numbers of Black people live, are places in which the state itself, and administrations and authorities of various kinds, constantly intervene, *always* in the interest of influencing what happens on the ground in the direction which *suits them*, but rarely in order to strengthen justice and equality for the ordinary citizens who live in these harassed communities — especially if they also have the 'misfortune' to be Black. That is the underlying 'message' of this Report. It is the message which anyone who has been attentive to what has been happening between Black people and the police in communities like this up and down the country in the past seven years will not fail to have grasped. As the Report clearly shows, it was also the context in which Colin Roach died. It was the reason why those people from the local community who held public demonstrations in favour of a public inquiry came, as the evidence here suggests, to be treated by the police like common criminals.

The Report presents a wealth of evidence, independently collected and fairly summarised. It will strengthen the political will of people in Hackney and elsewhere not simply to accept as gospel what those in power say and do, just because they are the powerful. This is a lesson which many ordinary people, especially those in the Black communities, have already worked out for themselves, for they have consistently supported the Roach family in their search for justice. They have sustained an active campaign of resistance around this and related issues. They have, by their own efforts and organization, made the holding of an unofficial inquiry possible and helped to provide the material means and the political support to have its Report made available to a wider public. Their efforts over the several years since Colin Roach disappeared into the entrance hall of Stoke Newington police station could, of course, be undone in an instant, as it was undone before, by a press and media treatment which, in its haste to accept official versions of events, however improbable, revealed its contempt for ordinary people. Fortunately for us all, there are other ways of getting at the truth. In the absence of a public and official duty to discover the truth at whatever cost, it is at least some comfort that ordinary people are still willing and able to take action for themselves.

Professor Stuart Hall
Adviser to Independent Committee
of Inquiry into Policing in Hackney

Chronology of the Campaign Following the Death of Colin Roach

1983

January 12   Death of Colin Roach in Stoke Newington police station.

14   Demonstration outside police station by local Black and white youths. 8 arrested.

17   Second demonstration outside police station by local youths. 17 arrested. Roach Family Support Committee (RFSC) formed at meeting called by Hackney Black People's Association and attended by 150 people.

18   Inquest into the death of Colin Roach opens at St. Pancras Coroner's Court. Immediately adjourned until 18 April.

22.   First demonstration organised by RFSC. 22 arrested.

27   Commission for Racial Equality calls for public inquiry into policing of Hackney.

February 3   RFSC writes to Home Secretary asking for a public inquiry into the death of Colin Roach, and the surrounding circumstances.

12   Second demonstration called by RFSC. 9 arrested.

18   Funeral of Colin Roach attended by over 300 people.

Hackney Council for Racial Equality (HCRE) publishes dossier on policing in the borough.

Ernie Roberts M.P. tables early day motion in Parliament calling for a public inquiry.

Hackney NALGO passes resolution calling for members to 'break links' with police.

March 2   Home Secretary replies to RFSC agreeing that a full and independent public inquiry is necessary but saying that this is what the inquest will provide.

12.   Third RFSC demonstration. 24 people arrested including James Roach and Councillor Dennis Twomey.

Campaign Against Racism and Fascism publishes in *Searchlight* a dossier of incidents of police racism in Hackney, 1971-83.

April 18   Inquest opens at St. Pancras Coroner's Court and is adjourned immediately. Coroner applies to the High Court on the issue of the venue.

30   High Court rules that Hackney Council and the Greater London Council have no power to compel the coroner to change the venue of the inquest, but suggests that a larger venue be found.

May 14   Fourth demonstration organised by RFSC. No arrests.

June 6   Inquest opens at Clerkenwell County Court.

17   Jury returns majority (8-2) verdict of suicide.

20   Jurors write to Home Secretary criticising police handling of the case especially their treatment of Mr. and Mrs. Roach.

28   Home Secretary replies saying that he is referring the jurors' letter to the Police Complaints Board.

1984

February 12 *Mail on Sunday* reports that the officers in the Colin Roach case will not be disciplined.

April 9 Police Complaints Board informs inquest jurors that no further action is to be taken.

1985

April 13 Independent Committee of Inquiry into Policing in Hackney launched by RFSC.

Introduction

This document is the result of a year long inquiry into the death of Colin Roach, and the context in which that death occurred: the policing of one inner city London Borough in recent years.

The background to the inquiry is well known: Colin Roach, a young Black man, died in the foyer of Stoke Newington police station on the 12 January 1983 from a single gunshot blast through the mouth. This death, and the police reaction to it, immediately sparked huge resentment in the community. This resentment was particularly strong in the Black community: police-Black relations in Hackney had for a long time been tense and Stoke Newington station had developed a reputation as a dangerous place for Black people to be.

Several public protests and demonstrations followed the death, and a campaign was quickly formed, based, as its name, the Roach Family Support Committee (RFSC) suggests, around the family itself. The RFSC quickly formulated as one of its main aims: the establishment of a full public inquiry into the circumstances of the death, the background to it, and the events that followed. This demand was backed by Hackney Borough Council, and numerous national groups and individuals, including the local M.P., Ernie Roberts.

Public inquiries into police related matters are rare in this country. There have been only two in this country since 1970, both set up under section 32 of the 1964 Police Act, and both presided over by Lord Scarman: the 1974 inquiry into the Red Lion Square demonstrations and the death of Kevin Gately, and the 1981 inquiry into the Brixton 'disorders' of the same year. Legal advice to the RFSC from Lord Gifford QC, suggested that such an inquiry in the Roach case, and the surrounding circumstances, would be appropriate under section 32 of the Act. (We publish Lord Gifford's advice in Appendix 3).

However, as with so many earlier calls for an inquiry into police-related deaths or deaths in police custody, the RFSC's and others calls for a public inquiry were turned down by the Government. Instead, Government ministers urged the public to accept the inquest as a full and proper inquiry. This claim was made despite the now well-known deficiencies of the workings of the inquest system, particularly where police-related deaths are concerned, and the fact that no inquest can ever inquire beyond the immediate cause of death. Even the Coroner in the Colin Roach case, Dr. Douglas Chambers, felt obliged to point out to his court that although he was holding an independent inquiry in public, this did not constitute a full independent public inquiry of the kind sought by the RFSC and others.

By refusing any inquiry, the Government's position, backed by certain sections of the media, represented an attempt to limit the explanation of the death to that of the action of one individual, whom the police, as we shall see, had already pathologised as "mentally ill".

But the issues raised by Colin's death went far wider. Only a few months before the death, a full meeting of Hackney Council had voted that there be an independent public inquiry into policing in the borough. There had been many such calls over the years in Hackney. The RFSC continued their campaign for a full inquiry. They did so, not only because they were unhappy with the June inquest verdict of "Suicide" but because they felt it was crucial to understand the history leading up to Colin Roach's death, particularly in terms of police-Black relations in Hackney.

The RFSC therefore decided to set up an independent committee of inquiry themselves and applied to the former Greater London Council for financial assistance to do so. This was granted and an independent committee of inquiry started work in April 1985. RFSC had decided that none of the invited members of the Inquiry should have an involvement in Hackney politics or police matters. However, those of us appointed have a wide range of work and community-based experience between us — in the church, law, politics, community action, research and writing. We are three women and three men. The majority of the Inquiry is Black. Professor Stuart Hall acted as adviser to the Inquiry and the Inquiry was also assisted by two part-time researchers and an administrator.

The terms of reference of the Inquiry, drawn up by the RFSC, were as follows:

> 1: To investigate and report on the nature of policing trends and developments in Hackney during the post-war period (1945-1984) and to consider in particular:
>
> a) The death of Colin Roach and surrounding circumstances
>
> b) Stoke Newington police station
>
> c) The relationship between the police and the Black community
>
> 2: To make recommendations for the consideration of the relevant agencies.

Sticking broadly to these terms of reference, we have divided the report into two main sections. The first deals with what we would call the precipitating factor — the death of

Colin Roach, and related events like the demonstrations after his death and the policing of those demonstrations, the role of the media and council; and the nature of the inquest and inquest aftermath. The second section of the report traces the history of policing in the borough of Hackney, and looks in more detail at relations between the police and Black people in the 1970s and early 1980s when considerable case material and evidence and fresher memories were made available to us. There is a particular examination of the history of Stoke Newington police station. (Although 1984 was set as the limit of our inquiry we have, in fact, gone beyond this as it seemed important to take account of developments which were taking place as we carried out our investigations).

It is worth briefly explaining our methods, how we set about collecting and collating information. After initial discussion and research, we set out to gather evidence from groups and individuals in Hackney. We twice advertised widely in the press, particularly the Black press, quoting our terms of reference and requesting written submissions and oral evidence (either as a follow up to written submissions, or from people who had not wanted to send written material). We heard oral evidence from November 1985 to April 1986, mainly at Hackney Town Hall (which is relatively central and accessible) and at Hackney Law Centre, over the road from the Town Hall. Members of the Committee also visited the Saxon Road Youth Club in Bow, with which Colin Roach was associated, and the Harambee II project for Black youth in Hackney. On both occasions we took the opportunity to talk to both staff and users of the projects. The Committee has also had recourse to previously unpublished material and to original research carried out by the workers for the Inquiry.

Wanting to take evidence from as wide a range of people in Hackney as possible, we several times approached the Metropolitan Police, both in Hackney and at Scotland Yard level, to ask them to come and talk to us. It is a matter of great regret that the police consistently refused to have anything to do with us. We publish some of the relevant correspondence on this in Appendix 4.

We have been struck over and over again by both the consistency of evidence presented to us, and the depth of feeling of those presenting it. The terms of reference required us to go beyond mere recitation of this evidence and to make recommendations. We do so in the conviction that policing problems in the borough do not stem from the actions of ill or misguided individuals but that the problem of policing in the borough lies in police priorities, the structure of the force, and the relationship (or lack of one) between the local force and the community it is supposed to serve.

We believe this document is important. It is certainly unique: to our knowledge, it is the only study to collate so extensively the experience of the policing of one community. Yet, although a specific study in that sense, we also believe it is of much wider significance, touching as it does on the ever more crucial issue of the policing of the inner-city.

We wish to conclude by offering our sincere thanks to all those who submitted evidence to the Inquiry or otherwise assisted its progress. We are particularly grateful to Stuart Hall for his advice and assistance; Gareth Peirce and Mike Mansfield, solicitor and barrister respectively for the Roach Family, for their detailed help and for supplying us with a wealth of information; and to INQUEST, who supplied us with a transcript of the inquest into Colin Roach's death. We must also acknowledge the excellent work of our researchers, Michael Medas and Patricia Tuitt, and our adminstrator, Maureen Pascal, whose contributions to the work of the Inquiry went far beyond what could reasonably have been expected.

Rev. David Moore (Chairperson)
Merle Amory
Melissa Benn
Fara Brown
Paul Gordon
A.B. Ngcobo

Independent Committee of Inquiry into Policing in Hackney.

Part I

The Colin Roach Story

Photograph: David Hoffman

"Colin Roach before his death".

Chapter 1

The Death of Colin Roach

1.1. Colin Roach died from a single shotgun blast to the head on the night of Wednesday 12 January 1983, in the foyer of Stoke Newington police station. The police claim that they heard a bang and found Colin's body sitting against the side wall in the outer lobby of the station, in an area which could not be seen from the reception desk. A sawn off single barrelled shotgun was apparently found lying across the floor from him.

The question of how, why and by whose hand Colin Roach met his death has never been satisfactorily explained to his family, friends or the Black community. In this chapter we examine all the facts surrounding Colin's death, drawing not only on inquest evidence, legal and police statements, but also on the oral and written evidence submitted to the Inquiry. The fuller picture that emerges is one which, we think, challenges the 'official' explanation of the sequence of events that led to Colin's death and the aftermath.

Colin : The Last Few Months

1.2 The circumstances of Colin's death were, by any standards, unusual. We therefore felt it was vital to find out more about Colin — the person — and events in the last few months of his life.

1.3 Colin Roach was a Black man, aged 21, who lived in Bow, east London. The Committee of Inquiry heard evidence from Colin's family and several of his friends. The picture that emerged was one of a quiet and well-liked young man, who in the words of one friend had 'everything going for him' at the time of his death. Some friends described him as a 'very outgoing person' who 'knew what he wanted'. To their knowledge there was 'nothing wrong with him'. Others mentioned his generous nature and the importance he placed upon his relationship with his family and with close friends:

> If a friend did him a wrong he would get really upset about it.

Colin was a tailor's cutter, but he had been made redundant some time previously. He lived at home with his family, whom one friend described as: "very close and very supportive". He was actively looking for work, he was keen on sports and was thinking of going to France with friends at the time of his death, either for a holiday or to seek work.

1.4 It appears that the only element of Colin's recent past that was in any way out of the ordinary was the short term of imprisonment he had served in December 1982 at Pentonville prison. In November, Colin had been arrested by police officers from Clerkenwell police station and charged with theft (of a wallet) and possession of an offensive weapon (a penknife). Although he had no previous convictions, apart from a minor charge of possession of cannabis, he was convicted at Clerkenwell Magistrates Court and sentenced to three months imprisonment. He entered Pentonville prison on 9 December 1982, appealed successfully against his sentence and was released three weeks later, on 29 December. On his release his family noticed that the experience had left him slightly depressed. According to his sister, Pauline, one thing that was "really noticeable" about Colin after his release was that "he couldn't keep still". Mrs. Roach, Colin's mother, described Colin's behaviour after his release as "anxiety" rather than "depression". Yet although as Pauline told the Inquiry "Colin didn't want us to worry", she was worried enough to call the doctor on 1 January 1983.

1.5 At this point it is necessary to comment on the possible explanations for Colin's "anxiety", which became apparent in the two weeks following his release from prison and prior to his death on 12 January 1983. Firstly, according to the evidence of Colin's family and friends as well as his solicitor, it had come as a surprise that Colin received a prison sentence at all. It was also his first time in prison. However, there are *two* possible 'deeper' explanations than this for Colin's distress. One explanation is concerned with Colin's medical condition from 1 January until his death, using the evidence of his family and the doctor(s) who treated him. The other is concerned with events which took place during Colin's three weeks in prison. The inquest into Colin's death was, as we observe later, given some evidence about the first of these explanations but *almost none about the second explanation.* Before looking at the 'medical' explanation for Colin anxiety from 1 January onwards, we have considered evidence regarding Colin's prison experiences. As early as the day following his release (30 December 1982) he took a close friend, Joe Joseph, into his confidence.

What Really Happened to Colin in Prison?

1.6 The inquest revealed only the bare facts: between the 16 and 22 December, Colin had shared a cell with a white prisoner, David John Chapman: he had noticed that Colin had apparently had an argument with the occupant of the cell next door and then subsequently asked him (i.e. Chapman) about the procedure for going on 'rule 43' (solitary confinement) without indicating why he wanted to know. Both the Coroner and the police investigators failed to locate or name the prisoner(s) with whom Colin had a disagreement. However, Joe Joseph, Colin's friend told the Inquiry that:

> When he got released from prison he came up to see me. It was obvious that he'd suffered a lot in there; that he must have been under a lot of pressure . . . He'd had a bit of aggravation with a couple of people in there . . . He asked me if we could help (NB — Joe had a twin brother — Jim, who also knew Colin) and we told him that we'd do our best but then he went away and when he came back for some reason he said that he couldn't tell us who the people were . . . Apparently they were supposed to have been after him . . .

Joe Joseph then went on to describe his attempts to get Colin to give him further details:

> ...I asked him who the people were and did he know them and he said yes, he did know them and that he could speak to them but he didn't want to tell us their names, and that it could bring aggravation down to us... if we helped him as such...
>
> There were three mates, three guys who used to hang out together all the time, Colin said. He had an argument with two of them and an actual fight with one of them (NB – the latter was the inmate of the cell next door)...

Colin told Joe Joseph this story on 30 December. However, two days later, on 1 January 1983, Colin's family, who were *not* aware of these details called the doctor. Accordingly, we now consider Colin's medical condition following his release from prison.

1.7   The Roach family's doctor, Dr. Elizabeth Cox, gave evidence on this area at the inquest. Prior to his time in prison, Colin had very rarely needed to see a doctor. He had had no physical ailments of any significance in the past. All Colin's family and friends emphasised to the Inquiry that Colin did NOT have a "history of mental illness", although this allegation was made in press reports which followed his death. Dr. Cox did not know Colin or his family, but was practising at the family doctor group practice.

1.8   According to Dr. Cox's testimony at the inquest, her surgery was closed at the time of Pauline's telephone call on 1 January 1983. It was therefore a 'relief' doctor, based at Lea Bridge Road with the G.P. relief service, who called that Saturday evening at the Roach home. The relief doctor, whom Dr. Cox was not able to identify by name at the inquest, appears to have seen Colin, who felt that he had an earache. The doctor, however, diagnosed that Colin had a cold and was suffering from anxiety, and prescribed 'Tranxene', a mild drug specifically for anxiety, for 3 days.

1.9   Dr. Cox herself visited the Roach household on Tuesday, 4 January in response to a telephone call from Pauline

Roach, and then on the Thursday 6, Friday 7 and Monday 10 January. On the first two occasions she said that she stayed for fifteen minutes, on the last, which was the only time she met or spoke to Colin, for twenty minutes. On 4 January Dr. Cox diagnosed Colin on the basis of information she said had come from his mother and sister (Pauline). Dr. Cox decided to prescribe 'larazepan', a slightly stronger tranquilizer, and said that she would visit on Friday (7 January). However, following a telephone call from Pauline on Thursday (6 January), she visited that day. According to notes made by Dr. Cox, and read out at the inquest, Colin's relatives had informed her he had been "out all night" driving Pauline's car and they were worried because he had been "hearing voices". On the basis of this information, although she had not yet seen Colin, she concluded that his condition had taken on a "psychotic aspect" and prescribed a daily dose of 300mg of Chlorpromazine (a drug very similar to largactil, which is used in prisons). However, according to the evidence submitted to the Inquiry by Pauline Roach, Colin never "heard voices" and had only been out on the Wednesday night for "about an hour".

1.10 Dr. Cox, who admitted during cross-examination at the inquest that she did not have any psychiatric qualifications, said that on the following day (Friday 7 January) she discussed Colin's case with a consultant psychiatrist from St. Clements Hospital, Bow. This psychiatrist, Dr. Walker was, she explained, supervising her treatment of Colin, although it was not clear from her evidence whether this supervision began before or after she prescribed the even stronger drug largactil for Colin. On the Friday she had also visited Colin's home, again without finding him at home, and had been told that his condition had improved. Colin had, she said, taken his dose of three 100mg tablets, and she believed that the treatment was working, as he was said to be eating and sleeping normally. On the following Monday evening (10 January) she visited and finally met Colin. She told the inquest that he told her he was "no longer" hearing voices, during the 20 minute conversation which they had in the living room, where Colin was watching a video. His mother was also present. Dr. Cox said that Colin asked her about the effect of the drugs he was taking, which was making him sleep too much, and she suggested that he could lower the dosage from 300 to 200mg per day from Thursday (13 January) onwards. Colin also agreed to her suggestion of a home visit by the psychiatrist, "eventually", although according to Dr. Cox Colin was "reluctant" even to see her.

1.11 It may be questioned how much of Colin's prison experience and subsequent worries were clear to the doctor at the time. She told the inquest that he was "upset" and "had a lot on his mind", but had given her no details "except that prison upset him". Dr. Cox, who told the Roach family's barrister at the inquest that he had never heard of the expression 'the liquid cosh', meaning largactil, also acknowledged that it had not occurred to her to contact any social worker or probation officer whom Colin might have seen while he was in prison in order to find out whether the problem stemming from prison was real or imaginary. She had been expecting, however that the visit of the psychiatrist, which was to have taken place, would show that the symptoms Colin's relatives were said to have described to her on 6 January would in the end prove to be "only an episode". She told the Coroner that she had been "shocked and surprised" at the news of Colin's death because she had seen no previous life threatening behaviour or ideas expressed by him. She went on to tell Mr. Mansfield (the Roach family's barrister) that depression was not a necessarily suicidal sympton. When asked what might be such a sympton, she said that "the biggest thing is what the patient himself says". However, she agreed that there was no sign of either a sucidal intention or the symptoms which she had described as a "psychotic episode" based on what she heard on 6 January and in Colin's conversation with her on 10 January. She also agreed that had she believed Colin to be suicidal, she might well have recommended hospital treatment. However, as described above, she agreed that he could reduce his medication and recommended a home visit by the psychiatrist.

1.12   Colin did not live long enough to receive that home visit. Yet in the period leading up to the day he was seen by Dr. Cox, 10 January, he had told Joe Joseph a little more about his prison experiences:

> On a visit that Colin had, the guy had one as well on that same day, they were in the visiting room together . . .
> He said that during the visit . . . he knew that they were talking about him . . . The guy was on a visit with his mum and . . . kept pointing Colin out (ie. to her —) When he got out the woman became involved. But I said to him "Well surely nothing's going to happen . . . Maybe it's just an argument", but he was saying no, that they were going to take him out, as in kill him, put his lights out, so like I said, we all got a bit concerned, but he wouldn't let us help him . . . They were on remand. He didn't give us any indication of where they came from or when they'd be out, but he just said they'd arranged . . through the geezer's mum, for these things to take place . . .

1.13   It appears that worried as he was, Colin at first intended to face this predicament alone, as it was only he who had been threatened. According to Joe, he was "a little edgy" rather than scared. However, on the weekend 8-9 January 1983, three days before his death, "everything came to a head".

> On the Friday he was alright . . . He came back the next day and wouldn't tell me anything. It was obvious that something had happened between the day he left me and through the night . . . He said that he had to get these people before they got him, because "Now they're saying that they're going to involve my family" . . . That's what brought it to a head, because at first it was all on him . . . He didn't mind facing it himself . . . He had to 'see' them, whether he meant 'see' them to communicate and try to get the problem sorted out or 'see' them as in 'deal with it'. He was . . . extremely scared and worried about them getting to his family . . . I've never seen Colin scared in the seven years that I knew him . . . and he said "They said they're going to get you, Joe. They said they're going to get you the way they're going to get me — with a bullet.

1.14   It must be emphasised that we have no evidence that Colin revealed any of his predicament to his family. As Pauline told the Inquiry "Colin didn't want us to worry".

1.15 On Monday, 10 January the day on which Dr. Cox paid Colin her one and only visit, Colin seemed to Joe Joseph (who saw him that morning) to have "calmed down a bit". Colin and Joe arranged to go out with two sisters whom they knew, Denise and Donna Carlow, to see a film on the Wednesday night. Colin and Joe discussed the idea on the Monday and it was agreed with the girls themselves (who both lived nearby) on the Tuesday evening when Colin and Joe visited them. In her evidence to the inquest, Denise Carlow said that Colin spent much of the time during the Tuesday visit sitting in a chair playing with her baby. He said little but when asked why he was quiet remarked only that there was nothing wrong. Joe Joseph recalls that Colin seemed perfectly alright at the end of the evening.

The Events of Wednesday 12 January

1.16 The last day of Colin's life, Wednesday 12 January began normally enough. By all accounts he spent much of the day at home. His father saw him in the morning when he left for work at 6 a.m. Colin was still asleep. His mother told us that he went out during the morning to nearby Victoria Park and returned. However, the most important event for Colin that day seems to have been the birth the previous night of a baby to his younger sister Valerie. The baby had been born in Mile End hospital, which was not far away. Colin bought some flowers and went out in the early afternoon to visit her with his elder brother Patrick. (Patrick and Pauline did not live at the Roach home, whereas Colin's two younger brothers and his younger sister, Valerie, did).

1.17 It was Colin who arranged for photos to be taken at the hospital. By all accounts he was overjoyed at the birth. He told Valerie during the visit that he would see her in a couple of days, on the Friday. Several eye witnesses who gave evidence at the inquest also saw Colin on the Wednesday buying the flowers on his way either to or from the hospital. Nothing unusual was noticed. Colin's father (James Roach) next saw him at 5.30p.m. when he returned from work. Colin told him about seeing the baby. At about 7p.m. Colin and his younger brother Darren left the house to get a video film.

They returned and the family together watched the video, followed by the remainder of 'Dallas' (which was on between 8.10 and 9pm) and the Nine o'clock news (9-9.25pm). By the time that the news was finished, according to Mr. and Mrs. Roach, Colin had been upstairs, changed his clothes and had come down, saying he was going out. This was about 9.30. At the time that he left his father said that Colin was not carrying any sort of bag. This is a significant fact in the light of later evidence.

1.18   It is not possible to say where Colin went immediately after that. We know he was not driving, however. We do know that he met another friend — Keith 'Nestor' Scully — in Joe's flats, about a twenty minute walk from Colin's home. (Scully was at that time sitting in his car, a gold Mercedes). Colin's presence at Joe's flat is probably not surprising considering he had arranged to go with Joe to see Denise Carlow that night.

1.19   Keith Scully (a white friend who knew Colin through their common acquaintances, the Joseph twins) may have been the last known person to see Colin alive. He was certainly the last of Colin's friends to see him that night; therefore his role in the events of 12-13 January is an important one. Keith Scully, however, declined our invitation to give evidence to the Inquiry. The account which follows is taken from the statement he gave to the family's lawyers *before* the inquest:

> I sat in the car and shouted up to Joe's flat for him. I then saw Colin walking through the flats. Colin walked up to the car... He was carrying a sports bag which was a dark colour — reddish brown with a shoulder strap and handle. I had not seen him with that bag before. One side of the bag was chequered. The bag was being worn across his shoulder. There was a towel hanging out of the bag. It was a beige colour. It appeared clean. He never took the towel out of the bag the whole time I saw him and he kept the bag over his shoulder the whole time. *The bag did not look heavy or full up. It was not bulging. He could have got more things in it* . . .

NB: This statement, to which we will be referring several times, is not to be confused with the statement that Keith Scully gave to the police in Stoke Newington police station later that night, which was neither available to the Roach family's lawyers at the inquest, (due to the rule regarding disclosure of witness statements) nor was it available to this Inquiry.

1.20 In this statement Scully estimated the time of his meeting with Colin to have been 10.20pm (although in his testimony to the inquest he said 10pm). His statement goes on to say that Colin seemed "out of breath" although "he did not appear as though he had been running". Shortly after this, Colin and Scully met Jim Joseph, Joe's twin brother. Here there is a slight difference in recollection: Scully, in his statement and in the oral evidence which he gave at the inquest remembers that firstly, Colin got into the car (the front passenger seat) and that Jim Joseph, who was in Joe's first floor flat, shouted out that Joe wasn't there and called out for him to hang on, followed by Jim coming downstairs and getting into the car. However, Jim's account to this Inquiry was that he was in fact "walking along" nearby Joe's flats when Scully and Colin picked him up, as they were driving past:

> Colin was already in the Merc before I got in . . . When he picked me up he said to me "Where's Joe?" and I said "I think he might be at Denise's" . . .

In any event, both accounts agree that it was Scully who met Colin first after Colin had left his home, that Colin was carrying a shoulder bag and that the three then proceeded at Colin's request, to try and find Joe, in the Mercedes. Jim also told us that he had not seen Colin with this bag before: "It didn't look like the type of bag that Colin would have". His family concur with this. Jim was sure "the bag wasn't closed" that night, and also saw the towel, which was familiar to Colin's family.

The next part of the evening was spent by Colin driving around.

1.21 Between the time when the drive began, which was probably soon after 10pm, and 11.25pm when Scully alone (i.e. without Jim Joseph as a passenger) dropped Colin off near to Stoke Newington police station, a sequence of events took place which may not have seemed clear in the evidence heard at the inquest from Scully, the Carlows and the Josephs, particularly with respect to the question of *why* Colin, Jim and Scully were driving and *why* Colin was giving Scully (as the driver) certain directions. In the following section we have tried to present that evidence, and the additional evidence which we have received in a way which is as clear as possible with reference to what Colin was saying or doing, in order to ascertain the answers to these questions.

1.22 According to Scully's statement, Colin had said before Jim got into the car that he wanted a lift back to his house in order to collect his own car (a convertible Fiesta). However, once Jim was in the car Colin had "changed his mind" and began directing Scully on a route which took them first to Mile End Road (from Bethnal Green), then eastwards to the Bow Fly-over, through Canning Town, West Ham and Stratford, and then back along Mile End Road heading west. Jim Joseph told this Inquiry:

> On the night we were trying to find my brother, but we couldn't find him anywhere. We kept missing him . . . Every time we went somewhere, Joe had just gone and Colin didn't want to stay in the place . . . he wanted to keep on the move all the time. . .
>
> We'd be driving along and he'd say 'take this left' or 'take this right' — and that's what we did. We didn't argue with him, we just did it. The only time we said to him 'No Col, we can't do it' was when he wanted us to start jumping lights and then we said 'No, we'll get nicked' . . .

1.23 The reason for Colin's wish 'to be on the move' appears to be related to the fact that, as Jim explained, "He kept looking back". If this meant that Colin believed they were being followed, he did not say so in as many words according to either Jim Joseph or Keith Scully. However,

Scully knew nothing of the prison incident or of the account which Colin had given Joe Joseph, only four days earlier, that he had to "get" these people "before they got him". Scully's statement explains how he repeatedly asked Colin what was wrong, but Colin replied "I can't tell you". After Scully, Jim and Colin had returned from the part of their journey which had taken them to Canning Town, West Ham and Stratford, acting on directions which were being given solely by Colin, it appears from Scully's account that they returned to Bethnal Green because Colin had expressed concern for the safety of Joe. It will be recalled that Colin had already told Joe more detail than anyone else about the prison incident, and that Joe had been told by Colin that he also could be receiving a "bullet" from the people concerned. Jim Joseph told the Inquiry that: "He (Colin) definitely wanted to find Joe, because he came back. He just didn't want to hang around". Finding Joe, then, was the object of the drive that night.

1.24 Between 10.45 and 11.00p.m. Colin and his friends arrived at Denise's flat in Bethnal Green to look for Joe. In their evidence at the inquest, the Carlow sisters said that they were in the flat, with Joe, when they heard the sound of the car horn. According to Jim Joseph, Colin stayed in the car with Scully:

> I suppose because of the mood he was feeling in he didn't want to face the girls. So he sent me up to get Joe ...
> When I went up there and told Joe, that Colin was downstairs; when we got down there he was gone. So Joe now left Denise Carlow's and went looking for him ... I waited up there in case he came back ... Nestor (i.e. Scully) came back with Colin. Colin stayed in the car and Nestor came upstairs and told me he was looking for Joe. I said 'You've just missed him ...

According to Scully's statement, Colin had insisted that he drive off when Jim and Joe were in the process of running down the stairs to meet them:

> Colin then asked me to then stop and phone his dad to tell him that I would be around to get Colin's car keys. Colin had told me that he wanted me to go in and get the car keys from his dad, because he did not want to go into the flats ...

After this, Scully says that they searched in vain to find a phone box which was working, and at one point Colin asked to drive the Mercedes. He drove only for a short distance, after which Scully took over and the pair returned to Denise Carlow's, where, as described above, Jim Joseph was now waiting, his brother Joe having gone off on foot to look for Colin. Jim got back into the car with them and together they went to the Roach family's home, in Bow, in order that they could get Colin's car. This, according to Jim, was because Scully was "getting a bit fed up" with driving Colin around, so instead:

> I would have got in the car with Colin (i.e. Colin's Fiesta) and the two of us would have gone looking for Joe . . .

When the car stopped outside Colin's flats, Colin did not go into his house. Instead he gave Jim his jewellery and told him to "give it to his mum". He did not say why. He then asked Jim to go in and get his car keys. According to Mr. Roach, Jim also brought £40 to give Mrs. Roach, £20 of which was to be used to put petrol in Colin's car. Jim told the Inquiry:

> I gave James (i.e. Colin's father) the jewellery and asked James for the key. James said to me, "Where's Colin?" I said "He's outside" . . . James said to me "Let's go and get Colin". As we came out of the house to go and get Colin, Colin must have told my friend (i.e. Scully) to drive off . . .

1.26 Following this, Jim drove Mr. Roach in Colin's car to look for Colin. They could not find him at Denise's flat or elsewhere. Both Jim and Joe were now looking for Colin, however they were not to find him, as he was, unknown to them, on his way to Stoke Newington with Keith Scully, on a trip which would prove fatal.

1.27 According to Scully's statement, Colin told him to drive off from where they had stopped after telling Jim "that we would be driving up and down and that we would meet him along the road". Jim, however, told this Inquiry that Colin "was supposed to have stayed there" waiting for him. This discrepancy in accounts may only be accidental, but must be mentioned because it occurs at the start of the last period of Colin's movements that night, in which our only source of information is Keith Scully, the last person known to have seen him alive. They also spent a short while searching for Jim at various petrol stations nearby. Colin had now become "totally silent". When they reached the traffic lights at the junction of Bethnal Green and Cambridge Heath Road, Colin said to him "Take me to Bethnal Green police station". Bethnal Green police station would have been a short distance past the traffic lights on the left, in the direction they were travelling (west) from Roman Road.

1.28 There is some variation in the accounts which Scully gavce at the inquest, in his statement to the family's solicitor and elsewhere, although he was certain in each case that Colin initially asked to be taken to Bethnal Green police station, which was not far (about one mile) from his home. In an interview given to *The Times* (28/1/83), Scully is quoted as saying that Colin gave as the reason for wanting to go to Bethnal Green police station that:

> Someone's going to get me and I want to get in there to be safe . . .

However, he does not recall this remark in the statements which we have quoted already or in his inquest testimony. What Keith Scully recalls in all accounts is that after Colin asked him to take him to Bethnal Green he then asked him to take him to Stoke Newington, *in order to see Colin's brother, Patrick, who lived in that area.* The route, which was not familiar to Scully, was told to him bit by bit, in the same manner that Colin had been giving directions all evening. Eventually they turned out of Amhurst Road on to Stoke Newington High Street and Colin asked him to stop at the corner of Victorian Road and the High Street, which was the turning just before the police station (see map page 89), the turning which led to Patrick's place. Scully's statement describes Colin telling him "This is it. On the left here", after which he stopped the car:

Colin leant over and touched my arm. He said "I'll be all right here".[1] He then got out of the car. I thought he was going to walk down the side street we had stopped by. However, he didn't. He simply walked towards the police station. I waited. I saw him go into the police station.

I had kept the engine running and when he went into the police station, I drove on. I slowed down as I arrived at the police station to look inside (NB – at the inquest Scully said that he was travelling at about 5 mph then) I suppose it had taken me ten seconds from the time Colin had gone into the police station until the time that I got there. When I looked into the police station I couldn't see much. However, I did see a silhouette. He had gone through the wooden doors which were open, but he had not gone through the glass door. I could not see who it was. I decided to drive on. This was some time between 11.20 and 11.30 p.m. . . . I did not hear any bangs or other special noise.

I then drove on and did a right at the second set of lights. I went down the one-way system. I then saw a police car which had passed me as I had been waiting near the police station, which had then gone through the one way system, with its lights flashing. I assumed something had happened because when it had passed me it had just been driving ordinarily. I suppose I saw this car about 1½ to 2 minutes after I dropped Colin off.

1.29 Three points maybe added to this account. Firstly that the figure seen by Scully in the lobby did not turn around or wave to him, as pointed out in his evidence at the inquest. Secondly, in an account given to *The Times* Scully added that when he dropped Colin off, "No-one was near Roach, although in his mirror he saw someone walking up the street". Thirdly, the holdall, unfamiliar to Colin's family, which was to prove (at the inquest) too small for the shotgun which killed him to have fitted inside, was still around Colin's shoulder, according to Scully, when he left the car.

1.30 Scully's account identifies that Colin asked to be driven to Stoke Newington. It does not explain why he entered the police station. As far as available evidence tells us, Colin's only connection with Stoke Newington was his brother Patrick. It was stated several times before and during the inquest by the police that Colin had no connection with, and was not known at, Stoke Newington police station. As we shall demonstrate later, this contention is called into question by the police evidence concerning how rapidly they identified Colin's body. It is not improbable that the name of Patrick Roach was known to Stoke Newington police as he lived nearby and had had encounters with the police in the past.

1.31 Another consideration relates to Colin's state of mind that night. Based upon quotes from Colin which Scully was alleged to have repeated in the statement which the police took from him later that night, the Police barrister at the inquest suggested that Colin "was in a hell of a state, wasn't he?" Scully's reply was to say "No, he was just upset". However, while it is apparent that Colin's concern for the safety of his friend Joe Joseph and his concern that he was being followed are consistent with his reactions to the death threat which he had told Joe about earlier; it must be repeated that hardly any reasons were provided at the inquest for Colin's anxiety other than the medical diagnosis which had been made by a doctor with whom Colin did not discuss his prison experience. Colin clearly did not want to stay in one place for long during the drive, although he was not confused about the directions which he was giving to Scully in between their intermittent search for Joe Joseph. It was equally clear that Colin kept the details of the threat and the details of the route he wanted them to take to himself in the presence of, at least, Scully, who had not known him as well as the twins and was already tired of driving him around. According to Jim Joseph:

> ... Nestor (i.e. Scully) didn't know him that well ... Nestor couldn't really distinguish between how he was acting then and how he used to be from before ... He couldn't make head or tail of it ..

1.32 The fact that Scully "couldn't make head or tail of it" may or may not explain why he drove away from the police station at 11.30, leaving Colin. He told the inquest, in answer to the Roach family's barrister that although he had seen a figure standing in the lobby he was not going to run the risk of going into the police station, having had his own history of brushes with the police. He then returned to find Jim and Joe in Bethnal Green. According to Jim, who had by then driven Mr. Roach home in Colin's car and was now on his way to the sisters' flat:

> As I was walking back towards Denise's . . . same place where they picked me up before, I saw Nestor coming back. So I said to Nestor "Where's Colin?" He said "I dropped him off, he asked me to drop him off around Patrick's. But when I dropped him off I saw him walking towards the police station". So I said "What police station-?" He said, "The one at Stoke Newington" . . . So I said to Nestor "Well, we can't leave him there . . . we'd better go and get James (i.e. Mr. Roach).

1.33 Mr. Roach, Jim and Scully returned to the police station in the Mercedes at about 12.15 am. Jim continued by saying:

> When we pulled up there . . . the police station doors were closed and cordoned off with one of those orange tape things. Two policemen were standing outside the door . . .

1.34 They had pulled up just past the closed wooden doors. Jim told this Inquiry that the two officers "seemed to recognise the car". It was Mr. Roach who spoke to them first.

The Police Treatment of Mr. and Mrs. Roach

1.35 In this section we describe the events of the rest of that night as experienced by Colin's family and friends. The chapter on the inquest examines what occurred at the police station between the time Colin had been dropped off and 12.15 a.m. (about 45 minutes). Here we deal only with what happened to Colin's family and friends and what explanations were provided to them, the following morning as to what had happened to Colin.

1.36 According to Mr. Roach:

> We reached there at 12.15 . . . after I got to the front door, I met a policeman there. I told the policeman "I hear that my

son is here, Colin Roach". He said "All right, I've got to take you" ... He took me around the back (ie the rear entrance of the police station) and took me upstairs into one room. When they took me in the room there were two of them there and they started to question me... One went out and one stayed in there and kept questioning me, asking if Colin had any gun, what Colin was doing, I told them Colin didn't have a gun ... I said "I'm not on trial here". They kept me in there form 12.15 to 2.45am.

At 2.45a.m. they took me into one more room and started to question me again. I told them that I had only come to find out if my son was there: Yes or no. Then they told me that my son was dead. I said "How did my son die?" *They told me that he shot himself.* I said "My son doesn't have a gun — how did he manage to shoot himself?" They told me that he shot himself. I asked them, "Could I see my son?" They said "No" and they kept on questioning me at the same time. I went back and asked them again: "Could I see my son?" — "No" and they kept me there until 5a.m. Then they brought me downstairs. I asked them when I came downstairs — "Could I see my son?" They said "No". Three of them brought me home... and when they reached home they started to turn the room upside down, saying that they were searching for ammunition in his room ...

1.37 Mr. Roach told this Inquiry that he was questioned continuously both before and after he was told of Colin's death. He was *not* asked to describe his son or identify him. The exact words used to tell him that Colin was dead were, "I have a sad report for you ... Your son is dead". During the questioning, before this point (between 12.15am and 2.45am) he was told "Don't tell lies — you're telling lies" and at one point his statement was even torn up. It was later alleged at the inquest by the police barrister that Mr. Roach had said in his statement that Colin had been "hearing voices and mentioning voodoo" — this was also alleged at the inquest by Det. Chief Supt. Robertson. On both occasions Mr. Roach denied it in the strongest possible terms. Finally, it was alleged soon after Colin's death and during the inquest that Mr. Roach had been told of Colin's death at *12.45am.* This was not accepted by the inquest Jury, in addition to the fact that it is not borne out by evidence which we have received.

1.38 Meanwhile, Mr. Roach, it will be recalled, had left Jim Joseph and Keith Scully sitting outside the police station in the Mercedes at 12.15am. According to Jim, after ten minutes, the one officer remaining outside:

> — came over to us and said . . . "Did you know Colin?" So we said "Yes". They said "Was it you two who dropped him off?" — So we said, "Yes". They said "Could you come with us, please" — and me, too — I said to him I wasn't there (i.e. when Colin was dropped off) but they said "Were you with him tonight?" — I said, "Yes . . . when he came back (NB when Keith Scully came back to see Jim Joseph) and told me he had dropped him here, I went and got his dad . . .

1.39 Jim and Scully were taken into the police station via the rear entrance and brought into a ground floor charge-room. At this time, Scully recalled in his inquest testimony that "There seemed to be a lot of officers coming off duty making notes". First the two friends were questioned together in the charge-room for a period which Scully, in the inquest estimated to be about 15-20 minutes. Neither was asked to identify Colin Roach, nor provide any kind of detailed description. They were then separated. Keith Scully was questioned by D.C. Pointer, whose name he recalled at the inquest. Jim Joseph was questioned by D.S. McLellan, according to D.C.S. Robertson's evidence at the inquest. However, D.S. McLellan, neither presented a statement nor gave any oral evidence at the inquest. D.C. Pointer claimed at the inquest that Scully was questioned by him from 12.45am to 2.45am before being told of Colin's death. Keith Scully, at the inquest, recalled the time that he was told of Colin's death as 4.45am. During Scully's interview, after he had been separated from Jim, he was told to make a statement. He was not cautioned. He was asked to provide a detailed account of Colin's movements, which was nine pages long. During the questioning by D.C. Pointer, another officer brought a smoke-filled plastic bag containing a shotgun into the room and was waved out by Pointer, Scully told the inquest. However Scully was not, he said, asked to idenfity the gun and he was asked no questions about the gun or the holdall which Colin had been carrying. Eventually they told him of Colin's death in the following manner:

> At the end of the interview the officer went out. He then came back and said "I've got some good news and some bad news for you. What do you want first?" I said "Bad news". The police officer said, "Colin's dead". I was choked. I waited about half an hour. After that I said "How could there be any good news after that?" The police officer said, "You're not going to be charged". (Extract from Keith Scully's statement to the Roach family's lawyers).

1.40 In the case of Jim Joseph, who was questioned by two officers at first, and then one alone (who, according to the police, was D.S. McLellan), the questioning was slightly different, after he and Keith Scully had been separated:

> They were asking me . . ."Did Colin have anything with him when we dropped him off" . . . I said "Yes, a sports bag". They said "Do you know what was in the sports bag?" I said "How the . . . hell do I know? . . . What's all this about?" . . . They said "Look, son, if you don't answer the questions, you're in serious trouble". So I said "Where's Colin?" They said "He's with the doctor" . . . So all the time I'm thinking he's alive . . . They kept on and on about "What was in the bag?" . . ."How was he acting" . . . "Was there anything wrong with him?" I said "What do you mean, wrong with him?" . . . I said no . . . They were trying to say it as if I was lying . . . I said "He had some problems in the nick, but it was nothing too serious that he couldn't handle . . ." They kept this up for about 3-4 hours. . . I saw him writing what I was saying (supposedly) . . . he just made me sign it."

1.41 The police officer did not tell Jim the object behind the questions he was asking him until after the time when he told him that Colin was dead, (3-4 hours later):

> After I'd signed the statement . . . He said "Well its obvious you had nothing to do with it . . . but your mate's dead". "Colin's dead". I said . . . your're joking". He said to me "Do you think I'd joke about a thing like that?" . . . He just came clean out with it — "He's dead". I said "I thought you said he was with the doctor?" — He said "Yes, but the doctor's look-

ing at his wounds and all that, he's dead though" . . . I said "How come you waited this long before you told me?" He said *"We wanted to make sure you knew nothing about the gun"* . . . That's all they wanted to know about, just the gun . . . nothing else . . .

1.42 Although the statement had been completed now, Jim was also asked about the gun:

> They were going "Well, the reason why we're asking you all these questions is because Colin had a gun, and we want to know where he got it from". I said "What gun?" They said "He's got an old German shotgun" . . . I remember him saying that it was a rare type of gun, there wasn't much of this particular type of shotgun about . . . He made the point of saying . . . *it should be easy to trace* . . .

1.43 Jim was also told that the police had "never heard of anyone killing themselves in that manner before", by the officer who was questioning him. Before he was brought back downstairs to join Mr. Roach and Keith Scully, (who he says had already been dealt with, since "they had me the longest") Jim Joseph was told by this officer a sequence of events relating to Colin's death:

> *Apparently Colin walked in, asked for help or whatever . . . the desk sergeant said "No, we can't help you", and walked away, back into the nick . . . After he heard the bang he's supposed to have gone running in there . . .*

1.44 Colin was said to have walked up to the public enquiries desk and spoken to the officer, who was named by the police subsequently as P.C. Jackson. Jim was also told, while alone with the CID officer who had questioned him that the reason they had not allowed Mr. Roach to see the body was that the body was a "mess". In addition, Jim recalls that he was told that the desk officer was "in shock" from having "found" the body, and that this "shock" was given as the reason why Mr. Roach could not see the desk officer, which he *asked* to do after the questioning (downstairs) in the presence of Jim Joseph and Keith Scully.

1.45 Mr. Roach was taken home just before 5am by 3 police officers. Jim Joseph was dropped home by some other officers, who asked him to take them to Denise Carlow's flat, which he did. They interviewed her for about 10-15 minutes. Keith Scully had his hand swabbed at the police station and then he was taken outside to his Mercedes, which was searched, and samples taken and labelled by an officer who was probably D.S. Warwick. However, before he was taken outside, he said that:

> the police officer told me not to say anything outside *because the press might be there and he did not want them to hear anything,* however they weren't there ... (Extract from Keith Scully's statement to the Roach family's lawyers).

1.46   James Roach had been at Stoke Newington police station from 12.15a.m. to 4.45a.m. on Thursday, 13 January. He had not been told of his son's death until 2.45a.m. and when he left he had not seen the body or been asked to identify Colin in any way. He was offered no sympathy, condolences or refreshment. At the time that he had been told of Colin's death he was crying, yet the questioning continued regardless. Meanwhile, his wife, Pamela Roach, had been trying to contact Stoke Newington police station. She telephoned five times between her husband's departure and 5am: She told the Inquiry:

> I said I'm Mrs. Roach, I'm Colin's mum, we were told that he came into Stoke Newington police station. I know my husband is there, because his (i.e. Colin's) friends came home and took him to the station ... He said to me at the moment they're busy and no one is available to talk to me. Each time. Until about 4.30 a.m. ...

1.47   On her fifth telephone call :-

> I asked him, "What happened to my husband and Colin?" He said "I won't talk about it", my husband is alright and he will be coming home in a little while. I said "What about Colin?" He said they would discuss it when they got home — and put the receiver down ...

Finally, at 4.45a.m. the police telephoned Mrs. Roach and told her her husband had asked her not to go to work (which she normally did at that time).

1.48   James Roach returned, accompanied by three police officers (D.S. Pierce, D.C. Pointer and W.P.C. Maddison) just before 5am. No sooner had he told her that Colin was dead, when the officers asked to search Colin's room. According to Mr. Roach:

> "I took them upstairs, they asked me if they could see Colin's room... Two officers (Pierce and Pointer) began 'pulling out everything' turning the room 'upside down'. They claimed they were searching for ammunition."

When Mr. Roach told them to stop, they went next door, woke up Kevin and Darren, Colin's younger brothers, and told them that Colin was dead, that he had shot himself.

1.49   While this was happening Mrs. Roach had been left downstairs with the third officer, W.P.C. Maddison. She could hear the 'tumbling' upstairs — yet rather than try to console her, the officer grabbed her by the throat and pushed her down into her chair: Mrs. Roach told the Inquiry:

> she was left downstairs with me... I wasn't crying, you know I was too shocked to cry at the time... Then she kept me down in the chair for a while and she even pushed me back down on the chair — they deny it, but whether she meant it on good terms or not they still deny it...

1.50   After the 35 minute visit, the police officers departed. They had not found any ammunition, Colin's room was in disarray and no apology was offered for the way in which Mrs. Roach and her two sons had been treated. This only added to the other matters which had not been explained by the police. Later in the morning of 13 January, the reception which the family received when they returned to the police station added insult to injury. As yet, they had not been able to see or identify Colin's body.

The Next Morning

1.51   The newspapers of 13 January 'broke' the story of Colin's death. For instance, *The Standard* in a story entitled 'Shotgun suicide clue' claimed that 'a young Black man, found dead with a shotgun blast... is thought to have killed himself'. Even worse for the family, the story said that it was 'believed that he had a history of mental instablity'. Other papers, which came out in the morning also carried the story. One *(The Daily Mail,)* even named him, as 'Clive' Roach. It was in this climate that Mr. and Mrs. Roach, Pauline Roach, their solicitor Gareth Peirce and a family friend, the Tower Hamlets Councillor Dennis Twomey, visited Stoke Newington police station at about 10.30 or 11am on Thursday morning.

1.52   The visit lasted only ten minutes. The front of the station was barricaded off, and according to Gareth Peirce:

> We asked to see the head of the station and we were sent round the back of the station to a side room. A.D.I. Scott came along . . .

1.53   Scott said that the head of the station was at home and unavailable. Mrs. Roach recalls that:

> He didn't have time to talk properly for he was in such a hurry, but he had time when he went out — he was talking to the other officers and laughing . . .

1.54   Because the party of seven was received in a corridor, with only a wooden bench nearby, Dennis Twomey went into a TV room to fetch an extra chair, and:

> Scott came running after me and grabbed the chair out of my hand. He said, what did I think I was doing and that people . . . might need the chairs. There must have been about fifteen chairs in the room . . .

1.55   D.I. Scott then 'demanded' the names and addresses of all those who had arrived. Gareth Peirce explained in her evidence to this Inquiry that she:

> Told him that he was dealing with a bereaved family and one expected a minimum of sympathy or compassion or a bare minimum of politeness from him, and repeated that they wanted to know what had happened . . .

1.56   Mr. Roach asked why he had been made to give a statement before he was told of Colin's death. Scott replied that Mr. Roach was 'either confused or lying', he said that it was 'rubbish' and then 'fired off a number of assertions'. According to the notes made at the time by Dennis Twomey; this was the account Scott read out to them:

> Colin had left home at 8.30 with a holdall, met a friend with a car, asked for a lift, gone to see other friends... but the driver of the car had left Colin to speak to a friend because he said that Colin was 'rambling'. Colin asked him to go to Stoke Newington which he did. Colin then went into the police station foyer, shot himself. There are outer wooden doors inner glass doors: He was betwen the two, that a noise was heard at 11.25, there was no-one else there, but on hearing the noise an officer looked out of the window but the car had gone and that two C.I.D. men had seen Colin get out of the car. That there had been a doctor at the police station who was called to Colin, who was already dead, and the weapon had been a single barrelled shotgun...

1.57   After this time, Scott, said Mrs. Roach, was 'in a hurry', 'said he had to go to a meeting', and the party was forced to leave... Gareth Peirce told us that:

> We subsequently found out that the post-mortem was about to take place, and he must have been anxious to get to it. There was no suggestion to Mr. and Mrs. Roach that there was a post-mortem and that they might wish to have a pathologist present...

1.58   Mr. and Mrs. Roach agreed that the police at no time during the meeting acknowledged that they might be in a state of 'shock' — not only was Scott 'laughing' as they left, he was 'very aggressive' and 'extraordinarily callous'.

1.59   The account provided by Scott was hardly more detailed than the news stories of that morning about Colin's death. Colin's parents had been interrogated, kept from knowing of his death for over three hours, accused of telling lies and forced to make a statement before hand, they had been raided, searched and Mrs. Roach assaulted. They had not been asked to identify or allowed to see Colin's body, yet they were expected to accept that he had walked into a police station, not in his area, and shot himself.

1.60 Information had somehow been released in time to reach the morning papers, saying not only that it was believed that Colin had killed himself but also that he had a history of mental illness. This must have been done before Mr. Roach had been told of Colin's death. Colin's surname, at least had already been printed in one newspaper, which described him as 'Clive' this was actually before the family had been able either to identify him or to indicate whether they wished such information to be released. They were not to see the body until Friday, by which time Colin's friends, two of whom had already been detained and questioned along with his father, were also to react to the shock of his death. No effort had been made on the part of the Stoke Newington police to offer the family any form of condolence. Mr. Roach was not contacted in any way until they arrested him on 12 March.

1.61 Underlying everything was the fact that no plausible explanation of HOW Colin had died was provided for the family. The first question that Colin's father and his two younger brothers had asked when each told of his death (despite the appalling circumstances in which they were each told) was 'How could he shoot himself? He didn't have a gun'. When that is added to the question of WHY Colin would wish to shoot himself, it can be seen how the 'unanswered questions' arising from Colin's death would proliferate. Yet by the morning after Colin's death 'suicide' had become, and was to remain, the 'official' explanation of events: originating from the police, echoed in the press, and finally consolidated at the inquest.

Notes To Chapter 1:

1) In other versions of this account (e.g. *The Times*, 28.1.83) Mr. Scully quotes Colin Roach as saying 'I'll be safe here'. During the inquest he quoted Colin as having said both that he would be 'safe' and that he would be 'all right'.

Chapter 2

The Campaign For A Public Inquiry

2.1 Within one week of Colin Roach's death there had been two spontaneous demonstrations outside Stoke Newington police station after which a campaign had been formed in Hackney to seek an independent public inquiry into his death. The rapidity of the community's response owed much to the inadequacy of the 'suicide' explanation formulated by the police, the harsh policing of these and subsequent demonstrations, the immediate denial by the police of the Roach family's version of how they had been treated on 12-13 January and the significance of Colin Roach's death to a Black community that had experienced a history of oppressive policing.

2.2 Colin's family had been treated most callously by the police on the night of 12 January and the next morning on their visit to Stoke Newington police station. They were not invited to the post-mortem which took place that afternoon, 13 January, and did not see Colin's body until the afternoon of Friday 14 January. In her evidence to the Inquiry the Roach family's solicitor, Gareth Pierce, said that she tried repeatedly without success to contact the Head of Stoke Newington police station by telephone and did not get her calls returned until she first contacted the Head of community relations at Scotland Yard. Then, on Friday night a telephone call from Stoke Newington police station informed her that there would be a meeting at the station on Saturday, 15 January. In the Hackney Gazette of 18 January Commander Taylor of 'G' district was quoted as saying that this

Photograph: Humphrey Nemar

Black youths demonstrate outside Stoke Newington Police Station two days after Colin Roach's death (14 January 1983).

meeting was held to "defuse the situation" after the spontaneous demonstration held outside Stoke Newington police station on Friday 14 January.

2.3   The demonstration had occurred when Colin Roach's friends at the Saxon youth club in Bow had heard of his death via the news media. On 13 and 14 January several press, radio and T.V. bulletins had reported Colin's death as the apparent 'suicide' of a man believed to have a 'history of mental illness'. Some of Colin's friends told the Inquiry they were 'shocked' and 'surprised' to hear this news on Friday's early afternoon bulletin as they sat in the Saxon youth club watching TV. It seemed, they said "a bit far fetched" because Colin "had so much to live for". For instance they were aware at the time that Colin's sister had given birth on the day before his death and that he had been overjoyed about this. The events of Thursday afternoon were related to the Inquiry by a Youth worker at the Saxon club who had known Colin, Sylverius Thomas:

> Thames News told us the story, at about two o'clock — half two .. we wanted to find out exactly what happened ... so drew up placards ... we left the club with about 20-30 youths. It gradually got bigger. By the time we got to the police station there were about 80 or 90 youths outside. Black youths, white youths also ... We wanted to find out from the horse's mouth itself, from the person in charge of the police station, what had actually happened, and we didn't want any lies ... When we did arrive at the police station we found hostility from the police. We were told that we were obstructing the highway ... We were trying to get to the police station. We were told "no, you can't come in", because they had seen the crowd by then and after they felt threatened, they told us no. We asked for a superintendent ... we were told that he's not there, so we just stood by the left-hand side of the main entrance and we started chanting "public inquiry", "we want the truth" and so forth.

2.4   The outcome of the demonstration that afternoon was described by the Community Alliance for Police Accountability — Tower Hamlets (CAPA) in their written submission to this Inquiry:

> ... At one point, some people, feeling that "nothing was happening" to satisfy their demands sat down in the road to block the traffic. (The numbers taking part were considerably less than claimed in court by police) ... Demonstrators claim that at one point, about 50 police charged out of the police station, and began indiscriminately grabbing people; 8 people were arrested, charged with 13 offences. The demonstration broke in disorder and disarray, caused according to those people participating, largely by the actions of the police. 7 Black and one white person were arrested. At least four of those arrested, including the white youth, had known Colin well. One other had gone to the police station by appointment to see an officer there, and another had been job-hunting, and stopped on the opposite side of the road to look.

(A more detailed examination of the trials which followed the arrests on this and all subsequent demonstrations is made in Appendix 5, which is a further extract from CAPA's evidence to the Inquiry).

2.5   According to Joe Joseph (whom Colin Roach had tried unsuccessfully to contact on the night of his death) he was standing outside the police station during the demonstration when he was asked to come inside alone, after the police heard him say that his brother (Jim Joseph) had been with Colin on the fatal night. Inside the police station he was asked questions about Colin such as "what was troubling him?" which he refused to answer. He told the Inquiry:

> I asked them why it took so long before they let his father know (before the police told James Roach of Colin's death).
> ... they said ... "we couldn't tell his father straight away or get him to identify the body because it would have been too distressing for him".

2.6   The statement that the police "couldn't tell his father straight away" appears to admit that Mr. Roach was kept waiting for 2½ hours. However on the day after the demonstration, Saturday 15 January, D.C.S. Robertson was to claim that he had told James Roach of his son's death between 12.30 and 12.45 a.m. just after Mr. Roach's arrival at Stoke Newington police station. He made this claim in the meeting called by Commander Taylor to "defuse the situation" (after the demonstration) and it was a claim which would remain part of the 'official' explanation of Colin Roach's death thereafter.

2.7   The meeting of 15 January with community representatives did not succeed in defusing the situation at all for several reasons.

2.8   During the meeting the police made several claims which were not readily accepted. Both Commander Taylor and Detective Chief Superintendent Robertson, who was introduced as being in charge of the investigation, mentioned that they were satisfied no one else was involved in Colin's death and admitted to have said they were not seeking any other suspects in their first press release which Commander Taylor said had been at 1.30am on 13 January. However *they did not say what had satisfied them.* Taylor also claimed that the information in the press of 13 January that Colin had a 'history of mental illness' had not come from the police.

2.9   Robertson denied that Mrs. Roach had been gripped by the throat by a WPC during the police search of her home. He also read out some of the post-mortem report describing the nature of the fatal injury, saying that the coroner had authorised the release of the report, yet the Roach family (as pointed out in the meeting by their solicitor) had neither been told of the post-mortem nor given a copy of this report. In addition to this, as mentioned above, Robertson claimed Mr. Roach had not been kept waiting 2½ hours but had been told of Colin's death between 12.30 and 12.45am. Thus, the police had effectively restated their 'suicide' conclusion without explaining how they had arrived at it and denied any impropriety in their treatment of the Roach family and statements to the press.

2.10   Clearly, the protests were not likely to cease following this unsatisfactory meeting. On Monday, 17 January Colin's friends held another spontaneous demonstration outside

Stoke Newington police station. According to the evidence of CAPA, based on observations at the scene and later during the trials of the 18 people arrested:

> People had gathered outside the police station, had gone for a short march and had returned . . . Again demonstrators' evidence backs up the notion that there was a predetermined plan to charge from the station to effect indiscriminate arrests . . .

2.11 The situation by this time had become a cause of concern to many people within the Black community in Hackney. On the evening of 17 January the Roach family gave their permission for the Hackney Black People's Association (HBPA) to hold a public meeting in a community centre in Stoke Newington. The meeting was attended by over 150 individual and representatives of organisations. Speakers included Barnor Hesse and Lester Lewis representing HBPA and Councillor Dennis Twomey.

It is here worth noting that HBPA had in November 1982 initiated a resolution (which was subsequently taken up by Hackney Borough Council) that there should be an independent public inquiry into policing in Hackney. At that time HBPA had argued that "enough evidence of police wrong-doing and police violence against Black people" was available to necessitate such an inquiry. On 17 January several speakers emphasised that Colin Roach's death was only the latest incident in a history of such 'police wrong-doing' in Hackney. According to an article in the *Caribbean Times* of 28 January 1983 entitled 'Another cover up?',a speaker from HBPA told the meeting that some people in the community feared Colin Roach "might have been killed by the police or other people and that there was a cover up being stage managed". It was in this context that the meeting decided to form a support committee for the Roach family and passed a unanimous resolution calling for an independent public inquiry into Colin Roach's death, which became the main objective of the 'Roach Family Support Committee' (RFSC). It was also decided to hold a protest march in Hackney on the following Saturday, 22 January.

2.12 The demand for a public inquiry into the death of Colin Roach, originating as a slogan expressed in the spontaneous protests of 14 and 17 January and consolidated by the formation of the RFSC was to attract considerable support during the months following January 1983. The RFSC organised four major demonstrations in Hackney on 22 January, 12 February, 12 March and 14 May. These encountered increasingly severe police reactions leading to large numbers of arrests. A secondary role was played by many other organisations and individuals who wrote to the Home Secretary after passing motions or resolutions in support of a public inquiry. However, it was by means of peaceful demonstrations that many people in Hackney and the Black community in particular attempted to show their support for a public inquiry. This was not made at all easy by the police.

2.13 Before examining the experiences of those demonstrations, it is important to ask what sort of inquiry was being demanded. Although this was not spelled out initially by those involved, it was usually implied that it would be of the kind provided for in the Police Act 1964. Section 32 of the Act provides that the Home Secretary may cause a local inquiry to be held by a person appointed by him 'into any matter connected with the policing of any area'. The section also provides that such an inquiry may be held in either public or private, as the Home Secretary directs. Since 1964, there had been only two inquiries under section 32 of the Police Act 1964. The first, in 1974, examined the events in Red Lion Square on 15 June when anti-fascist demonstrators clashed with police and one man, Kevin Gately, was killed. The second was the inquiry into the Brixton 'Disorders' of April 1981. Both inquiries were headed by Lord Scarman.

2.14 In their letter to the Home Secretary, William Whitelaw, of 3 February 1983 the RFSC asked for an independent inquiry into "the death and circumstances surrounding the death of Colin Roach" which, it was argued "should be held in

Photograph: Humphrey Nemar

22 January 1983 demonstration

public and should have the sort of Black representation which has the trust, respect and confidence of the Roach Family Support Committee and the Black community". Some groups followed the RFSC by specifically calling for an inquiry into the death of Colin Roach, while others phrased the subject of the inquiry as 'Stoke Newington Police Station' or 'police-community relations in Hackney'. However it was clear from the community reaction to Colin's death that these subjects were all inter-related, so any inquiry set up into either of the latter two topics would have to include the death of Colin Roach. Similarly, the RFSC pointed out in their letter to the Home Secretary that "The circumstances surrounding Colin's death are wider than the fundamental and still inadequately answered questions of the how and why of his death". These circumstances, it was argued, included "the entire panoply of racist actions and attitudes exhibited by the police since 12/1/83".

It is worth adding here that to argue for a public inquiry into the death of Colin Roach presented another difficulty. In their evidence to the Inquiry, the RFSC told us that although the question of 'who killed Colin Roach' was their main impetus, to ask the more detailed question — 'how and in what circumstances did Colin die?' required that they "contest a definition which already existed, which was that Colin committed suicide". They pointed out that this definition had been based on a 'retrospective account' of Colin's death: Colin was identified as 'depressed' and 'mentally ill', therefore 'suicidal', yet to explain why a 'suicide' took place in a police station the account was "led back to mental illness as a justification". Challenging the illogicality of this account of Colin's death then, was also an essential element of the campaign.

2.15 The first RFSC demonstration held on 22 January passed off relatively peacefully until it attempted to disperse. According to the evidence of CAPA, based on the observations of volunteers at the scene and in court:

> The march, . . . ended at Stoke Newington Common with speeches, just after 4.00pm. Something like 100-150 people according to police, or 50 according to those participating, decided to go back to Stoke Newington Police Station to

picket it. It was in Stoke Newington High Street, and in the roads immediately near the Police Station off Stoke Newington High Street, that the arrests and violence occurred.

Piecing together the picture from witnesses' statements and evidence given in court, it would seem that a fairly large group of people, some running, most walking, were going up Stoke Newington High Street towards the Police Station. At least 2 serials possibly more, appeared from out of their large green Police vans near the police station and began to rush towards the people, most of whom turned and fled back down Stoke Newington High Street to avoid trouble. Then they were confronted by officers running towards them from the opposite direction, from the south. The police also blocked side roads, so that people who had run into them, or were already in them, trying to get out of the way, were trapped. Indiscriminate grabbing of people then occurred on a large scale, and several were assaulted, then, and later at the police station. 22 people were arrested — 21 Black and 1 white, 19 men and 3 women — 1 was a juvenile.

2.16 We were also told by several people arrested about their subsequent treatment. At least two witnesses told us that following the arrests they were taken into the rear courtyard of Stoke Newington police station where:

> There was queue to be 'processed' and have your photo taken with a polaroid camera by the officer who arrested you. (Extract from evidence to the Inquiry of Chas Holmes of RFSC).

The purpose of these photographs became clear on the next two demonstrations where some of the witnesses who gave evidence to the Inquiry are certain that the police had begun 'targetting' individuals for arrest as soon as they recognised them from previous marches.

The days following the demonstration on 22 January led to a full-blown condemnation of the demonstration in the Sunday papers of 23 January based on a story originating from a police press release, stating that people involved in the demonstration had been involved in the robbery of a jeweller's shop in Amhurst Way, Stoke Newington. This is

Photograph: David Hoffman

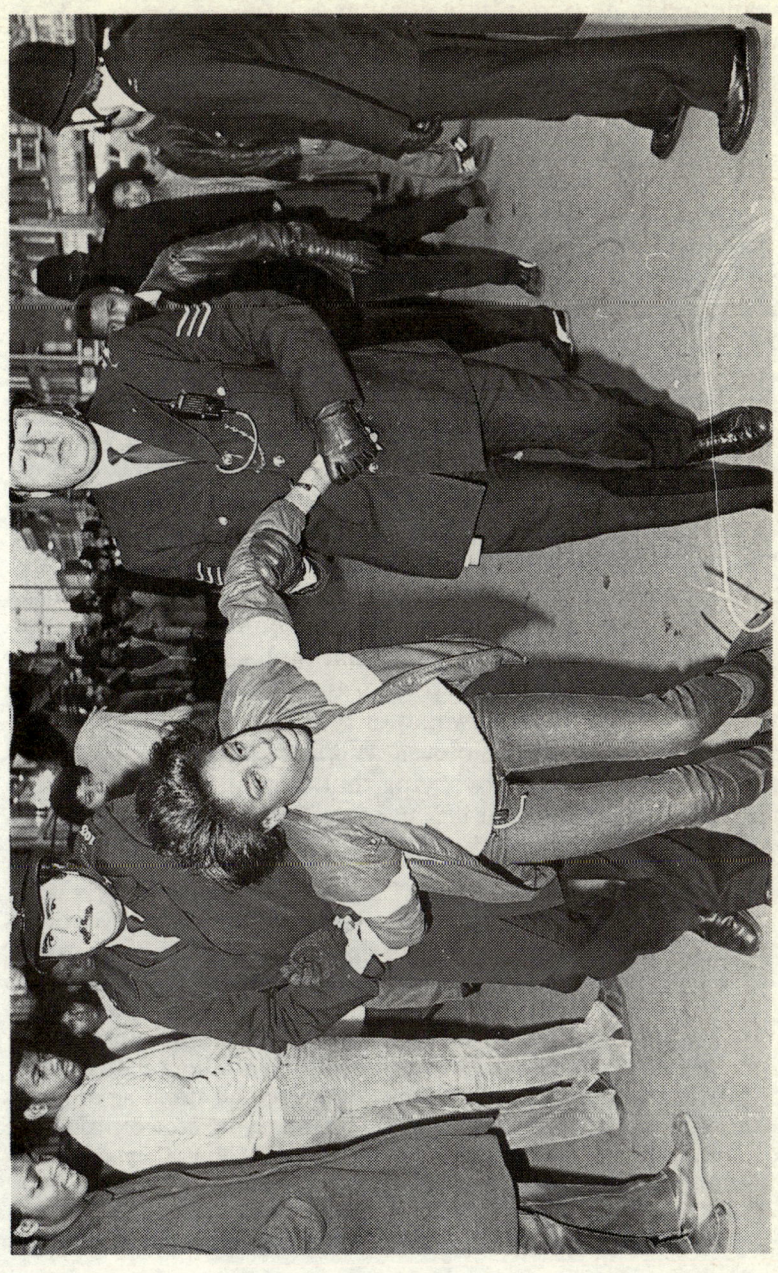

A young woman is arrested in Stoke Newington High Street, following the RFSC demonstration of 22 January 1983.

examined in more depth in chapter 4. However, when it was admitted by the police that the robbery had nothing to do with the demonstration, only one national daily newspaper carried this item of correction.

2.17 It was because of the indiscriminate arrests which followed the demonstration and the apparent attempt by the police to link the campaign with a criminal act such as the robbery on 22 January that questions were again raised about the intentions of the police. For example, a bulletin published by the RFSC offered the view that if the police and Government did not have something to hide, then they would not have responded in the way that they did. Shortly after that demonstration several things happened which suggested to some people that the police may have been hiding something. It was reported by Ian Haig of Hackney Council for Racial Equality (HCRE) in the press (*City Limits* 28 January 1983) that HCRE had received evidence from two Black men in their twenties, one of whom had said he had been 'questioned in Stoke Newington police station with a gun held to his head', the other that he had been 'visited in this house by police, who pulled guns on him'. It was also revealed (in the *Voice* newspaper of 5 February 1983) that a Black youth worker, Dolores Williams, claimed to have overheard police officers saying that they shot Colin Roach. The following statement is a sworn affidavit she made which was reproduced in another RFSC Bulletin:

> On Wednesday 26 January 1983 at about 8am I was arrested at home by officers from Stoke Newington police station. There were a number of plain clothes officers who came to my home together with one uniformed WPC. The officer in my case was D.C. Randall. I was taken to Stoke Newington police station together with Ian McNeil who was also arrested. While we were being booked in at the station at about 8.45am the officers who had come to my home were all standing around us. I was arrested on suspicion of receiving stolen property and the officers seemed to be annoyed that they had not found any stolen property at my home.
> One plain clothes officer said 'we killed Colin Roach because he would not give us the evidence we wanted'. His

Photograph: Humphrey Nemar

RFSC demonstration of 12 February 1983 reaches Stoke Newington High Street

colleagues laughed at this remark. Ian McNeil replied 'its no laughing matter'. The same officer said 'we shot him with a sawn off shotgun'.

That was the end of the conversation. Colin Roach was not mentioned again throughout the period of my detention.

2.18   The link between Colin Roach's death and the policing experience of Black people in Hackney was also made during February 1983 by the publication of HCRE's dossier of 40 cases entitled 'Policing in Hackney — a record of HCRE's experience 1978-1982'.

In one of these cases, that of the White family (which although it took place in 1976, only came to light in 1982, following a successful claim for damages in the Civil courts); a High Court Judge had condemned the "monstrous, wicked and shameful conduct" of the police, adding that there had also been an orchestrated attempt to mislead the court in order "to cover up" illegality and unjustified use of force.

2.19   The demonstration of 12 February according to CAPA, encountered still more 'trouble':

> The 'trouble' on this demonstration was, it became clear as the trials progressed, orchestrated by police on the Narrow Way, as the march, which had passed without incident, was nearing Hackney Town Hall on its return. (After sitting through the 12 March trials, some people began to wonder if this was part of a deliberate policy on the part of the police — to create disorder to discredit the march, as an even worse example of provocation and stage-management emerged from those trials.)

The Narrow Way, as its name suggests, is where Mare Street narrows, and it would have been, on a Saturday afternoon, quite dense with shoppers. There was thus the opportunity for police to create maximum disorder and effect. They blocked off sections of the marchers from each other; had several serials, or District Support Units, waiting in side roads at which point police officers swooped out, without apparently any coherent orders (or none that they could recall in court) to make arbitrary arrests.

The initial arrests, and treatment of the arrested people, provoked anger, and gave rise to further arrests. 9 people

Funeral of Colin Roach

were arrested — all male and all Black, two were juveniles at the time of arrest, though 1 later became an adult.

2.20   It was also in February and early March 1983 that some of the organisations and individuals who had written to the Home Secretary, asking him to set up a public inquiry into the death of Colin Roach received replies. All of these were negative. The RFSC, who had written to the Home Secretary on 3 February, received a reply from the Home Office on 2 March. Others receiving replies included the Commission for Racial Equality, Hackney Borough Council, Hackney Black Peoples' Association and Ernie Roberts, M.P. for Hackney North and Stoke Newington. Most of these replies by or on behalf of the Home Secretary, William Whitelaw, echoed what he had said in the earliest of them, written on 3 February to the Deputy Chairman of the Commission for Racial Equality, Clifton Robinson. In that letter, Mr. Whitelaw had said:

> I understand and share the concern that there should be a full, independent and public inquiry into this tragedy, but this is precisely what the coroner's inquest . . . will provide.

2.21   The statement that an inquest was equivalent to a public inquiry was to be contradicted on two occasions: By Dr. Chambers (the St. Pancras coroner) who told a community delegation on 21 March that the Home Secretary had been "wrongly or badly advised". And also by a High Court judge, Mr. Justice Woolf who, in a ruling on 30 April on the question of where the Roach inquest would be held, declared that "although an inquest is an inquiry which is to be held in public . . . it is not intended to be a public inquiry, using the phrase as referring to the type of inquiry Mr. Whitelaw had been asked to set up". It should also be noted that all those who had demanded a public inquiry into the death of Colin Roach had already pointed out that an inquest could not by its very nature act as the kind of comprehensive inquiry which was sought. For example, the RFSC when writing to the Home Secretary had made reference to "the bitter experience Black people have had in relation to the narrow terms of reference of coroners' inquests" and had cited the inquest into the 'New Cross Massacre' of 1981 as an example of their experience. It must also be noted that when Mr. Justice Woolf ruled that an inquest was not a public inquiry, the Home Secretary then argued, in a letter of 19 May to Chris Price M.P. that "it has never been my intention to suggest that an inquest and a public inquiry were synonymous". However, Mr. Whitelaw was still able to argue that it would be "premature" to make a decision on "any inquiry... until the inquest had been completed". This view and his earlier views that the inquest would provide a public inquiry may have been intended as a delaying 'tactic' to defuse the campaign.

2.22 This 'tactic' had one effect: Out of two Parliamentary Early Day Motions initiated in early February, demanding a public inquiry into the death of Colin Roach, the one which asked for the demand to be considered *after* the inquest (tabled by Stanley Clinton Davis, M.P. for Hackney south) obtained more signatures than the one which left out the time clause and simply urged "the Home Secretary to make an investigation into policing practices in Hackney — Stoke Newington" (tabled by Ernie Roberts, M.P. for Hackney North and Stoke Newington).

2.23 The third RFSC demonstration on 12 March 1983, began at Hackney Town Hall and its route took it past Stoke Newington police station. Again, it was on the way back from the police station to Hackney Town Hall that the march was attacked. According to CAPA:

> This was probably the most heavily policed of all the demonstrations — observers suggest that there were 2 police officers for every demonstrator, and photos certainly bear out the impression of rows of police, shoulder to shoulder, in an extremely oppressive presence. This was also the most complex and difficult march of which to obtain a clear picture ...

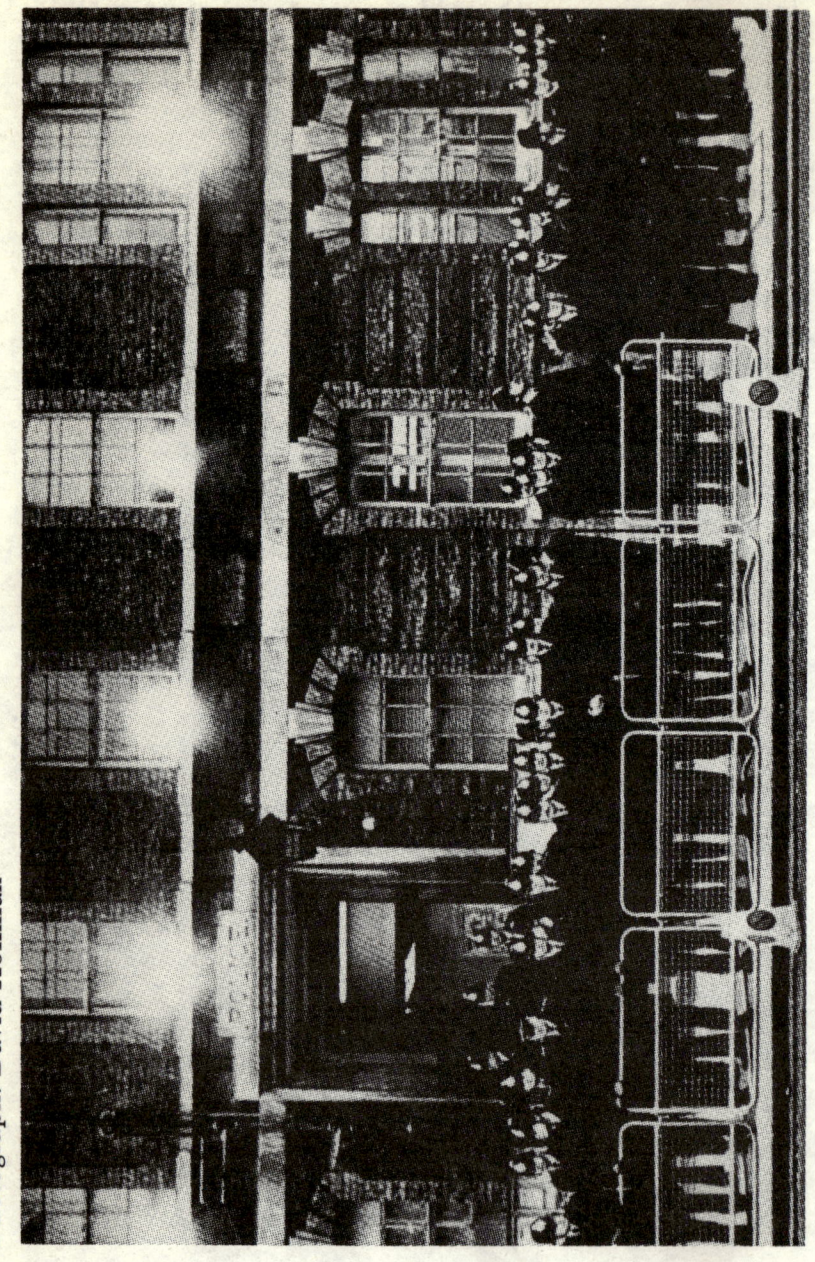

Photograph: David Hoffman

Stoke Newington police prepare for the arrival of the RFSC demonstration on 12

From observers' and independent eye witness accounts, as well as from evidence given in court, it would seem that there was a deliberate, planned decision to smash the march at its most populous point, and where there would be the maximum disorder created by police — Kingsland High Street shopping area. One is drawn to the inevitable conclusion that there was a well-organised plan for the following reasons. The police control vehicle at the head of the march moved ahead to allow a police carrier which had been in front it, (the large green coach which holds 20 men) to drop back and get between it and the body of the march. On the left hand side of the road, the cordon funnelled people into a narrower path, while on the right hand side, police had narrowed the width of the march, so that its extreme right hand edge was on the white line in the centre of the road. The right hand side of the road was kept clear, and while the above was going on, 3 or 4 white transit police transports sped down this alley, and positioned themselves to the front, middle and rear of the march, ready to receive persons who had not yet been arrested.

Police cleared a gap between the lorry and the rest of the march; at the front of the march, the march lorry was attacked — (there is no other way of describing it) by police. Some mounted the open-backed lorry to remove the people on it, while others smashed the driver's window and hauled him out (Dennis Twomey). People at the back of the march didn't yet realise that the front had stopped; people on the left hand side suddenly found themselves being squashed towards their right, and people started being grabbed. One piece of police brutality gave rise to anger, and further arrests on the left side, and in the area immediately surrounding the march lorry, police from the right hand side began to wade into the densely packed crowd, and plucked out random people for no apparent reason. Three people who were no part of the demonstration, but were just out shopping, were caught and arrested. James Roach was grabbed and manhandled in an appalling way; photographs show expressions of hatred, or glee, on the faces of the officers surrounding him — 4/5 initially, and 10/12 as he was being placed in the van. He was assaulted. It doesn't take a genius to imagine what the sight of his arrest did to the people nearby.

The Roach Family Support Committee banner was snatched by the police and dismantled. Mrs. Roach, who had been in the passenger seat next to Dennis in the march lorry, and who had caught a glimpse of her husband being dragged away, took the banner and with others, continued the march on foot, holding the banner in front of her. Throughout the march, many observers say police, from senior officers down, were extremely provocative and threatening to a number of individuals. They also seemed to get more tense as the march neared City Road Police Station, where during the course of the demonstration held outside there 4 people were arrested — 2 Black men and two white men.

2.24 Very little was ever written or said at the time about this demonstration in the media, despite the way in which it had been policed. We have selected some extracts from witnesses who were arrested at the time who gave evidence to the Inquiry in order to illustrate what took place more fully.

Mr. Roach was arrested when he enquired why officers were holding the mother of his five-year old godson down on the ground. He told us that:

> As quick as I said that, it was a set of them on my arm, one got me around my head, one punched me in my face and they took me and arrested me at the same time. When I saw the photographs I couldn't believe how many police could have one man and the man is not violent.

Sylverius Thomas had just observed a friend being "jumped on by six or seven policemen".

> I made one step from the spot and I just got jumped on... from there I saw Mr. Roach actually being arrested... I was... being held... spreadeagled... I was chucked on the seat (ie of the green police coach into which arrestees were being taken) ... I couldn't see in front of me, all I could see was my left hand side through the glass outside... One policeman had his... elbows on my throat... Another one had one of my arms. Another had another of my arms... There was one on my right leg, one was on my left leg. I was... trying to say to the policeman 'I'm not resisting your arrest, so why can't you stop choking me?' He was just laughing and calling us names (such as) 'Black bastard'...

According to another witness:

> Quite a few photographers were arrested on that day... before the march was broken up and the video crew which had

been following us was arrested also . . . that might seem to indicate that the police definitely didn't want many records of what happened on the day.

2.25 It seems clear that by March 1983 the oppressive policing at the demonstrations was exacting a heavy toll on the campaign. The trials of the defendants, who by mid March numbered over 80, were to last most of 1983. These trials required time and resources to deal with, whether fines for defendants not legally aided or for people to picket the court where the cases were being held. Where defendants were remanded in custody or given prison sentences, it took them off the streets making it more difficult to attend marches or meetings e.g. some bail conditions even required that they stayed away from Hackney. The legal attack upon the campaign was one reason for the formation in March 1983 of the Stoke Newington and Hackney Defence Campaign (SNHDC). In his evidence Ace Kelly of the SNHDC explained that:

> We saw that . . . to win the cases . . . you had to have good . . . solicitors, you had to get all your witnesses together. All the paperwork, all what is really basic, had to be done . . . On top of that you had to have the publicity . . .

2.26 The SNHDC in addition to campaigning for a public inquiry on behalf of the defendants, made a formal complaint to the Lord Chancellor about magistrate Michael Johnstone of Highbury Magistrates' Court who had heard many of the cases arising from the arrests made on demonstrations (these are examined in more detail in Appendix 5). In their letter of 19 May, the SNHDC cited details of nine cases in which Johnstone had shown "consistent hostility . . . against defendants" as well as "disapproval of anybody who participated in the demonstrations" and "blatant racism towards Black defendants". It was pointed out that Johnstone had consistently ignored defence witnesses' photographic evidence and glaring contradictions in the evidence of police witnesses. He had also shown a "refusal in all the cases to grant bail pending appeal against conviction".

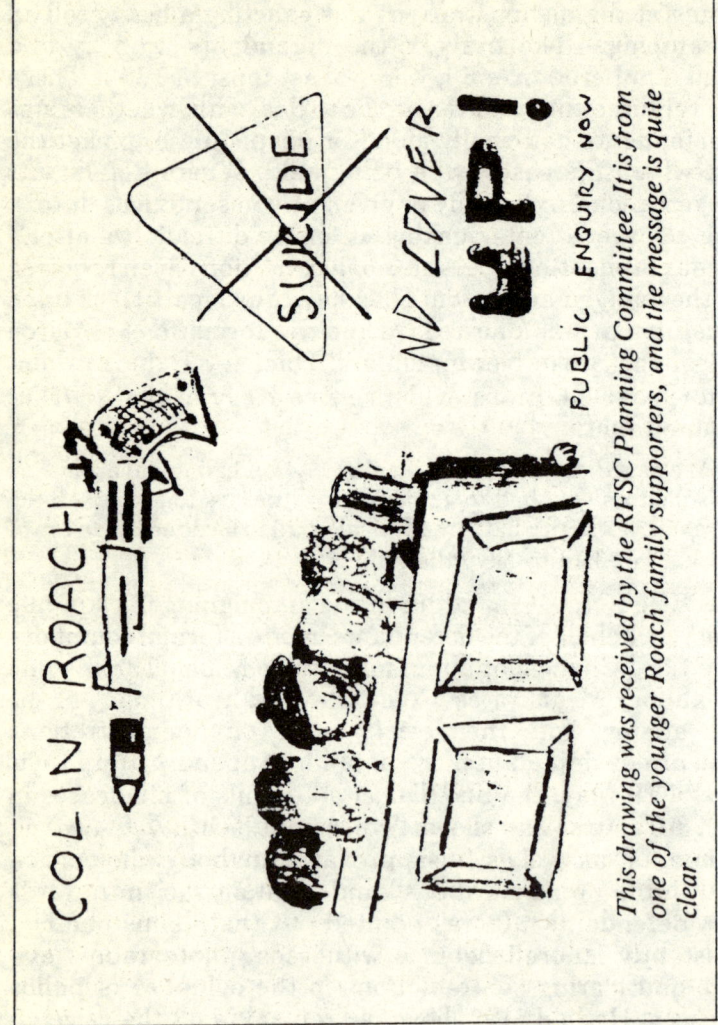

This drawing was received by the RFSC Planning Committee. It is from one of the younger Roach family supporters, and the message is quite clear.

2.27   The result of this complaint, which had ended calling for "the removal of magistrate Johnstone from these cases" was, according to Ace Kelly of SNHDC, that Johnstone "took one more case" before apparently being removed from the trials, although this was not formally admitted by the authorities to have been done.

2.28   By the time that the RFSC had held its fourth, demonstration, which was on 14 May, two months had elapsed. According to CAPA, the "entire demeanour" of the police had changed. Only two arrests were made and the police behaved "without provocation, rancour or brutality". Three reasons were suggested by CAPA for this. The first was the presence of a National Union of Journalists contingent which had followed the reports in the NUJ publication of journalists being beaten up by police on previous marches. Secondly, it had been announced during the week before the march that there would be a general election on 9 June. Thirdly, there was the presence of M.Ps (including Ernie Roberts) on the march. It was also pointed out by some of the other witnesses who gave evidence to the Inquiry that there was a higher proportion of white people among the marchers on 14 May and that this along with the presence of a BBC-TV film crew may have resulted in a different style of policing from that used on the previous demonstrations which were mostly Black in composition.

The Venue of the Inquest
2.29   Although it was not, strictly speaking, part of the campaign for a public inquiry, it is important to note that many of those who were calling for a public inquiry were also involved in the dispute which arose over the venue for the inquest into Colin Roach's death. The Coroner, Dr. Douglas Chambers intended to hold the inquest in the small St. Pancras Coroner's Court, but on 21 March he received a delegation from Hackney Council, and Hackney Council for Racial Equality who urged him to move the inquest to a larger venue because of the considerable public interest in

the case. Hackney Council even offered its council chamber. These requests were refused. In April the Greater London Council also urged that the inquest be moved and following this the coroner applied to the High Court for a hearing to settle the issue. At the hearing counsel for the Metropolitan Police said that the police did not oppose moving the inquest but they did object to it being transferred to Hackney Town Hall since they feared 'disorder' if the inquest was held there. On 29 April, Mr. Justice Woolf ruled that neither Hackney Council nor the GLC had any powers to compel the coroner to move the inquest but, he added, it ought to be possible to find a room larger than the small St. Pancras Coroner's Court without at the same time moving it to an 'arena'. Counsel for Dr. Chambers then announced that he was seeking permission to hold the inquest in Clerkenwell County Court which had seating for about 100.

The Police Precept

2.30   For its part, Hackney Council's Police Committee resolved in early February to withhold its annual contribution of 4 million to the cost of the Metropolitan Police — the 'precept'; a decision which was supported by a full Council meeting on 23 February 1983. The Council adopted the following resolution:

> That the Council take whatever steps are open to it to withhold the payment of the police precept both as an expression of anger at the state of policing in Hackney and with a view to bringing home to the Government the community demands for an independent inquiry into policing in Hackney.

In the event the Council was told by its legal advisers in March that it could not lawfully withhold the money and the precept was paid.

2.31   The gesture of withholding the police precept obtained much publicity. However, it is important to note that as with most of the 'supportive' actions made by organisations other than the RFSC, it was a gesture which *followed* rather than *led* the initiatives planned by the RFSC itself. A letter from the RFSC to all Hackney Councillors prepared for the Council meeting of February at which the decision was taken asked not only for them to vote to withhold the police precept but also to take a vote of 'no confidence' in Stoke Newington police and to 'break all links' with the police "unless and until" a public inquiry was held. Hackney Council never in fact passed the 'break links' resolution, although on 25 February the resolution was passed by the Hackney branch of NALGO after being put forward, also in response to the RFSC, by union members from the Council's Social Services department.

2.32 For the RFSC it must be said that neither the inquest nor the attention given to the inquest in the media was the main issue. However, as explained by Chas Holmes of the RFSC in his evidence to the Inquiry:

> It was always a battle for us to get... our point of view across ... The best illustration of that is the way that the inquest "became the issue": where to have the inquest, when it was... That was from the media side ... From the government side they were telling us we should wait for the inquest, the inquest will answer all our problems, whereas we had always said that the inquest will not answer our problems: That's why we're asking for an inquiry. So it was very difficult to put across what the campaign wanted and what the family wanted.

2.33 To give an indication of what the RFSC attempted to 'put across' at the time, it is worth noting the press conference of 14 April 1983 in which they argued that the inquest:

> Has always been an inescapable irrelevance. Whatever the verdict, our campaign for an independent public inquiry into Colin Roach's death will continue. In this sense there can be no 'good' or 'bad' verdict that can come out of the inquest, since it has no legal power whatsoever to consider, if necessary, matters of blame or guilt.

Photograph: David Hoffman

Colin's parents, Pamela and James Roach at RFSC's candlelight vigil outside Stoke Newington Police Station on the first anniversary of Colin Roach's death (12

The inadequacy of the coroner's inquest was emphasised by a speaker at the press conference, John Collins, the brother of Simeon Collins, who had died on 8 December 1982, also in Hackney. A verdict of misadventure had meant that his family: "came out asking more questions . . . than when we went in". As we show in the next chapter, this proved to be the case again with the inquest into the death of Colin Roach.

After The Inquest

2.34   The RFSC stated in a press release on 21 June 1983 that:

> The case for an independent public inquiry remains undiminished by the illogical and nonsensical verdict of suicide at Clerkenwell County Court yesterday — people who think otherwise simply do not understand the case.

The strength of the case for an independent public inquiry following the inquest is examined in more detail in Chapter 5 (the wider political context). Here it should be noted that shortly after the inquest the RFSC also obtained a favourable legal opinion from Lord Gifford QC on the prospects of challenging the new Home Secretary's decision not to hold a public inquiry (announced in answer to a 'planted' parliamentary question on *28 June*). This opinion is contained in Appendix 3. In addition, they promoted a resolution calling for organisations in Hackney to 'break links' with the police, with some success.

2.35   According to a Bulletin of the RFSC published in 1984, the rationale for the demand that:

> There shall be no links or co-operation with the police unless and until there has been an independent public inquiry into the death of Colin Roach and surrounding circumstances' (the 'Break Links' resolution) was as follows:

> When we look at previous Black people's struggle against the British State, we see that the State can wipe out a campaign:
> — by using the oppressive powers of the police;
> — by refusing to meet the demands of the campaign.

They know that by doing this, most campaigns will fade away, and will not permanently oppose the State. By permanent opposition we do not mean we just continue with the traditional means of campaigning in the hope that the State will have change of heart. We mean that we must change the way we relate to the State in order that we do register our permanent opposition. This is explained in our 'Break Links' resolution.

2.36 The RFSC also continued its campaign by launching (in July 1983) a petition to the European Parliament seeking its support for a public inquiry. The petition (which was not eventually successful) concluded:

> Given the history of racism and racist violence associated with Stoke Newington police station, the failure of the police to investigate crimes committed against Black people; the police tendency to form hasty conclusions . . . when investigating the murder of Black people; the fact that inquests in the United Kingdom have been falling into disrepute over the years . . . We . . . strongly urge Members of the European Parliament to support our demand for an independent public inquiry . . .

Chapter 3

The Inquest

> When we do go to that inquest they already have the verdict waiting. They're only going to go through everything to make it look good, but the verdict is already there on paper . . . (Mrs. Roach, quoted in March 1983).

> The Colin Roach inquest was one of a long line of inquests that have cast doubt on the independence of the coroner's jury from the coroner, and of the coroner from the police (INQUEST-United Campaign for Justice-extract from submission of evidence to the Inquiry).

> The jury didn't make up their minds — the coroner made up their minds for them, James Roach, quoted following the verdict on 21 June 1983.

3.1   The inquest proper began on 6 June 1983 in Clerkenwell County Court. It consisted of 6 days of proceedings held over a 2 week period. Evidence was heard from a total of 51 witnesses, of whom 16 were police officers from Stoke Newington police station, 11 were 'experts' in various technical, medical, forensic and pathological areas and 6 were friends and family of Colin Roach. On the final day, Monday 20 June, Coroner Dr. Douglas Chambers offered the jury of 6 white and 4 Black people the only summary of the evidence which they were entitled to receive and directed them to choose from 4 possible verdicts: Suicide, misadventure, unlawful killing or an open verdict. The jury retired at about

1.30pm. By 3.30pm the jurors had still not agreed on a verdict and they asked for further directions from the coroner. He said that he would accept a 'majority' verdict providing that the size of the minority did not exceed 2. The jury retired again and finally, at 4.43pm, returned a verdict of suicide by an 8-2 majority. All 10 members of the jury then wrote a letter to the Home Secretary, in which they stated that:

> As members of the jury, and having heard all the evidence in question — we fairly reached a decision of suicide but we are deeply distressed at the handling of the case by the police regarding the Roach family. We feel that the bereaved family were kept in the dark over the death of their son — and that the police were not sympathetic to the situation. We also feel that the case could have been investigated more professionally and extensively. We hope you will be able to look into the matter.

3.2   The response of the Home Secretary to that letter is examined in Chapter 5. Here we examine whether the inquest allowed the jury any 'fair' choice at all in reaching the decision of 'suicide', given that much of what emerged about Colin's death was from one source, police officers whom, in the jury's own words, had not investigated his death 'professionally' or 'extensively'. We also examine whether the English coroner's inquest is capable of providing an adequate forum to investigate the wider issues raised by controversial deaths, such as that of Colin Roach, given that as the law stands, the purpose of an inquest shall be directed solely to ascertaining:

> who the deceased was [and] how, why and where the deceased came by his (sic) death. [1]

There were already a plethora of 'unanswered questions' arising from Colin's death by June 1983. What remains to be seen is whether the inquest provided even a few answers, or whether it actually multiplied the unanswered questions.

3.3   Finally, certain key issues emerge out of inquest evidence. These we examine under the following headings:

'When did Colin die?' 'Where did Colin die?' How did Colin die?' 'Could Colin's death have been witnessed?' 'What was the police's reaction to Colin's death' and what was 'Colin's state of mind?'

Inquests — An Overview — Part 1

3.4 According to the evidence submitted to the Inquiry by INQUEST:

> "The coroner's system is an ancient procedure for investigating sudden deaths, which developed long before modern methods of policing and forensic medicine. Nowadays, any suspicious death is investigated before the inquest by police and forensic scientists, and the inquest gives the impression of being a rubber stamp for conclusions that have been reached before it begins. This is particularly unsatisfactory where the conduct of the police is itself in question. It is true that the family of the deceased and any other 'properly interested persons' have the right to be represented and to ask questions and that where the death occurred in police or prison custody and in certain other cases, the final decision is made by a jury. These democratic features of the inquest are important, but their practical significance is reduced by a number of procedural defects, all of which were present at the Colin Roach inquest".

Following a detailed examination of the Colin Roach inquest we will discuss the limitations of inquests in general and the wider issue of inquest reform. As an introduction, these general issues may be usefully summarised as follows:

1. The democratic features of the coroner's inquest are in general overshadowed by a number of procedural defects which make it inappropriate to deal with certain categories of deaths.

2. In his conduct of an inquest the coroner is particularly dependent on the police investigation of the death and the witness statements which this investigation provides.

3. Witness statements taken by the police are privileged and need not be shown to the legal representatives of the family of the deceased or to any other interested party.

4. The coroner has much more discretionary power over the conduct of the proceedings than a judge in a criminal trial and is the only person permitted to sum up the evidence before the jury. The scope for the jury to challenge his interpretation of the evidence is therefore limited.

5. The findings of an inquest can be expressed only in a limited range of standardized verdicts which may not adequately express the 'cause' of death.

6. Interested parties, such as the family of the deceased, do not receive legal aid for representation at the inquest.

Some Discrepancies in Police Evidence

3.5 According to their evidence at the inquest, no Stoke Newington police officer witnessed the death of Colin Roach. However, the nature of that evidence is at times contradictory, and this raises significant questions about the whereabouts of several officers at the time of Colin's death.

First, at least 4 police officers who were named as having been involved in the events of that night by other officers did not appear at the inquest and a statement was produced from only 1 of the 4. Second, it appears that out of 15 officers who did appear at the inquest ranging from constables to a Chief Inspector and a Detective Chief Superintendent, all but one, a Detective Sergeant, did not make any notes whatsoever on the night of the shooting. Yet, some, including the officer who said that he found Colin's body claimed to have a 'vivid recollection' of events. In other cases, the police appear to have suffered from a collective loss of memory, forgetting events, times, the contents of the statements which they wrote after the events, and whether other officers were with them at particular times. What is most significant is that their evidence does not give a satisfactory answer to 'where', 'when' or 'how' Colin Roach came by his death, yet as shown later it gave sufficient cause on more than one occasion for those observing the inquest, including Mr. and Mrs. Roach, to accuse police officers who were giving evidence of 'telling lies'.

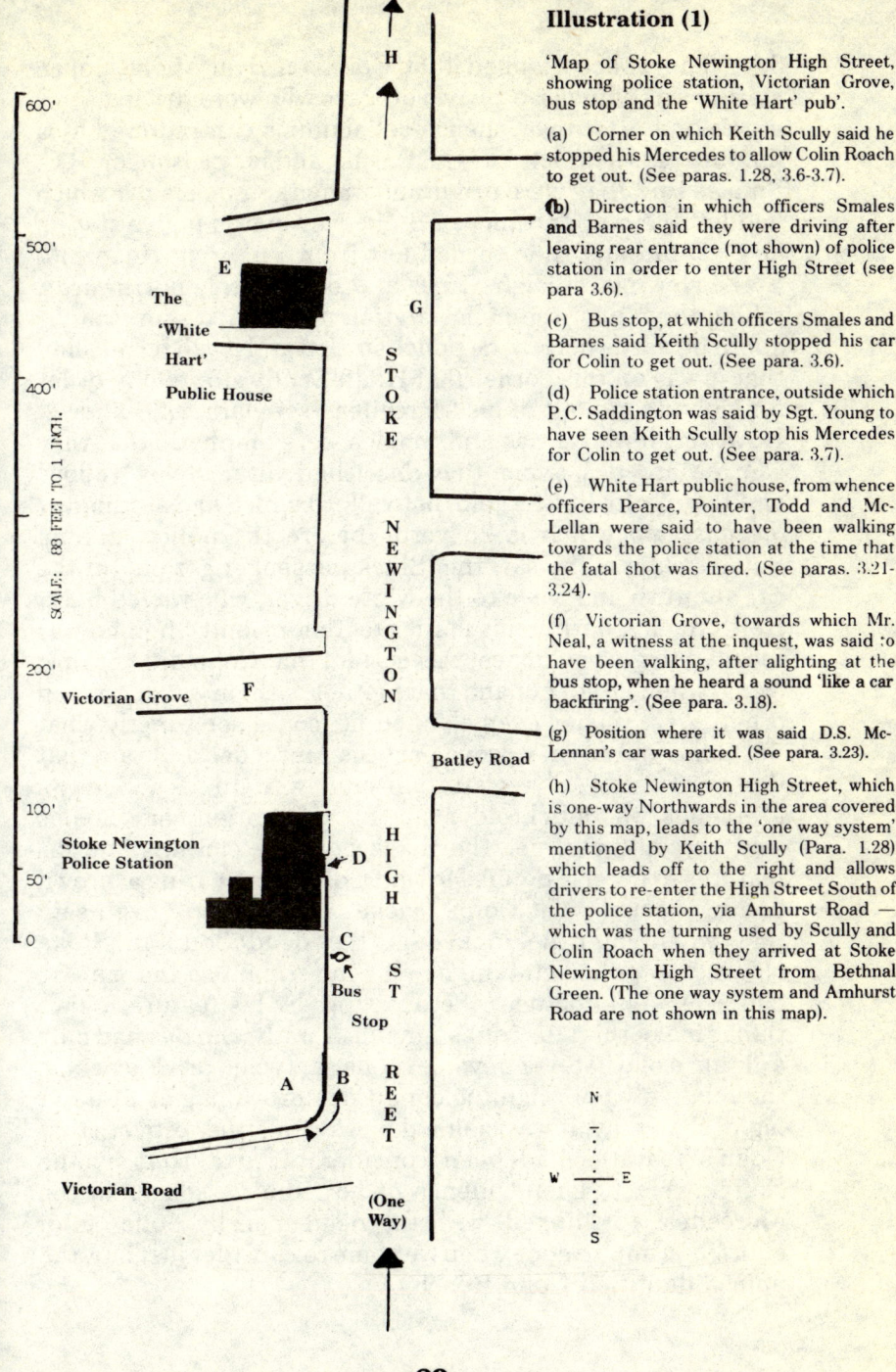

Illustration (1)

'Map of Stoke Newington High Street, showing police station, Victorian Grove, bus stop and the 'White Hart' pub'.

(a) Corner on which Keith Scully said he stopped his Mercedes to allow Colin Roach to get out. (See paras. 1.28, 3.6-3.7).

(b) Direction in which officers Smales and Barnes said they were driving after leaving rear entrance (not shown) of police station in order to enter High Street (see para 3.6).

(c) Bus stop, at which officers Smales and Barnes said Keith Scully stopped his car for Colin to get out. (See para. 3.6).

(d) Police station entrance, outside which P.C. Saddington was said by Sgt. Young to have seen Keith Scully stop his Mercedes for Colin to get out. (See para. 3.7).

(e) White Hart public house, from whence officers Pearce, Pointer, Todd and McLellan were said to have been walking towards the police station at the time that the fatal shot was fired. (See paras. 3.21-3.24).

(f) Victorian Grove, towards which Mr. Neal, a witness at the inquest, was said to have been walking, after alighting at the bus stop, when he heard a sound 'like a car backfiring'. (See para. 3.18).

(g) Position where it was said D.S. McLennan's car was parked. (See para. 3.23).

(h) Stoke Newington High Street, which is one-way Northwards in the area covered by this map, leads to the 'one way system' mentioned by Keith Scully (Para. 1.28) which leads off to the right and allows drivers to re-enter the High Street South of the police station, via Amhurst Road — which was the turning used by Scully and Colin Roach when they arrived at Stoke Newington High Street from Bethnal Green. (The one way system and Amhurst Road are not shown in this map).

3.6 The police claimed that Colin's arrival at the police station was witnessed by two officers who were driving away at the time. However, their recollection is contradicted by a number of other factors. D.C. Barnes and his passenger, P.C. Smales said they were driving an unmarked police car which had left the rear entrance of Stoke Newington police station at 11.25pm and then turned left from Victorian Road into Stoke Newington High Street in order to drive northwards, taking them past the police station itself. Victorian Road is about 60 yards before the police station and it will be recalled that it was on this corner that Keith Scully stopped in order for Colin to get out of his Mercedes. (see para. 1.28 above). However, both Barnes and Smales were emphatic that they saw a Mercedes, which they described variously as 'yellow' and then 'gold' (it was gold, not yellow) which had stopped *at the bus stop* which is 25 yards before the police station. Smales claimed he saw the 'Black passenger get out' of the car and turn and wave to the white driver, who waved back. Keith Scully, both in his earlier testimony and when he was recalled to give evidence, was certain that Colin did not turn round when he got out and that neither of them waved to each other. P.C. Smales even claimed he 'could see exactly what was going on' as they drove past the Mercedes and said that the car was an 'S' registration or newer. In fact, Scully's Mercedes was much older, an 'L' registration car. Smales said he could also see the Black person's clothing and his features in precise detail. He said Colin was wearing a 'brown bomber jacket'. Yet Colin's jacket was grey. He even said that when later he looked at the dead body in Stoke Newington police station, he recognised him as the man he had seen standing near the bus stop 'by his features'. Two things make this story questionable. Firstly, Smales had only a glimpse of whatever or whoever he saw while driving past in the relatively poor lighting conditions prevailing at 11.25 at night. Secondly, it was claimed by several other officers that Colin's features had been considerably distorted by the shotgun blast. This evidence of how the passenger in the Mercedes was 'linked' with the dead man by police is of enormous importance when we come to consider just how the police identified Colin Roach.

3.7 There are more anomalies in this particular account. D.C. Barnes was unable to explain how his written statement said: 'I saw the Black passenger get out' of the car, when at the inquest he said he did not see him get out, and that 'The most I would have seen was the door opening'. In addition to this, Barnes says he was driving an 'unmarked blue Avenger' when he passed the Mercedes, prior to receiving a message to return to Stoke Newington police station just after 11.30pm. Scully however, said in his statement to the Roach family's lawyers that after dropping Colin off, he saw 'a police car... with its lights flashing', a car which he said had passed him when he was stationary at the corner of Victorian Road. Since the officers who claim to have seen him and Colin were driving an unmarked car with 'no siren', how could Scully later have described it as a 'police car' with 'flashing lights?' Unless, of course, the car in which Barnes and Smales were driving was not the car which passed Scully and Colin Roach.

The question remains, if these officers really saw Colin and Scully, how could their memories be so inaccurate about the colour and position of the car when it had stopped, the 'waving' between its two occupants after one had got out, and the colour of Colin's jacket, when Smales was equally sure he had a good enough view based on a glimpse from a car travelling at 25mph at night to be able to recognise the dead man in the police station 'by his features?' Another officer (P.C. Saddington) was said by Sgt. Young to have told him that he had seen the Mercedes stop *in front of* the police station and this was the version initially released to the press by the police. These discrepancies were not explained by the inquest.

When Did Colin Die?
3.8 The question of exactly when Colin died is not clear. P.C. Jackson claims he was standing behind the counter in the front reception area of Stoke Newington police station when he 'heard a bang' and saw a 'dark object' strike the outer glass doors of the lobby. Then:

> I went through the first set of glass doors and as I looked towards the main entrance I saw the body of a young coloured

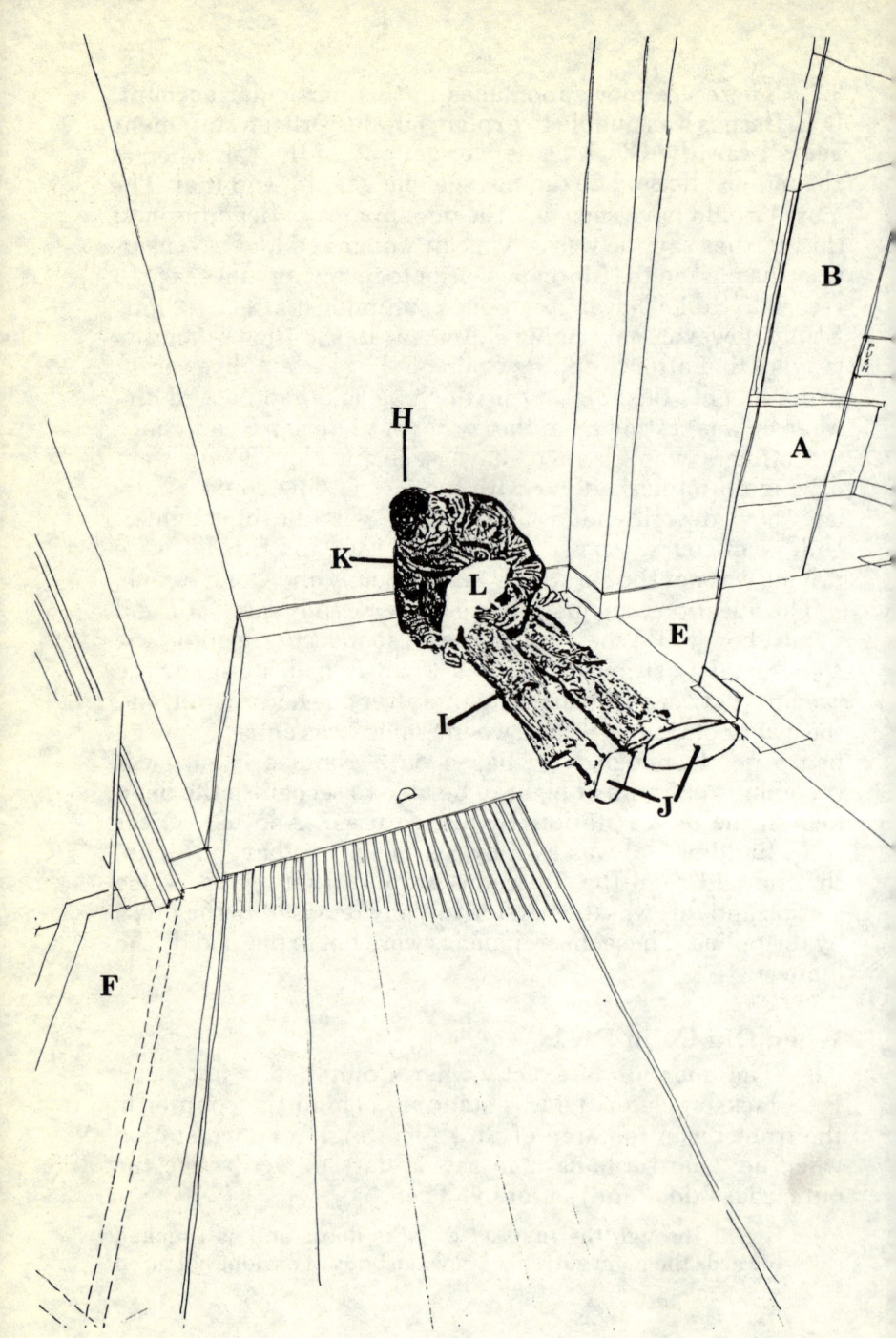

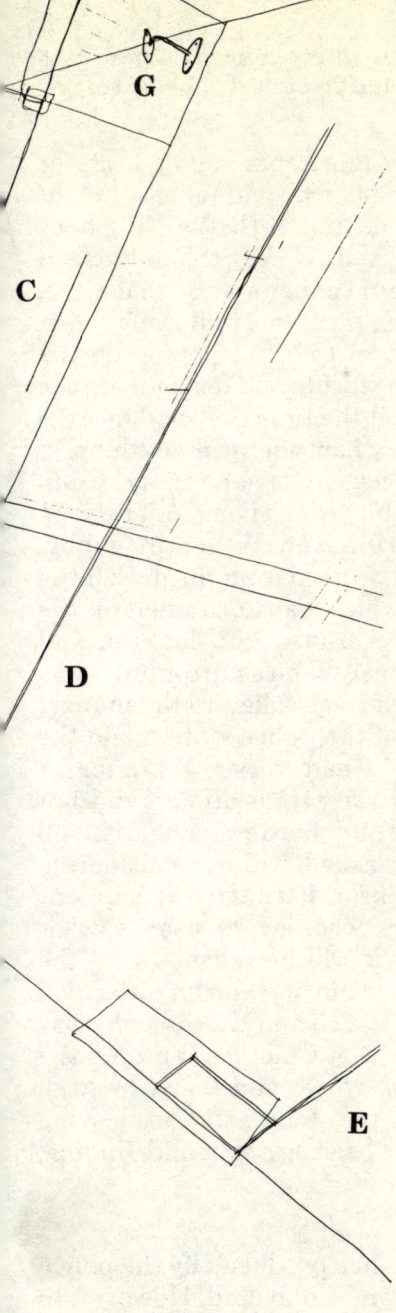

Illustration (2)

'The view into Stoke Newington police station from the North, showing Colin Roach's body lying against the South wall of the outer lobby and the two sets of glass doors/glass partitions situated between Colin and the reception counter'.

(a) Reception counter behind which P.C. Jackson said he was standing when the shot was fired which killed Colin Roach. (See para. 3.8).

(b) Inner glass doors dividing reception area from inner lobby.

(c) Inner glass partitions.
(d) Outer glass doors dividing inner lobby from outer lobby
(e) Outer glass partitions.
(NB: P.C. Jackson said that he saw a dark object strike these doors when he heard the bang. See para. 3.8)

(f) Doorway to Stoke Newington High Street (wooden doors not shown).

(g) Wall-mounted holder for mirror designed to allow officer behind reception counter to view outer lobby and street entrance. (See para. 3.8).

(h) Body of Colin Roach, in position he lay when police photographs were taken, at 1.30am on 13th January 1983. (See paras. 3.9-3.11 and 3.19).

(i) Note jeans creased or puckered at knees. (See para. 3.11(c)).

(j) Rubber soled training shoes. (See para. 3.12(d)).

(k) Leather jacket.

(l) Towel lying on top of, and obscuring, holdall bag which is strapped over Colin's right shoulder. (See para. 3.19).

man. He was sat on the floor to my right. His head was slumped forward and there was a great deal of blood coming from his mouth and nose . . .

Jackson was not sure whether this happened at 11.25 or 11.30pm. Although he claimed he had a vivid recollection of events, he said he had made no notes that night about anything because he was 'not asked to'. Yet the uniformed officer in charge of Stoke Newington police station that night, Inspector Dickins, who also made no notes, told the inquest that making notes was the duty of the first person on the scene. Two civilian witnesses, one inside and one outside the police station were more sure that the time they had heard a bang was 11.30pm although they had not seen anything.

The position in which P.C. Jackson says he found Colin was in the only segment of the lobby which could not be seen directly from the front desk. However, the entire lobby, station entrance included, could be seen from the desk if the desk officer looked in a mirror which was positioned on the wall to his left for that purpose. Both P.C. Jackson and Smales claimed there had previously been a mirror but it was now out of action. P.C. Lewis, who was called to the inquest solely to present a set of plans of the police station and the surrounding area, claimed that he had worked there for 23 years and *never* seen such a mirror. Other officers did not recall a mirror, either working or out of order, being there on the night. The question has to be asked, without considering *how* Colin died, could P.C. Jackson have seen it happen? Another, connected question is whether Jackson saw or spoke to Colin before he died? It will be recalled that the C.I.D. officer who later questioned Jim Joseph on his arrival at the police station with James Roach and Keith Scully was to say, according to Jim Joseph, that Colin had entered the police station, *spoken to the desk officer* and then 'the desk officer walked away' back into the police station, leaving Colin standing at the desk, before hearing a shot and 'finding' Colin.

'Where Did Colin Die?'

3.9 There was no positive evidence produced by the police at the inquest to say exactly 'where' Colin died. However, to claim that he shot himself requires he did so in such a way as to end up in the position where he was found (see illustrations 2 & 3). But that position, sitting against a wall with his legs stretched out in front of him, is almost impossible to explain. Unless, of course, Colin was 'propped up' by someone else after he was shot in a convenient corner out of the direct view of the front counter. Colin's eventual position could not be accounted for by either of the two pathologists who gave evidence at the inquest, Dr. Peter Vanezis and Dr. ian West, the former working for the police and the latter engaged by the Roach family to conduct a second postmortem. Neither could his position be accounted for by the ballistics expert from the Metropolitan Police laboratory in Lambeth, Mr. Kevin O'Callahan.

3.10   Mr. O'Callahan was asked how he thought the shooting could have occurred. He said "We, in the Metropolitan Police, have never had either a murder or a suicide of this type". He was asked where Colin had been when he was shot, and replied: "We don't jump to conclusions about things of that sort". He was then asked to say if the shooting happened in the position where Colin was found. He said: "It isn't possible to say, I have no experience of this kind of injury". When asked if Colin's body had been moved after the shooting, before ending up in the position shown in the photographs, he replied. "Commonsense says that it must have been moved".

These answers reflected the difficulty experienced by one witness in explaining Colin's position. Dr. Vanezis, the first pathologist to have been involved in the investigation, was asked if the body had been moved before it was examined in the lobby and replied: "The officers told me otherwise".

3.11   The conclusions of these experts on the position in which Colin had been in prior to the shooting, *if* he did shoot himself, were as follows:

a) Mr. O'Callahan was very unsure, but at one stage ventured the opinion that Colin had been "directly at, or above" the position in which he was found;

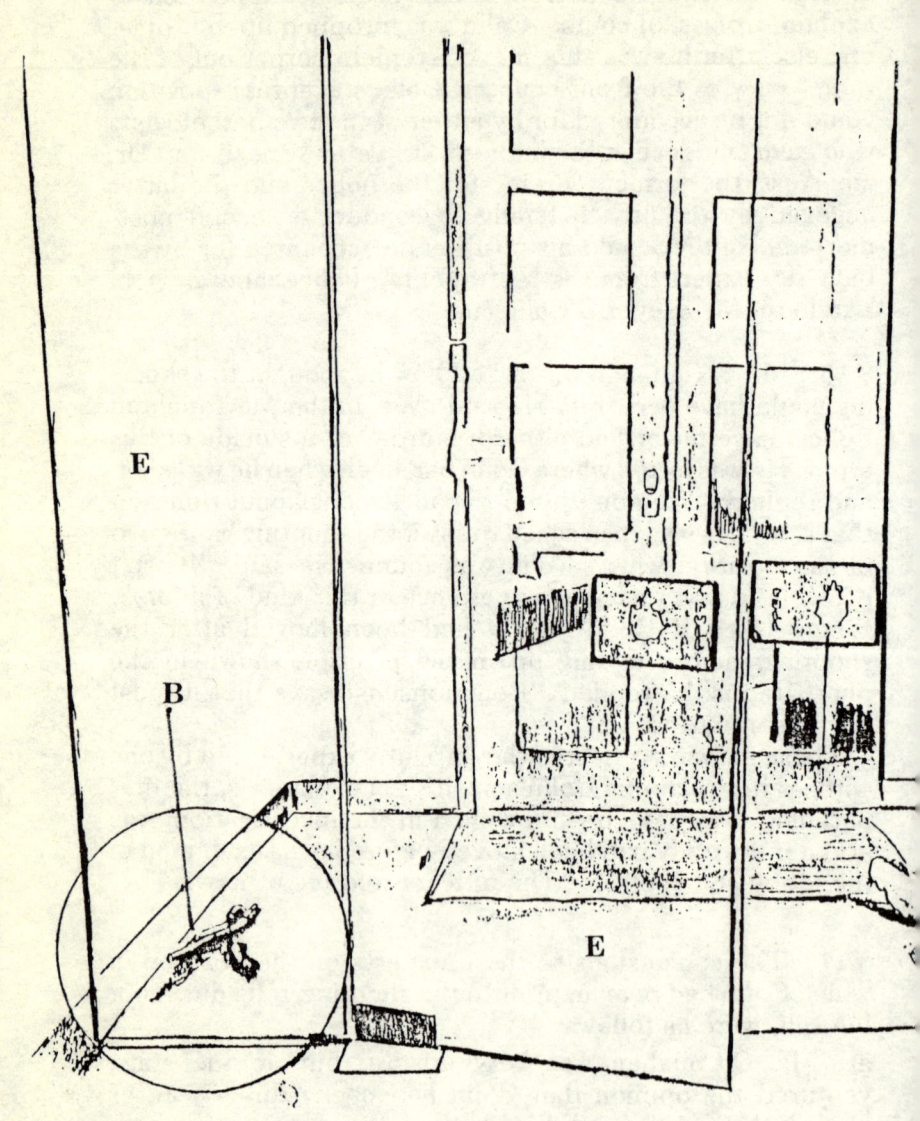

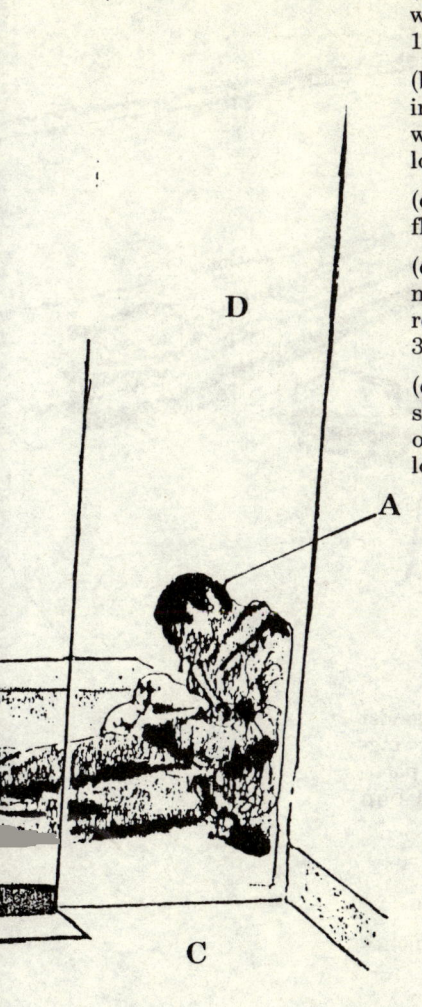

Illustration (3)

'The view towards the outer lobby of Stoke Newington police station from the West, showing Colin's body, the shot gun and the wooden street doors'.

(a) Colin Roach's body, in position he lay when police photographs taken (1.30am on 13.1.83). (See para. 3.19).

(b) Shot gun, circled for emphasis, lying in two pieces in position where police say it was found, next to North wall of outer lobby. (See para. 3.15-3.16).

(c) Flooring: linoleum above wooden floorboards. (See para. 3.12(d)).

(d) South wall of outer lobby, on which no marks or bloodstains found from alleged recoil of Colin's head backwards. (See para. 3.12(c)).

(e) No marks from alleged recoil of shotgun away from Colin were found either on the floor or on the North wall of the outer lobby. (See para. 3.12(a)).

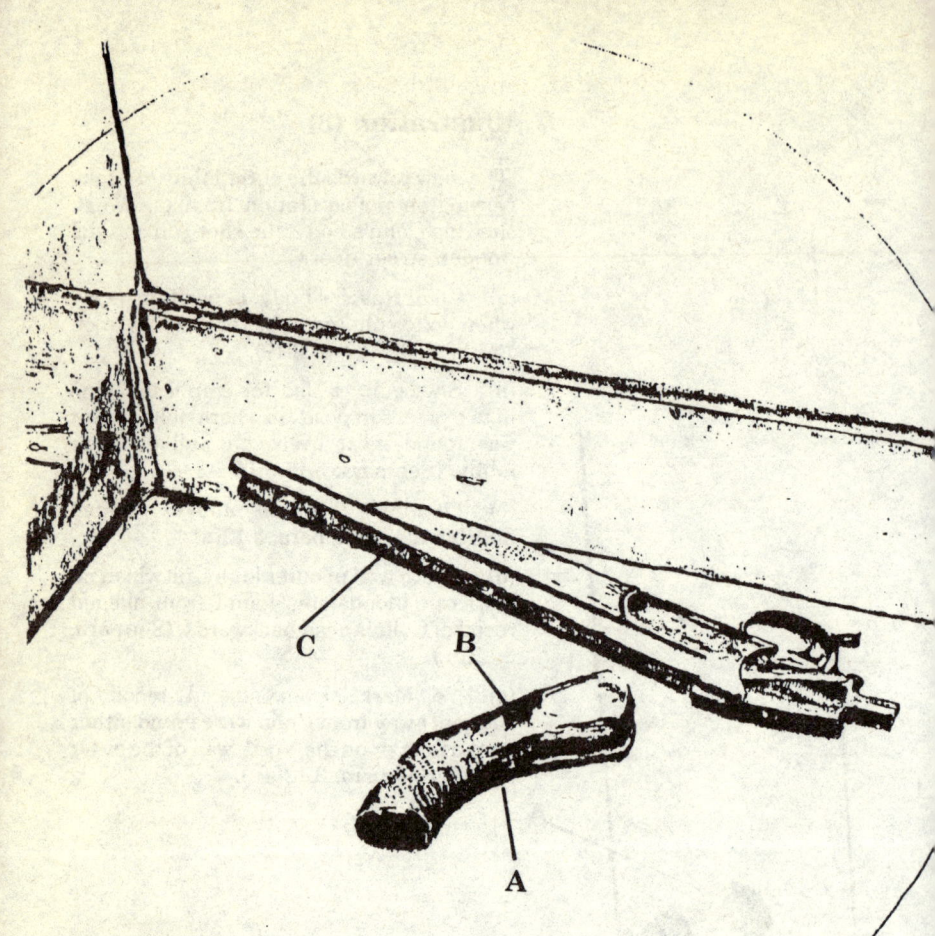

Illustration (4)

'Magnified view of shotgun, lying against North wall of outer lobby of Stoke Newington police station, next to outer glass partition and opposite (not shown) of Colin Roach'. (See para. 3.12).

(a) Stock.

(b) Sellotape holding stock together.

(c) Gun barrel, sawn off to 15¼ inches length (original length 28¾ inches).

b) Dr. Vanezis thought Colin might have been standing or sitting, perhaps 2-3 feet away from the wall, but he said he "couldn't be sure".

(c) Dr. West thought Colin was "either standing or crouched", but not sitting, and that in any case he would have fallen back against the wall and slid down it. However, Dr. West found it "unusual" that Colin's jeans were creased at the knees while his legs were pointing forward. He said it suggested that the legs had not been straight before the shooting. Yet he thought if the knees were even slightly bent before the shot was fired, it would result in the legs crumpling up when he fell backwards.

3.12 These conclusions show how difficult it was to prove that Colin had shot himself in such a way as to end up in the position he was 'found'. However, opposite the seated figure of Colin was the shotgun. Clearly, if Colin shot himself, the recoil of the gun away from him would have determined the eventual position of both his body and the gun. Tests were carried out by Mr. O'Callahan on the same weapon and videos of these tests were shown to the inquest. Yet tests showed that if the backward movement of the gun was unimpeded it would recoil on average 17ft before hitting the floor when fired 5ft 10 inches above the ground, and just over 10ft before hitting the floor when fired 2ft 6 inches above the ground.

Mr. O'Callahan agreed that in the relatively shorter distance across the police station lobby (which was 11ft wide) it would have hit the opposite wall or the floor after having been fired by Colin. He also agreed that a gun recoiling in this manner would make a mark on the wall or the floor, as it had done in each of the experiments carried out.

However:

(a) There were *no* marks anywhere on the floor, the glass doors or the opposite wall of the police station lobby, consistent with the recoil of the gun away from Colin.

(b) There were no injuries to Colin's finger or thumb having been caught by the trigger guard of the gun as it flew away from him.

(c) There were no injuries or bruises found by either pathologist on the back of Colin's head, and no marks found on the wall behind his head, consistent with his head being thrown backwards by the force of the shot gun blast itself.

In addition, there were two other reasons why Colin's position sitting against the wall was not explicable by the idea that he shot himself:

(d) Colin's legs were stretched out in front of him and he was wearing rubber soled shoes. With these shoes on he could not have 'slid' into his final position because the lino-covered floor, on which no slide marks were found, would have impeded the motion of his feet.

(e) The position in which the towel was found lying on Colin's body was, said Dr. West, "inexplicable".

3.13 Thus, Colin's position in the lobby is inconsistent with him having shot himself with the gun found opposite him. *The inquest did not provide a satisfactory answer to the question of where he had been shot, but it clearly left open the possibility that another person had fired the shot and then placed Colin and the shotgun on opposite sides of the police station lobby.*

How Did Colin Die?

3.14 The next question to be answered is 'how' was Colin Roach shot. Both the pathologists concluded that he died as a result of a shot gun blast fired inside his mouth, with the tip of the barrel just past his teeth.

For the following reasons, each pathologist concluded that the injury had been *self inflicted:*

Dr. Vanezis:

1. There were no "external injuries" found on Colin's face consistent with the gun having been fired outside the mouth, or forced into his mouth.
2. The injuries inside Colin's mouth caused by the blast were "symmetrical".

Dr. West:
1. The fact that the gun was fired inside the mouth with the muzzle beyond the teeth, without injuries to the lips or teeth other than those caused by the shot gun blast.
2. The lack of "signs of a struggle" to show that Colin had been "restrained" or kicked and punched on the head, chin, chest, hands or knees.

3.15   However, there are a number of flaws in these conclusions:

(a)   Both pathologists based their conclusions on the fact that they had *not* found things which they assumed would be found in a homicidial shooting.

(b)   Neither pathologist had ever heard of a suicide being carried out with a sawn-off shotgun before whether in their experience or in the text books.

(c)   Neither pathologist, as said earlier, could explain the position of the body and the straightened legs, in a way consistent with a 'suicide'.

(d)   Neither pathologist, when asked, could preclude the possibility that another person had put the gun in Colin's mouth, if his mouth was opened 'willingly'.

(e)   Dr. West stated in his written post-mortem report that it was impossible to tell whether or not Colin had been conscious at the time that the shot was fired.

Thus it appears that their conclusions of suicide by no means made killing by a third party out of the question, and were based on 'social' rather than scientific clues. In his evidence to the Inquiry, Mr. Mansfield, the Roach family's barrister, told us that he believed both pathologists had been: "Unwilling to contemplate anything other than suicide because they couldn't quite figure out what else could have happened".

3.16   With these factors in mind, it is necessary to consider whether the 'social' explanations used by the pathologists to conclude 'suicide' were borne out by the evidence about the shotgun itself.

The conclusions which can be drawn about the shotgun are as follows:

(a)   No fingerprints were found on any part of the shotgun which killed Colin Roach, yet Colin had not been wearing gloves. It was agreed by Mr. Grant, a police fingerprint expert who tested the gun, that the 'normal reasons' why prints might *not* be found did not apply to the smooth surfaces of the gun's barrel and of its wooden butt. (These reasons were that the surface was too greasy, too rough or too small to leave prints).

(b)   However, there was 'no sign' that the gun had been wiped clean of prints. No fingerprints were found on the smooth plastic surface of the fired shotgun cartridge, or on the two unfired cartridges which were allegedly found in Colin's jacket pocket.

(c)   The shotgun could not be forensically linked either to the holdall which Colin was carrying or to the towel found on top of the holdall which had been seen by his friends inside the holdall. Mr. Phillip Toates, the police scientist who tested them, found several hundred microscopic fibres on the gun, but was unable to find any which matched those of the towel or the inside of the holdall.

(d)   No-one was ever traced from Colin's family or friends to suggest that Colin ever had a gun, would have known how to obtain a gun or how to use one. As shown later in this chapter, the police admitted that they made no investigations in the London area to ascertain the origin of the gun which killed Colin.

(e)   When tested several times during the inquest, witnesses were unable to fit the sawn-off shotgun into the holdall which Colin had been carrying, without the barrel protruding by 2-3 inches, once the wooden butt of the gun had already been removed. If the gun was 'broken' into its loading position, the shape of the bag was crunched up and visibly distorted when seen from the outside with the zip closed. Furthermore, the zip could not be kept closed to prevent the barrel from protruding again. Yet both Keith Scully and Jim Joseph, who had been with Colin on the night of his death, saw no gun inside the holdall, sticking out or otherwise distorting the bag's shape. In fact as shown earlier (see para. 1.19) they both said that the bag 'wasn't closed' and that the towel was visible inside.

The fact that the gun could not be scientifically linked to Colin Roach had a dramatic effect on the inquest following an incident which took place on Friday 17 June, the day on which D.C.S. Robertson, the chief detective of 'G' district, who had headed the investigation into Colin's death, was giving his evidence (NB: D.C.S. Robertson was the most senior C.I.D. officer present at Stoke Newington police station on the night of January 12/13).

The lawyers representing the Roach Family, Gareth Peirce and Mike Mansfield saw a curious event taking place involving D.C.S. Robertson and P.C. Smales. According to Mr. Mansfield:

> One lunch hour, Gareth and I walked back into the court... and we found Robertson... trying to get the gun into the bag.. Clearly if the gun had come from inside the police station it was something they probably hadn't thought of until that moment in time, and suddenly decided they'd better go and see if it would fit, and found that it wouldn't...

3.17 When the inquest resumed, Robertson was giving evidence. The following exchange took place:

Mr. Mansfield: At lunch time today, did you come here into this court with the object of putting the gun into the bag? Why?

D.C.S. Robertson: I did this because of the theory we have been discussing about the position of the deceased's hands. I thought it might save time.

Mr. Mansfield: Well, Superintendent, did you find a way?

D.C.S. Robertson: No.

Mr. Mansfield: It doesn't fit without protruding, does it? Had you ever tried to do it before? Had it ever occurred to you to try this until now?

D.C.S. Robertson: No, I was told in a phone call from the laboratory that it did fit.

Mr. Mansfield: Who were you told by? When did this phone call come? How were you told that it fitted?

D.C.S. Robertson: I don't know. I'm sorry. I can't recall.
(At counsel's request, another demonstration was made in which it was attempted to get the gun into the bag)
D.C.S. Robertson: I agree that if its assembled it won't go in.
(Extract from transcript of the Colin Roach inquest provided as evidence by 'INQUEST').

This incident raised further questions: how can the police claim to have investigated the shooting if they had not even established that Colin Roach had brought the gun into the police station? Was it possible, as suggested by Mr. Mansfield that 'the gun had come from inside the police station?' *It has already been seen that the inquest did not establish where or when Colin died with any degree of certainty — 'how' he died had only been answered to the extent of proving that a shot gun blast had killed him.* The forensic evidence relating to the gun and the fact that Colin would not have been able to have carried it without it being visible or to have left his fingerprints on it when it was fired, suggest that 'suicide' as an explanation is highly questionable. When this is considered with the unusual position in which Colin's body was found, it makes suicide not only appear improbable but leaves open the possibility that the fatal shot may have been fired by another person. The Inquiry therefore felt it was necessary to look at exactly what was going on when Colin died, how police officers accounted for their movements at the time and the ways in which the police claimed to have reacted to his death shortly afterwards.

BULLETIN No.
of the Roach Family Support Committee

WHY AN INQUEST IS NOT ENOUGH

The standard argument used by op- tion of the evidence. The family's solicitor it finds that he was unlawfully

Could Colin's Death Have Been Witnessed?

3.18   P.C. Jackson, who said that he found the man lying in the lobby, was joined by P.C. Bruce. Bruce then said he ran out into the High Street (see map page 89). Jackson went shortly afterwards and saw Bruce chasing and apprehending a man who had just turned the corner into Victorian Grove. This man, Mr. Martin Neal, told the inquest that he had got off a bus and walked 10 feet past the police station entrance heading northwards when he heard a sound like a car backfiring. Neither Jackson or Bruce said that they saw anyone else outside. Sgt. Young, the station officer, had been at his desk in the office behind the counter at which Jackson was standing when he heard the shot. He said he looked immediately out of a bay window into the High Street looking north. He claimed:

> 'I would have been able to see a person getting away. The area was deserted.'

By the time Jackson came back into the station entrance, another officer, P.C. Saddington, had also come to the lobby to observe the man lying there. He, like Bruce and Young, had been in the station office behind the front counter when they heard the shot. Yet in the time between Jackson finding the shotgun victim and his return, with Bruce, from outside the entrance, something had apparently altered which cannot be explained.

3.19   Jackson told the inquest at first that he had seen a rolled up towel behind the head of the person he found in the lobby. Then he said that on his return from the street the towel "had fallen into his lap" and was no longer rolled up. How could the towel have fallen from behind Colin's neck and unrolled itself at the same time? Mr. Marriage, the police barrister, absolutely refused to let Mr. Mansfield see this officer's statement. However, the coroner eventually read out part of it. The rolled up towel was described as being 'on his left shoulder' and there was nothing about it 'falling' into his lap. Jackson then claimed that the towel had rolled from behind the neck to the left shoulder and then fallen, somehow.

Yet according to P.C. Saddington, who apparently entered the lobby after Jackson and Bruce, the towel "As far as I remember, was hanging from his right shoulder". The mystery is compounded by D.C.S. Robertson, who did not see the towel when he said he examined the body at 12.30am. He said he only found out about it from Jackson. Yet by 1.30am when the body was photographed the towel had returned and was in the position which Dr. West was to describe as "inexplicable" as the result of any self-shooting. It was surely even harder to explain how Colin could have shot himself and fallen into a position where a rolled up towel was wedged behind his neck or balanced on one shoulder. Since all the police officers were certain that they touched nothing, how could this towel have moved around, unassisted?

3.20 Another related change in the scene of the crime seems to have occurred with the position of Colin's body. In the photographs (see diagram of body) he is leaning slightly to the right. However:

(a) Dr. Hannah Striesow, who examined Colin between 11.40 and 11.45, was certain that he was slumped over *further* at that time than he is in the photographs taken later.

(b) Inspector Dickins, who said he saw Colin at '11.30 or 11.35" also said that the body was slumped more to the right than in the photographs.

(c) D.C. Pointer, who claimed he saw Colin at 11.35 said: "The body was more *upright* than is shown in the picture".

How is it possible for a dead man to lean over, sit himself up again and then lean over into a position which is higher than his original position, without any assistance? Why would it be necessary to 'adjust' his position for the photographs which were going to be shown to the pathologist who would have to decide how the death had been caused?

3.21 The question of who was outside the police station when the shot was heard at or just about 11.30 is interesting. Sgt. Young, who said the street was deserted, seems to have missed Mr. Neal, who had walked a few feet past the doors when Young looked northwards, in the direction he was heading. There were three witnesses in a police waiting room who also looked out of a front window. These were friends of a rape victim who was at that time being examined by Dr. Striesow. We refer to them as Ms. A, B and C. They all looked out when they heard the noise, which they described respectively: like a champagne cork being opened, like somebody throwing a metal ashtray, like a metal cabinet falling.

Each of them recalled seeing a middle-aged white man in a raincoat, standing across the road looking towards the police station. It appears that Sgt. Young did not see him, either. Who was this man and what connection might he have had with Colin's death? The police took his description from these women, who gave evidence at the inquest. What was done with that information?

3.22 In order to attempt to answer these questions it is necessary to consider yet another group of police officers who claimed to have been in the vicinity at the time of Colin Roach's death. D.C. Pierce and D.C. Pointer were the two C.I.D. officers who claimed to have been off duty, somewhere in the High Street outside the police station, between 11.10pm and 11.35pm, without hearing or seeing anything. They said they walked to the White Hart pub, situated some yards North of Stoke Newington police station, (also on the left of the High Street and just after the Victorian Grove turning), at 11.00pm. They apparently did this in order to speak to two other off-duty officers in connection with the rape investigation. The other two they named as D.S. McLellan and D.C. Todd. These officers, unlike Pierce and Pointer, did not submit statements or give any oral evidence to the inquest, although at least one of them, D.S. McLellan, was named by D.C.S. Robertson as having been the main officer questioning Jim Joseph, who arrived later that night with Colin's father James Roach and Keith Scully.

Why did they not give evidence and how can D.C.S. Robertson, who was in charge of the investigation, not have known the names of the C.I.D. officers who were there on the night?

3.23 According to D.C. Pointer, it took three minutes to walk from the police station to the pub. They had been inside and emerged talking to the other officers. By 11.10 Pierce, Pointer, Todd and McLellan were standing on the pavement outside the pub. At 11.20, Pointer said they crossed the road to look at McLellan's car which was parked opposite the pub. He said they were 'killing time' until the doctor had finished with her examination of the rape victim at the police station. Pierce and Pointer claimed they left McLellan locking up his car and walked or strolled back to the entrance of Stoke Newington police station, which they entered at 11.35. They knew this because each one said that they looked at their watches and signed the duty book. However, by 11.35, there was a shotgun victim sitting in the lobby of the police station. Pierce and Pointer claimed they were able to enter the front doors (wooden street doors) at this time, even though several officers claimed to have 'sealed' the venue by locking the doors from the inside just after the shooting. What is most incredible is that during their stroll from the pavement opposite the pub to the station entrance, between 11.20 and 11.35:

(a) They did not see Colin Roach arriving at the station, nor did they see Scully's distinctive Mercedes driving away. Scully said that he drove on between 11.20 and 11.30 (see paragraph 1.28). The road was one way, so he would have driven past anyone who was positioned north of the station in the direction of the White Hart.

(b) They neither saw nor were seen by P.C. Smales and D.C. Barnes, who claimed to have driven past the police station at 11.25, northwards.

(c) They neither saw nor were seen by PCs Jackson and Bruce, even though P.C. Bruce ran half way as far as the pub, to Victorian Grove, in order to catch Mr. Neal, whom they did not see either.

(d) They were not seen walking towards the police station

by Sergeant Young when he looked out of the window at 11.30.

3.24 Pierce and Pointer said that they heard no noises, yet someone standing in the position of the man in the raincoat would probably have heard a noise in the same way that Mr. Neal did. Who was the man? If he was not one of the C.I.D. officers, how could he have gone unnoticed by five policemen? If he was, did he have anything to do with the shooting?

3.25 Once again, the rule against disclosure of police witness statements to the interested parties at the inquest hindered the Roach family from conducting their case. This was because the two detectives gave their evidence on the fifth day of the inquest, after all the other witnesses who had not corroborated their story had already given evidence. Mr. Mansfield had not been able to cross-examine any other witness on the alleged presence outside Stoke Newington police station of D.S. Pierce and D.C. Pointer because he did not know what Pierce and Pointer were going to say. He told us:

> If I'd known at the beginning that I was going to have at the end of the inquest detectives who were going to say that just by coincidence they were off duty, and just by coincidence they happened to walk down the road to the police station and just by coincidence they ... walked in the front ... lobby at just after the shooting itself — Then I would have asked a lot of questions of the earlier witnesses.

With reference to Ms. C, who was in a waiting room at Stoke Newington police station with her two friends when she looked out of the window at 11.30, he said:

> If I knew detectives were going to come along and say they'd walked down the street I would have asked the woman whether she'd seen three men, or two men, or one man approaching the police station, dressed as they claimed they were dressed, off duty ...

The last of the unanswered questions about the detectives

has already been suggested by D.C. Pointer's description of the body (see paragraph 3.20) which raised the possibility that he saw Colin Roach before P.C. Jackson. In Mike Mansfield's words:

> *The question that still remains to be answered is — Were those detectives really off duty in a pub up the road or were they inside the police station.*

The Police Reaction to Colin's Death

3.26 The reactions of the police to the shotgun death appear odd if it is believed that they did not know Colin Roach, did not see him killed and did not know who killed him. Moreover there is one startling fact at the centre of their reactions. *They defined his death as 'suicide' before 11.33pm, and from that time to the inquest, did not consider any other possibility.* The inquest heard evidence from two ambulance men from the Tottenham ambulance department: Messrs. Ian Elliot and Christopher Lambert. At 11.33pm the driver of the ambulance, Mr. Lambert, received a telephone call from central ambulance control saying *"We have received two emergency calls stating that a man has shot himself* at Stoke Newington police station. Will you deal?" The questions raised about the reactions of the police are as follows: How were they sure the person was dead? What efforts were made to save him if he was not? How did the scene of the crime 'change' as described earlier? How did they identify the body as that of Colin Roach when formal identification by his parents was not allowed until 36 hours later? Why would they not allow Mr. Roach to see the body, even if somehow they already knew it was Colin Roach? Did they conduct a serious investigation into the death, which they defined as suicide within 3-8 minutes of it happening? If not, what were they doing?

3.27 The first question relates to the state in which the police found Colin. Between the time the shot was heard, 11.25 or 11.30pm according to P.C. Jackson, and the arrival in the lobby of a doctor at 11.40pm, 10 police officers claim to have gone to see the shotgun victim in the lobby. These were

P.C. Jackson, Bruce and Saddington; Sgt. Young, D.C. Barnes and P.C. Smales, D.S. Pierce and D.C. Pointer, D.I. Dickins and C.I. Clapton. None said they were certain that the man was dead but none, equally, tried his pulse to check if he was still alive. D.S. Pierce "shouted" at him to try and revive him. Most of these officers made a point of saying that they had touched nothing in the lobby, Colin included. P.C. Jackson, who found Colin, had not called a doctor because "in the rush of events I didn't think of it". D.C. Barnes, who said he entered the lobby at 11.35pm and "set the ball rolling" in the investigation as the first CID officer there, said that calling a doctor was not his responsibiilty. D.C. Pointer who was with D.S. Pierce, when he (Pierce) "shouted" at the gun victim said he did not call a doctor initially because "it didn't spring to mind straight away". While D.S. Pierce told the inquest that "I didn't try his pulse because *I didn't want to move him*".

Finally, D.C. Pointer found his way to the surgeon's room, which was also on the ground floor. Dr. Striesow was taking a blood sample from a rape victim. W.P.C. Maddison, who was with her, said that Pointer asked for a doctor to attend the "shooting", without saying whether the victim was dead or alive. Dr. Striesow did not come immediately. She waited until Maddison had gone, with Pointer, to see Colin and then returned, telling the doctor that he looked "dead or injured". Even then, it was, according to Maddison, "a few minutes" later when the doctor finally left what she was doing and went to the lobby. The doctor's notes said she began her examination at 11.40p.m. She claimed it took 4-5 minutes to try his pulse and reflexes and certify him dead. When the 2 ambulance men arrived at 11.45p.m. she was still examining him. They were sent away after being informed he was dead.

3.28   P.C. Scott and Sgt. Young had both phoned for an ambulance from the station office after the shot was heard. They both told the ambulance service a man had "shot himself", before 11.33pm. Yet neither of them claimed to have seen the body by then. They were acting in response to officers Jackson, Bruce and Saddington. No CID officer claims to have been at the scene until 11.35 p.m. at the earliest to investigate how the shooting had happened. How then could two uniformed officers conclude it was a suicide at a time when the man had not even been pronounced dead and was sitting in a position which, as it was said earlier, looked as if he had been propped up against a wall? When Sgt. Young was on the telephone calling an ambulance, P.C.s Bruce and Jackson were still outside the police station. If they really were searching for suspects or witnesses who might have been involved, would it make sense for Sgt. Young to conclude the man had shot himself before they returned?

It has been mentioned that the scene of the crime changed itself around in a way that could not be explained by police officers, all of whom "moved nothing". Three of them claimed to have "sealed" the lobby by locking the outer wooden doors from the inside: Sgt. Young said he did it, without being able to recall if he did it before or after Jackson and Bruce came back inside. D.S. Pierce, who had not been seen by Bruce or Jackson in the street, claimed that he told P.C. Saddington to lock the doors after he arrived at 11.35pm. C.I. Clapton who said that when he returned to the police station *after* the shooting, the time was either 11.40, 11.25 or 11.20pm, claimed that he was the one who "made sure" that lobby was sealed. 10 officers altogether claimed they visited the scene before 11.40pm, 6 of whom came from outside the police station.

3.29   There are a number of questions raised by the police investigation into the death of Colin Roach which makes it difficult to explain how they identified him and categorised his death as a suicide almost immediately. Prior to the arrival of D.C.S. Robertson, the most senior CID officer at (he claimed) 12.25 a.m. no effort was made to identify the body or determine how his death had occurred. D.S. Pierce and D.C. Pointer did not look in the dead man's pockets to find any identification, and D.I. Scott, who would have been the most senior CID officer before Robertson arrived, did not question the civilian witnesses at the front of the police station on what they had seen through the window at 11.30p.m. The two senior uniformed officers present from the initial period before the doctor examined Colin until Robertson's arrival, C.I. Clapton and Inspector Dickins, claim to have played no part in the investigation. Clapton's reasons for this are odd for an officer who was in charge of Stoke Newington and three other stations. First, he claimed his job was merely to "wait for the CID" because it was a "suspicious death". Then he said he was not interested in how the shooting had occurred because "it was similar to other incidents". When questioned further as to whether he had seen other shotgun suicides in the Metropolitan Police, he replied "yes". This appears to contradict the experience of the police ballistics (see para. 3.10) as well as the experience of the two pathologists, none of whom knew of any previous suicides by means of a sawn off shotgun. Clapton did not even remember what time Robertson arrived and took over the investigation.

3.30 When D.C.S. Robertson arrived, *his* version of events is as follows: He arrived at 12.25a.m. was briefed upstairs by D.S. Pierce, in the company of D.C. Pointer, D.C. Barnes and D.I. Scott. This briefing was interrupted at 12.27-28a.m. by the arrival of three men who said they had dropped Colin Roach at the police station. Robertson had meanwhile been told minutes earlier, by D.S. Pierce, that Smales had identified the dead man "by his features" as the person whom he had seen arriving at the police station at 11.25pm. Robertson then ended the briefing session and directed Pierce, Pointer and McLellan to interview the three men separately. Then he spent "five minutes" examining the body, the lobby and some time examining the outside of the police station and the Mercedes. By 12.45am, he had been told that the three men had described Colin and he then "made the assumption that the body was that of Colin Roach" and told Mr. Roach that he believed his son was dead. Mr. Roach, though "distraught", was "co-operative" and left Robertson's office at 1.30am after telling him Colin had been "hearing voices" and "mentioning voodoo".

3.31 D.C.S. Robertson's version of events was challenged by James Roach, (who protested during the inquest at some of Robertson's testimony), as well as by the inquest jury, who firmly believed, as they put it in their letter to the Home Secretary, that the bereaved family was "kept in the dark over the death of their son". In particular, Robertson's evidence was challenged by the following (see also paras. 1.36/1.39):-

(a) Mr. Roach maintains that he was not told of the death of his son until after 2.45am on 13 January and that he never said that Colin had heard "voices" or mentioned "voodoo", yet he was questioned before and after 2.45am on "whether Colin had a gun", made to give a statement and accused of telling lies.

(b) Mr. Roach did not give the police a description of Colin or what he was wearing, nor did he describe the towel and holdall Colin was carrying because he had not seen Colin leave the house and Colin had not acquired the holdall until later when he met Keith Scully.

(c) Jim Joseph and Keith Scully did not provide, nor were they asked to provide a detailed description of Colin Roach. They were not asked about Colin until they were separated following the 15-20 minutes in which they were questioned together in the charge room. If they arrived at 12.27am as D.C.S. Robertson maintains, they would not have been questioned separately until *after* 12.45. Therefore, D.C.S. Robertson cannot have heard a description of Colin Roach from Colin's friends prior to 12.45am.

3.32 If we accept James Roach's version of events, it must then be asked whether it took the police until 2.45am to be certain that the body was that of Colin Roach. Was there any part of his questioning which was intended to identify the body? This hardly seems likely, because when he asked on a number of occasions to see Colin he was refused. That would have been the only sure way to identify the body and the fact that he was refused indicates that the police knew Colin's identity before Mr. Roach even arrived. The question asked of Jim Joseph as he sat with Keith Scully in the Mercedes outside Stoke Newington police station shortly after their arrival at 12.15am, by a police officer, was: "Did you know Colin...?" which suggests Colin was being spoken about as if already dead. It must be questioned again how D.C.S. Robertson claimed to have identified the body. P.C. Smales produced the account that he had glimpsed Colin's face as he turned and "waved" to Keith Scully at 11.25pm and then recognised the dead body as the same man "by his features". As shown earlier, this account is contradicted by Scully, by the lighting conditions in which he saw Colin being dropped off and by the injuries to Colin's face. It was mainly on the basis of Smales' account that Robertson claimed the dead man was linked with the Mercedes and its passenger.

3.33   It is also alleged that the return of the Mercedes, this time containing James Roach, Keith Scully and Jim Joseph, was linked with the earlier sighting and the dead man by the "description" that the three arrivals provided of Colin. Yet the police did not ask for a detailed description of Colin and they did not see fit to look in the pockets of the dead man until the post-mortem the following day. Formal identification by Mr. and Mrs. Roach was only achieved one day after that, on 14 January. An important piece of evidence which suggests that the police had not only seen, but spoken to and found out the name of Colin Roach before his death is provided by what was told to Jim Joseph 3-4 hours after his arrival and questioning by the C.I.D. officer (named by Robertson as McLellan) who did not attend the inquest:

> ... apparently Colin walked in, asked for help or whatever... the desk sergeant said 'No, we can't help you', and walked away, back into the nick ...

It is clear from the evidence we have heard that the police knew the identity of Colin Roach very soon after and possibly before his death. It is also clear that their investigation of the scene of the crime and questioning of Mr. Roach and Colin's friends had no relation to this identification process. Why then was it necessary for P.C. Smales to say that he alone identified the body as that of Colin Roach on the basis of the glimpse he claimed to have had of Keith Scully's "Black passenger" getting out of the Mercedes?

3.34   How did the police categorise Colin's death as 'suicide' and for what reason? Officers Young and Scott appear to have told the ambulance service before 11.33pm that "a man had shot himself". Inspector Peter Dickins, in charge of Stoke Newington police station, said he made up his mind that it was suicide "in ten minutes" after seeing the body at 11.30-35 p.m. C.I. Clapton, in charge of Stoke Newington and three other police stations within 'G' district, admitted under cross-examination that he "might" have told Sgt. Young to give the Scotland Yard Press Bureau the information that the man had "shot himself", before 2am. D.C.S. Robertson admitted that the Area 3 Press Officer, David Grangecroft, had been told by "the uniformed officers and me" to give the Press Bureau a certain statement. D.C.S. Robertson told the Coroner that this had been done at 1.30am but then told Mr. Mansfield it was at 1.50am. The statement added to one which had been produced at 12.40am describing how the police had found the shotgun victim, described at that time as "a Black man in his twenties", declared:

> At this stage the police are not seeking anyone else . . .

3.35   Under cross-examination D.C.S. Robertson was unable to explain why the press statement had been released or why it said that Colin had a history of mental illness. He could only say it was not intended for publication, and further that:

> Unfortunately a reporter mistakenly — not I'm sure through wickedness — published the statement.

However, he was not able to explain the use of the name "Clive" Roach and how it had appeared in an edition of the *Daily Mail* of the next day (13 January). Neither could he explain how there was any name in a statement which claimed the man had not been formally identified because his face had been blown away. Another revealing part of Robertson's evidence related to the press conference held on 15 January at which he, Mr. Grangecroft and Commander

Taylor had all been present:

"Mr. Mansfield: At the conference on Saturday Commander Taylor denied that the police said that the deceased had a history of mental illness, is that not right?

D.C.S. Robertson: Sir, what we said was not a press statement.

Mr. Mansfield: Well that may be, but no one ever said 'we're sorry we told them'. The facts remain that you did tell them and they did publish. You never experienced any regret did you? You could have corrected it the next day or are you expected to be completely dumb in the presence of a commander? . . .

D.C.S. Robertson: I was very busy at the time. I can't even recall if I even knew then that the statement was marked 'not for publication'.

Mr. Mansfield: Oh come on! The press officer was there too. Can I put to you another possibility? The thing makes no sense unless you didn't want the public to know that it was you who were putting it out. Was this then the object — to prevent the public knowing and to blur any resulting issues?

D.C.S. Robertson: No, not at all, absolutely not. "

3.36 Were Mr. Mansfield's questions suggesting the real reason for the police reactions to Colin Roach's death? To answer that we must consider all the steps in their investigation of the death. First, they made no real effort to ascertain whether Colin was dead or merely injured, refused to touch him and took some time to fetch a doctor. Second they preserved rather than examined the scene of the crime. One area of the gun, the inside of the sellotape holding together the previously split wooden butt, was never tested for fingerprints and the lack of marks in the lobby, indicating the recoil of the gun from Colin, was noticed, but ignored by D.C.S. Robertson who said he "became more convinced" it was suicide throughout the night. Third, there was no real attempt to identify Colin by looking in his pockets or allowing his father to see his body. Despite the press release which claimed that "formal identification" was not yet available, the police admitted that they knew by 12.45am who he was. Fourth, there was no attempt to notify Colin's next of kin once he had been positively identified. James Roach was only told the news of Colin's death when he refused to answer any more questions at 2.45-3am, yet police had known Colin's identity at least 2½ hours before. Fifth, there was no logical reason for giving the press Colin's identity and the notion that he was mentally ill and had killed himself *before* the Roach family were told, unless it was done in the anticipation of dispelling blame from the police for his death.

3.37 Did the police investigation turn up any results at all? The only exhibits which were discovered by police were a gun, a fired cartridge, two unfired cartridges, and a bottle of tablets which had been prescribed for Colin Roach. The police carried out extensive investigations in Worcestershire, Wales and Scotland, from the importation of the gun in 1979 to its sale in December 1980 by a Welsh farmer. They carried out no local investigations in the Stoke Newington, Hackney or Bethnal Green areas to trace its history from 1980 until 1983. D.C.S. Robertson, D.I. Scott and D.S. Pierce were totally unable to explain why this had not been done. Then there were the cartridges: No less than three individuals were said to have found the two loaded cartridges in Colin's jacket pocket at the post-mortem. They were P.C. Clayton, the exhibits officer, who was "on his honeymoon" during the inquest, D.S. Warwick and Dr. Venezis, the pathologist (which was odd, because pathologists do not normally search clothing). However, it was demonstrated quite dramatically at the inquest that the pocket of Colin's jacket was so stiffened with blood that it would have been almost impossible to "find" them as suggested. There is also the fact that no other part of Colin's clothing was said to have been searched. As far as the tablets were concerned, they were taken from James Roach while he was being questioned and never returned. Yet he had not said to the police that Colin was under medical treatment — how then can they have known that these tablets would be needed to help 'prove' Colin mentally ill at the inquest?

Was there something in the Police Station that the Police didn't want Mr. Roach to know?

3.38 The police investigation into Colin Roach's death was a most unusual one. They assumed or were aware from the start that he was dead and made no attempt to see if he was alive. All but one officer claimed to have "made no notes" following the incident. They interrogated Colin's father and two friends but this questioning seemed designed to find out things that were 'wrong' with Colin. Despite the fact that one friend was the last person known to have seen Colin alive he was not (according to D.S. Pierce) treated as an "actual" suspect or given a caution. No effort was made to use the three three people being questioned to identify the body, although it appears that the body was identified rapidly in some way. Instead, time was spent by the police searching for information which could 'prove' that Colin was mentally ill. The press were informed long before the Roach family of a version of the death which placed the maximum amount of blame on the deceased and none whatsoever on the police. Before they even began their investigation into the death the police had explained it as a suicide and in their investigation no enquiries were made in London as to the source of the gun.

3.39 During the course of the inquest Mr. Mansfield questioned the nature of the police investigation. He asked D.C.S. Robertson why James Roach had been kept in the police station and questioned for several hours before being told of his son's death. Mr. Robertson denied that this was what had happened. Mr. Mansfield then asked why James Roach had been refused access to the body. Mr. Robertson replied that he had felt "protective" and wanted to "minimise the anguish". The following exchange then took place:

Mr. Mansfield: Was there some thing in the police station that you didn't want Mr. Roach to know?

D.C.S. Robertson: Absolutely not!

Coroner: I don't see the relevance of your questions.

Mr. Mansfield: There is a connection between the police station and the death that isn't being revealed...

D.C.S. Robertson: That allegation is totally and utterly false!

Mr. Mansfield: The family are very disturbed about the investigation and want to know whether it was a truthful investigation... If this is a suicide and that is all it is, about the simplest, most humanitarian thing is for the father to have been shown the body and to have been taken home in a police car to his wife to explain the situation.

Coroner: That sounds to me more like a complaint against the police. If Mr. Roach had been kept at the police station until Christmas time it wouldn't have affected the cause of death.

Mrs. Roach (from public gallery): You're biased! You don't want the truth to come out!

(At this point the Coroner adjourned the inquest and the jury was dismissed from the court).

The Coroner might not have been able to see the relevance of Mr. Mansfield's questions but, as we said at the beginning of this chapter, the inquest jury was later to criticise the police investigation saying that "the bereaved family were kept in the dark over the death of their son".

Colin Roach's 'State of Mind'

3.40 Within hours of Colin Roach's death the police had issued a statement to the press claiming that "he had a history of mental illness". Colin's family and friends in the evidence submitted to this Inquiry have made it quite clear that Colin was not known to have a history of mental illness. Prior to our examination of the Coroner's summing up and the eventual verdict, it is necessary to consider the extent to which evidence relating to Colin's state of mind shaped the proceedings of the inquest. In other words: how the issue of Colin's state of mind was placed on the agenda of any future investigations from the time that the police issued the press statement, a mere two hours after his death.

3.41 It was described in Chapter 1 how Colin had experienced some 'anxiety' during the 2 weeks following his release from prison. Two distinct explanations or ways of attempting to understand this anxiety were mentioned — first, Colin's reactions to his prison experience and what he regarded as a threat made to his life; second, the nature of Colin's 'medical condition' as diagnosed by Dr. Cox. Neither of these explanations was complete in itself *but it is important to note that the evidence submitted to us by Joe Joseph regarding the 'death threat' was largely unknown to Colin's immediate family or to Dr. Cox.* In addition it should be noted that the police investigation did not trace the prisoner (in the cell next door) with whom Colin had had a fight, although the fight was mentioned both by Colin's former cell mate David Chapman (who gave evidence at the inquest) and Joe Joseph. The evidence to this Inquiry suggests that the 'death threat' was an outcome of the fight. Therefore, the first explanation, the 'death threat', was one which, if sufficiently investigated, may have changed the 'medical' diagnosis of Colin's behaviour at the time.

What did the Inquest reveal about Colin's 'Medical Condition?'

3.42 Dr. Cox also told the inquest that prior to meeting Colin (which she did on Monday 10 January) and without Colin having seen a psychiatrist, she had diagnosed that he had suffered a "psychotic episode" solely on the basis of a report which she said Colin's family had given her i.e. that he was "hearing voices". It will be recalled that in evidence to this Inquiry they denied having told her this. However, it remains significant that when Dr. Cox finally was able to meet Colin she was certain that he exhibited no suicidal tendencies.

3.43 The evidence we have received reveals significant factors which suggest Colin's state of mind was *not* suicidal. First, the way in which Colin was reacting to the prison incident and the perceived death threat was not at all irrational. Indeed, his friends (the Joseph twins) wanted to help him face the individuals whom he said were threatening him, but were not told their identities because in Colin's opinion that would put his friends at risk.

The second factor is that a number of witnesses have told us that, on the day of his death Colin was overjoyed at the birth of a baby to his younger sister Valerie and that he had been making plans to travel to France. This does not seem to be the behaviour of someone who had serious thoughts about suicide.

3.44   If the evidence concerning Colin's state of mind which we have considered indicates that he was not contemplating suicide, then it must be asked whether *any* of the evidence available to the inquest indicated that Colin's state of mind was suicidal. In order for an inquest to return a verdict of suicide it must be proven that the person intended to kill himself or herself and that he or she actually did it. The first element, the intent to take one's own life, is what concerns us here. Was there anything in the inquest which appeared to suggest that Colin intended to kill himself?

3.45   Another witness to be asked about Colin's state of mind at the inquest was Colin's father, James Roach. Mr. Marriage put to James Roach a statement he was alleged to have made during his questioning on the night of Colin's death in which it was claimed he had said Colin was "hearing voices" and "mentioning voodoo". Mr. Roach denied this both then and later when D.C.S. Robertson, during his evidence, repeated the allegation. Dr. Cox was also emphatic that Colin had never mentioned "voodoo". Indeed the very use of the term, according to one observer of this and other similar inquests, is suspect:

> This comes up time and time again when you get young Black people — it has certainly come up in the Michael Martin case in Broadmoor — if you want to damn some young person who has died in those circumstances, you say they were mentally ill, they believed in voodoo. When they are talking about voodoo, they are not talking about voodoo as a

religion. They are talking about Hollywood 'B' movies. You can see the police mind working: Oh he's a nutter, isn't he? What do nutters do? They hear voices. Oh, he's a Black man, therefore ... It was transparently obvious that this was what they had done. (Extract from evidence to the Inquiry by David Leadbetter of 'INQUEST').

3.46   Mr. Roach also told us that he had taken a container of tablets for Colin to the police station on the night of 12 January. The police took these tablets from him without asking what they were for, or whether Colin was unwell. The tablets were produced by Mr. Marriage, the police barrister, during the testimony of Dr. Cox. He then claimed that the number remaining in the bottle indicated that Colin had not been taking his full dosage at the time of his death. He also drew the court's attention to the minor traces of cannabis found in a sample of Colin's blood after his death and attempted to get Dr. Cox to agree that a combination of cannabis and largactil could produce "psychotic symptoms". Dr. Cox was not sure, saying she knew too little about what she described as "cannabis-induced psychosis". She then admitted to Mr. Mansfield that she did not know of a single case in which the taking of cannabis had led to suicide. However, both the "voodoo" allegation and the argument about "cannabis-induced psychosis" may well have affected the perception of the jury in considering Colin's state of mind.

3.47   The two examples above of Mr. Marriage's questioning show that it was not difficult for the meagre evidence about Colin's state of mind to be exaggerated in a particular direction. We find it alarming how easily the label 'psychotic' was applied to Colin Roach by Dr. Cox prior to her meeting with him. It is also a matter of concern that she then prescribed — the drug largactil — one which has been widely criticised for its use in prisons, where it is known as the 'liquid cosh'. There was not the time or opportunity for Colin to see a doctor with psychiatric qualifications before he died and it is also a matter of concern that very little was known of the reasons for his anxiety by the doctor who used the term 'psychotic' and prescribed him largactil. The link made by the police barrister between the taking of cannabis and psychosis is also alarming because it invokes a dubious concept which (like 'West Indian psychosis') has been challenged as racist, by groups and individuals in the Black community. These wider issues which are raised by Colin's treatment are dealt with in Appendix 6 ("Black people, misdiagnosis and mental health").

3.48   The evidence we have considered does not suggest that Colin had a suicidal state of mind. Admittedly it is very difficult to define a suicidal state of mind. In this area coroners and their officers, as research has shown, regularly rely upon subjective inferences and a particular range of social clues in any definition of a death as suicide.[2] But none of these could be applied to Colin's death. For example, "suicide" is regarded almost by definition as being a "solitary act".[3] It is apparent then that the choice of a police station (not a secluded location) would be incompatible with a suicide attempt, according to this social clue. Further, another traditional social clue, the suicide note (or any other indication that Colin intended to take his own life) was conspicuously absent. Usually in inquests on deaths where there are few obvious clues which support the judgement that the deceased *intended* to take his or her life and *succeeded*, it is highly unlikely that a suicide verdict will be returned.

However, whether the jury would decide that Colin Roach had killed himself was dependent on the way the Coroner summed up the evidence. Clearly without 'hard' forensic evidence to say that Colin definitely fired the shot, the Coroner's interpretation of Colin's state of mind would be of crucial importance.

The Summing-up and Verdict

3.49   The Coroner summed up the evidence, which had been heard, on 20 June 1983. Dr. Chambers began by addressing the jury on the purpose of the inquest. He told them it was not a trial and that its object was to find out who the deceased was, how, when and where he came by his death, as laid down in the Coroner's Rules. He said he had made 130 pages of notes, but that he did not propose to review every single piece of evidence. With this in mind, he did not choose to review the inconsistencies in the police evidence with regard to time and place. He told the jury that he believed all officers had given accounts "which are to the best of their knowledge correct". He said nothing about the fact that many officers could not corroborate each others whereabouts at the time of the shooting or explain the movements of the towel and the body as evidenced from their descriptions and the photos. All he said about the towel was: "You will recall that Mr. Scully told us that the bag was unzipped and the towel visible". Neither did Dr. Chambers remind the jury that it had proven impossible to fit the gun into the bag despite the highly irregular attempt made by D.C.S. Robertson during one lunch time. He even said that:

> The evidence about the gun, what you saw demonstrated is that it is possible to get it into the bag.

As to the whereabouts of 2 key groups of officers Dr. Chambers said:

> I suggest that the uniformed officers sitting inside do not seem to have had time to take part or the opportunity to have any relation with Mr. Roach's death. The 2 detectives have been examined . . . they were seen in the streets, it doesn't show they were anywhere else at the time. I am sure the evidence implicates no-one else.

3.50 At one point, the Coroner pointed out that he was really only concerned with the scientific part of the evidence. He spoke of the pathologists' conclusions of suicide without dwelling for long on the disagreements between them as to how it happened. But he admitted:

> The difficulty is, there is nothing to tie Colin Roach to the gun.

This was followed by the comment that:

> I should say negatives don't prove anything . . . It doesn't mean for example, that the gun wasn't handled . . .

This was an interesting comment. Especially since his opinions expressed earlier had been based on negatives, for example the evidence did "not" convince him anyone else was involved and he had "see nothing" to suggest that the uniformed officers might have been involved.

3.51 Another area of evidence discounted by the Coroner was the conflict between the police version and the Roach family's version of what time they had been told of Colin's death. The Coroner said that he did "not accept that any witness here has not told the truth" — and he believed that police officers "wouldn't want to perjure themselves".

It seems, therefore, that the Coroner's mind was made up. The police had not told lies; they had not been involved in Colin's death and it was possible that Colin had killed himself even though the 'scientific evidence' which he saw as "important", was unable to link the gun to Colin.

3.52 After reviewing the evidence in this manner, Dr. Chambers told the jury the verdicts they could return: suicide; misadventure; unlawful killing; and open verdict.

3.53 To return a verdict of suicide, or simply that Colin Roach shot himself, Dr. Chambers told the jury, they had to be satisfied that the actual cause of death was "uniquely self-inflicted". He told the jury that it was his duty to remind them that there was a presumption in law against suicide and there must be some "positive evidence — either direct or in the form of a very strong inference" to enable them to take such a view. However, he went on to say that in his experience "Nothing is done out of the blue" and mentioned that people who committed suicide often suffered some "psychiatric illness" or were "disturbed" by an "episode" in the past. He said he thought there was 'no doubt' that Colin had suffered such an "episode" before his death.

3.54 On a verdict of unlawful killing Dr. Chambers told the jury that they might consider that someone else might have entered and inflicted the wound but he added that "in the time scale it happened . . . it seems to have been premeditated action on the part of the deceased". He added that he thought that "no other person was involved".

Photograph: David Hoffman

Outside St. Pancras Coroner's Court, James Roach, Barnor Hesse and Pauline Roach give RFSC's response to the inquest verdict (20 June 1983)

3.55   On a possible verdict of misadventure, Dr. Chambers described a scenario in which Colin Roach had shot himself by accident after either cleaning the gun, preparing to fire it, or not realising that it was loaded. It appeared that he considered this a possible verdict.

3.56   The jury could return an open verdict, Dr. Chambers said, if they felt they had not heard enough evidence to make up their minds one way or another, but he went on to say that "from what we have heard it would seem an open verdict would be wrong" and made the remark that a great deal of work had been done on the preparation of the case.

3.57   The jury retired for two hours and returned to ask the Coroner whether it might return a majority verdict. The Coroner advised them that a majority verdict should be returned provided that the minority did not exceed two, but he again made some remarks indicating his own views saying that "the question of suicide must arise" and that: "The presumption is always against suicide but you may think on the facts you heard that this is the only possible verdict..."

3.58   The jury returned an hour later to declare a verdict of suicide by a majority of 8 to 2. The announcement of the verdict was greeted with uproar in the court, making it clear that Colin Roach's family and friends, as well as many of those involved in the campaign for a public inquiry, did not accept this.

Conclusion

3.59   The inquest into Colin Roach's death left unanswered a number of important questions and issues:
— the gun was never scientifically linked to Colin Roach;
— no fingerprints were found on the gun, or fibres from either the holdall or the towel which Colin had been carrying.
— the gun could not be concealed in Colin's holdall.
— police did not try to trace the origin of the gun in the London area.

- no less than three individuals claimed to have found the unfired cartridges in Colin's pocket.
- two pathologists were unable to explain the position of the body.
- the report of the police pathologist had been altered at least twice.
- there were unexplained changes in the position of Colin's body and of the towel he had been carrying.
- the inquest was unable to provide consistent explanations of the whereabouts of a number of police officers at the time of Colin's death.
- at least four officers named as being involved in the events of the night did not appear at the inquest.
- there was no explanation for the speed with which Colin's death was explained by police officers as 'suicide'.
- there was no explanation for how Colin's body was identified without allowing his father to see the body.

3.60 At the very least a major failing of the inquest, was that it did not *prove* that Colin Roach committed suicide. As we have seen, the police explained the death as suicide from the start and their apparent investigation of the death was circumscribed by this explanation. As we have also seen, the Coroner steered the jury strongly towards a verdict of suicide and away from either verdict which might have in any way implicated the police — unlawful killing or an open verdict. It is necessary at this point to consider the legal position on the verdict of suicide. According to evidence submitted to this Inquiry by INQUEST, it is an important legal principle, which has been upheld many times in the High Court, that there is a *presumption against suicide*. Suicide, according to case law, "must be affirmatively proved"; not by an "attractive possible theory", nor because it seems on the face of it to be a "likely explanation" nor — and this is especially pertinent in the Colin Roach case — "by a process of exhaustion or ruling out the likelihood of other explanations". Although it originated when suicide was a crime, "this principle remains valid and reflects a humane concern for the mental anguish which a suicide verdict can cause for the family of the deceased".

The arguments provided by INQUEST are very important here and are well worth consideration at length:

A few weeks before the Roach inquest began, the Lord Chief Justice, in quashing the verdict of suicide on the Italian banker Roberto Calvi reiterated the words of his predecessor in an earlier case which would he said, "serve as an appropriate reminder" to the jury:-

"I would impress upon coroners that if they find themselves compelled to return an open verdict, that is not in any sense a reflection upon them. It does not suggest that they are not doing their job properly, or are insufficiently perceptive. There are many, many cases where there is real doubt as to the cause of death and where an open verdict is right, and where anything else is unjust to the family of the deceased."

Applying these principles to the Roach case, a strong case exists against the verdict of suicide. We have noted the unsatisfactory nature of the evidence as to Colin's mental state, and it seems unnecessary to dwell on the weaknesses of the evidence linking Colin with the gun. The medical evidence — even if one accepts Dr. West's perhaps overconfident deductions from a handful of earlier cases — at most shows the relative unlikelihood of murder, rather than affirmatively proving suicide. The case law shows the importance of this distinction.

The Coroner did tell the jury of the presumption against suicide, and referred briefly to the Calvi case. But he did everything possible to point the jury towards a verdict of suicide, and away from an open verdict. He twice expressed the "personal opinion" that no one but Colin was involved (we might imagine the judge at a criminal trial expressing the "personal opinion" that the accused was guilty). He did "not accept that any witness here has not told the truth" — a fatuous remark in view of the stark conflict between James Roach's evidence and that of the police. He told the jury that coroners in general do not like open verdicts and it would be "wrong" to return an open verdict after "the amount of work" that had been done — most of it by Mike Mansfield who was obviously aiming for an open verdict. There can be little doubt that this all helped to ensure that the jury returned the "right" verdict, but it also robbed that verdict of any legitimacy in the eyes of the family and the wider community. (Extract from evidence to this Inquiry by INQUEST)

3.61   In the light of this and all we have considered so far, it is our firm and considered view that the correct verdict at the inquest should have been an 'open' one.

In our view it was wrong for the Coroner to have 'steered' the jury towards a suicide verdict. Against the background of evidence which this Inquiry has considered we contend: *The inquest proved neither that Colin actually fired the shot that killed him nor that he intended to take his own life; and that it would have been virtually impossible for Colin to have killed himself under the circumstances identified.*

3.62   If Colin shot himself the gun must have found its own way to the police station, because he could not have concealed it in his holdall. The gun must then have wiped itself clean of his fingerprints, because he was not wearing gloves. Further the gun must have chosen not to recoil after he fired it as no marks were found on the walls or floor, prior to placing itself on the opposite side of the foyer. In order for Colin to have shot himself and end up in the position where he was found his legs must have straightened themselves after he died (instantaneously) and his head must have prevented itself from marking or being marked by the wall against which his body was found leaning. Moreover his dead body must have found some way to move a rolled up towel from his neck to his shoulder to his lap, before his body leaned itself more upright in time for the police photographer's arrival. Clearly, the absurdity of this process of reasoning which arises from evidence collated to support a suicide verdict is implied in that verdict.

Inquest: An Overview — Part 2

3.63   There are a number of other areas relating to the coroner's inquest which have been highlighted as worthy of consideration:

3.64   *The role of the police:* to a large extent the Coroner is dependent upon the police for any interpretation he may form of the death before the inquest begins. If the police are also a party to the inquest, as they clearly were at the Colin Roach inquest, other interested parties such as the family of the deceased may be at a disadvantage. The police prepare the report for the Coroner, including statements by potential witnesses while the Coroner's officer, who often attends the post-mortem and views the body on behalf of the Coroner — as happened in the case of Colin Roach — is always a serving or former police officer. In the Colin Roach case, the Coroner's officer was a police officer serving in 'G' district, where Stoke Newington police station is located.

3.65 *The witness statements:* under the Coroner's rules, no person has a right to see statements submitted to the Coroner for assistance in his enquiries. On the first of many applications by Mr. Mansfield to see the witness statements taken by the police (including in 21 cases, from police officers) and which were available to the Coroner and to counsel for the police, Dr. Chambers refused, citing the ruling made in the Blair Peach case that the statements were the property of the police and could not be disclosed to anyone else without breach of confidence or trust. A concession was later made by Mr. Marriage by which Mr. Mansfield was allowed to see a copy of *some* of the statements just before a witness was to give evidence. These statements were taken back immediately after the witness had given evidence. As INQUEST put it:

> The number of times Mr. Mansfield referred to the statements reflects their crucial importance from an advocate's point of view. Armed with the statements, counsel can anticipate roughly what a witness will say, can spot discrepancies between what she/he says in court and his/her previous statements, and can judge which witnesses would best able to deal with particular matters — thus saving a good deal of time, doubtless to the satisfaction for the Coroner. It is particularly unfair that, in a case where the police are involved, one side should have these advantages and the other not. (Extract from evidence submitted to the Inquiry by INQUEST)

3.66 *The rules of evidence:* these apply in other courts but do not apply to inquests. Thus hearsay evidence is admissible. It is easy to appreciate why this should be so: since the main protagonist in the events under investigation — the deceased — cannot testify, it would unduly restrict the search for truth to exclude evidence of what she/he said while alive. In the Roach inquest, however, an important part of the evidence was what might be called 'double hearsay': the alleged statements of James Roach to the police, and of Mrs. Roach to the family doctor, that Colin had talked of hearing voices.

3.67 *The power of the Coroner:* the Coroner not only has absolute discretion as to which witnesses will be called to give evidence at an inquest and in which order, but he can also determine how witnesses may be questioned and can disallow any question he regards, as not relevant or not proper. Thus, for instance, Dr. Chambers decided that it was not "relevant" for Mr. Mansfield to question D.C.S. Robertson on the length of time for which James Roach was questioned before being told of his son's death. The jury clearly regarded this as relevant since they complained to the Home Secretary about the fact that "the bereaved family were kept in the dark over the death of the son".

3.68 *The summing up:* the area where the power of the Coroner is seen most acutely to dominate the inquest is in his summing-up to the jury. No one, other than the Coroner, is allowed to address the jury as to the facts and the jury does not hear a concluding interpretation of the evidence from the lawyers representing the parties involved. The only summary they hear is that of the Coroner who concludes by offering a choice of standard verdict. In the Colin Roach case, the Coroner was able to steer the jury towards a particular verdict.

Other inquests in which Coroners have summed up the evidence in such a way as to give rise to criticism that juries were mis-directed include those of Blair Peach, Simeon Collins and the first inquest into the death of Roberto Calvi.

3.69 *Juries and riders:* with certain categories of deaths including those in police or prison custody the Coroner is obliged to sit with a jury. However the jury, as one Coroner has written "is almost entirely circumscribed by the discretionary powers of the Coroner".[4] Juries do not often rebel against the choice of verdict which may be suggested in the Coroner's summing-up speech. They were until 1980 allowed to add 'riders' to their verdicts (specific recommendations designed to prevent future fatalities). However this right was abolished shortly after the Blair Peach jury added riders which were not at all acceptable to the Coroner and which effectively implicated the police in a way in which the verdict had not done. The letter to the Home Secretary by the Colin Roach jury may to some extent be regarded as an unofficial 'rider' to the verdict of suicide.

3.70 *Legal aid:* legal aid is not available for representation at inquests, although provision for it was made in the Legal Aid Act 1974. Had it not been for the willingness of solicitor Gareth Peirce and barrister, Mike Mansfield to waive their fees, the Roach family would have had to find several thousand pounds to ensure proper legal representation. The police, on the other hand, had all their legal fees met ultimately from rates and taxes. This situation inflicts an unjust disadvantages on many families of deceased persons.

Bibliographical Notes to Chapter 3

1. Coroner's Rules (1984) rule 36 (1)
2. See — Steven Taylor: 'Durkheim and the study of suicide' (MacMillian 1982).
   See also Maxwell Atkinson: 'Discovering Suicide' (MacMillan 1978).
3. Quoted from J. Maxwell Atkinson: 'Societal Reactions to Suicide: The roles of the coroner's definition' ppl79/80 in Cohen (ed). 'Images of Deviance' (Harmondsworth Penguin (1971)).
4. Quoted from the York Coroner, Anthony Morris, in "Legal Action" (August 1984).

Chapter 4

Colin Roach and the Press

4.1 It has often been shown that the media may not be impartial in relation to the events which they portray, despite the wishes of some journalists to maintain a 'balanced' or 'objective' approach to their work. One reason for this is that a newspaper or a news bulletin must inevitably select certain stories for coverage and reject others. Dramatic events such as a shooting and events with 'negative' consequences, such as arrests following a demonstration, must already have been selected as having 'news value' before we hear about them. Once a story is selected as having such news value, the story must present what are then selected as the 'key' facts from what is known. It is also regarded as important by those who believe they are presenting news objectively that 'fact' is kept separate from 'interpretation' although this is not always achieved.

4.2 Before we look at how the press dealt with the death of Colin Roach and some of the related issues, it is worth commenting that the media bear a special responsibility in what they report because, as well as providing information, they may well influence events, both because others will think and act upon the information they make available and because they establish in people's minds the important 'first impressions' of an event. Where an event has not been witnessed and is not able to be explained fully, for instance 'Who shot Colin Roach?' the first impressions given by the media are likely to have a powerful effect on contesting explanations which are debated after the event. Such first impressions are formed on the basis of facts and interpretation and, in the case of Colin Roach, it is necessary to see whether one particular interpretation of how he died — suicide — was kept separate from the known facts of the case or whether this interpretation came to be presented — and accepted — as one of the key facts.

In this chapter we examine the daily (mainly national) press during two periods:

(a) from 12 January 1983 until the inquest,
(b) during and after the inquest of 6-20 June 1983.

The Death of Colin Roach

4.3   Three national newspapers reported the death of Colin Roach on 13 January, the day after the death itself, with another two carrying reports on 14 January. On the 13 January *The Guardian* reported that a man had been found shot dead in Stoke Newington police station, that police had heard a shot and "found the man dead with gunshot wounds to the head and a sawn-off shot gun by his side". A similar story appeared in *The Sun* which added that the man was Black and in his twenties and had arrived at the police station "a few minutes earlier in a yellow Mercedes car". The paper also quoted a police spokesman as saying "No one saw the shooting, so we do not know exactly what happened. We are not sure whether the man shot himself or whether someone else was involved".

4.4   Neither of these stories suggested any interpretation as to the cause of death and limited themselves to straightforward presentation of the facts. However, the facts in these stories had been supplied by the police, the sole source of information.

4.5   On the following day, however, (14 January) *The Times* carried a short item saying that police were trying to identify the man found dead in the police station, adding that "Scotland Yard said that no crime was involved", while a *Daily Telegraph* item said that "A coloured man with a history of mental illness walked into Stoke Newington police station . . . and shot himself through the head".

4.6 All these stories, the only ones in the national newspapers tell of the "gun death" and all were based on information supplied by the Metropolitan Police Press Bureau. There are, however, significant differences between them. Only *The Guardian* and *The Sun* reported the story free of any added interpretation about the cause of the death, with *The Sun* making clear that the lack of any explanation was a police view. The other papers, however, presented fact mixed up with interpretation: *The Telegraph*, presented a view of the event as "suicide" as if it were a straightforward and uncontested fact.

4.7 The different ways in which the different papers reported the death show how the same 'facts' as supplied by one source — in this case the Metropolitan Police — can be used in different ways. While the claim that Colin Roach had a history of mental illness also emanated from the police and had disingenuously been marked "for background only — not for publication" clearly this did not prevent two newspapers from publishing it.

4.8 Apart from *The Guardian* and *The Sun* reports, the overall impression created by these initial reports was that Colin Roach's death was the result of suicide.

What is important to see is whether this impression was allowed to persist as subsequent events unfolded.

The first spontaneous demonstration, held by Colin's friends, on 14 January, was announced by the following headlines:

Police hurt in riot by mob *(Daily Express 15/1/83).*
Two police hurt in clash with protestors
(Daily Telegraph 15/1/83).
Eight held in demo at Black man's death
(Guardian 15/1/83).

4.9   *The Express* reported how "Two policemen were hurt yesterday when a mob besieged a London police station where a 21 year old Black man is believed to have shot himself two days ago". *The Daily Mail* reported that a "riot" involving a mob of more than 100 youths, had laid virtual siege to the police station. The youths, the paper said, were complaining about the death of a man who had walked into the police station and "shot himself dead with a sawn-off shot gun". Similarly, *The Daily Telegraph* in its report of the "clash" repeated its earlier story that "a Black man with a history of mental illness killed himself with a single barrel sawn-off shot gun".

4.10   These reports of the first protest demonstration were to set a certain tone for the reporting of all future demonstrations around the Colin Roach case. Thus on 18 January *The Guardian* reported "19 held in death protest" and on 22 January, the day of the first march called by the RFSC, *The Daily Telegraph* and *The Daily Mirror* both reported on the cancellation of police leave as a result of the march.

4.11   The demonstration on 22 January was widely reported in terms of "violence" and "looting" which were alleged to have occurred:

Violence erupts after demo
(Sunday Telegraph).

Demo ends in looting
(Mail on Sunday).

Twenty held in death demo riot
(Sunday Express).

22 held as youths march on police HQ
(Sunday Times).

Mob loots gems in demo raid
(News of the World).

Black demo gang loots jewels shop/Violence after police station protest
(Sunday People).

4.12   All these papers (apart from the *Sunday Telegraph*) reported on the breaking of a jeweller's shop window and the theft of jewellery, while, some *(Sunday Express, Sunday Times, Mail on Sunday,* and *News of the World)* spoke also of charges by demonstrators against police or police barricades.

4.13   The news stories of 15 and 23 January reveal a particular slant to the reporting of the public protests at a death which, to the Black community in Hackney and to Colin's friends and family, had not been explained at all. The description of the first spontaneous demonstration as a "riot" or a "clash" in some newspapers was repeated after the RFSC demonstration of 22 January as the "violence" or "riot" of a "mob" or "gang". Within these news bulletins there was practically no suggestion of why protestors were demanding a public inquiry into the death and refusing to accept the police version of events. However, there was much said about the apparent "violence" and "crime" of the protests, even in the 'quality' press, which tended to emphasise the numbers of arrests (e.g. *Sunday Times* and *Observer,* 23 January) primarily as being significant. We know from witnesses who described both these demonstrations that the violence did not occur out of a "riot" or "charges" by demonstrators but out of the decision to make indiscriminate arrests by the police.

4.14   As for the extensive and lurid descriptions in the Sunday papers of 23 January of the looting of a jeweller's shop, the following small item appeared in Paul Foot's column of the *Daily Mirror* of 26 January:

> The Sunday papers were full of a story of a 'demo mob' who broke away from a protest march about Colin Roach to rob a jeweller's shop. Scotland Yard confirmed on Monday that this information (which came originally from Stoke Newington police) was incorrect. The raid on the shop was at 3.23pm before the march occurred.

4.15   However, the fact that the large amount of unfavourable national press coverage of the marches outnumbered items such as these proved to be the case throughout most of the campaign. In the words of one member of the RFSC:

> It became the sort of situation where if we had a demonstration or if we organised something and there were arrests, it was news. If there weren't arrests we weren't doing anything .(Chas Holmes)

4.16   This meant in practical terms that a demonstration which was not characterised by any arrests such as the London-wide march on the 14 May, received a tiny amount of national news coverage. Yet the most 'violent' of all the demonstrations, (12 March), which the police broke up in a most dramatic and brutal way was only covered by a few 'quality' papers (*Guardian, Times, Telegraph*) and mainly because of the fact that Mr. Roach had been arrested. The single demonstration receiving the highest amount of press coverage had been the one on 22 January, covered by seven Sunday newspapers, quoted earlier as well as four of the national dailies on Monday, 24 January. It is also noticeable that stories which contained the most inaccuracies obtained all of their information from the police. The only 'eye witness' account was that of the owner of the jeweller's shop. This is perhaps why according to another member of the RFSC:

> All that materialised was the fact that arrests had been made, not how the arrests had come about. (Maurice Hesse)

The Campaign for a Public Inquiry

4.17   There was more to the campaign than protest marches ending in arrests and it was not entirely the case that the Colin Roach affair was only 'newsworthy' to the press when it seemed to be linked with 'violence' or 'criminality'. The last week of January 1983 saw Hackney M.P. Ernie Roberts, make public his concern about the breakdown of relations between police and public as well as his support for an inquiry. Also in that week, the GLC responded to RFSC, via Hackney Council, to a request for a modest grant of £1,500 to assist the campaign. On 27 January it was this item which made front page news in two national newspapers, *The Daily telegraph* and *The Daily Mail,* while Ernie Roberts' story was only reported on the inside pages of the *Daily Express.*

4.18   The difference in importance accorded to these stories by the press highlight a significant point. Ernie Roberts had made detailed comments to the media, pointing out how the death of Colin Roach was the latest phase in a steadily worsening relationship between police and the local Black community. The sensational headline attached to this story by *The Daily Express* ("Race Riot Peril") was misleading to say the least. The breakdown of relations mentioned by Ernie Roberts concerned conflict between the police and the community rather than between the Black and white communities. However, it is important to note that prior to this time most national daily newspapers had said nothing to relate the community's reaction to Colin Roach's death to the history of policing in Stoke Newington.

4.19   The remarks made by Ernie Roberts reflected closely what was being said by the Black community and the RFSC who did not have ready access to the media.

4.20   These elements of background to the Colin Roach campaign contrast with the two stories on the same day about the "GLC Cash". Neither story gave any information about the history of poor police/community relations which had led to the demand for an inquiry or even the reasons why the RFSC were questioning the 'official account' of Colin's death. Instead, *The Daily Mail,* in a story entitled "Row over GLC cash to fight police", reported that "Black activists" were to receive £1,500 to protest over the death, it quoted "furious opponents" of the GLC's "Left-Wing leaders" who accused them of "fostering discontent" among Black people against the police and claimed that the grant had been given against the advice of the GLC's legal advisers.

4.21   In a similiar story entitled "GLC cash for death inquiry", the *Daily Telegraph* said that the grant was to be used to "fund a campaign for a public inquiry into the death of Colin Roach, who shot himself at Stoke Newington police station". The impression of Colin's death as a suicide based on an interpretation supplied by the police, had now been established as 'fact'. Although *The Telegraph* also stated that

Ernie Roberts had called upon the Home Secretary to set up an inquiry, it is clear that "the GLC cash" was the main element of their story as it was in *The Daily Mail*.

Background To The Campaign

4.22 Several other articles appeared in the national press between January and the inquest in June which examined what they considered to be the background to the Colin Roach issue. *The Daily Mail* which had reported on the GLC cash on 27 January, devoted an editorial and a background feature to the Colin Roach campaign on the following day. In the editorial entitled "Irresponsible" *The Mail* criticised the CRE and others who were demanding an inquiry. Such demands, the paper said: "Can only further fan local passions and pander to prejudice". In the accompanying feature article entitled "Prison secret of a man in shooting — he was a mugger not long out of jail". *The Mail* "revealed" that Colin Roach had only just been released from a three month sentence in Pentonville Prison. The story was clearly intended to smear those campaigning for an inquiry by linking them to a man with a criminal record. The story also, of course, affirmed the popular stereotype of the "Black mugger" and in doing so almost implied that his death was only to be expected. This kind of background feature began a campaign of abuse which continued with Professor John Vincent's weekly column in *The Sun* on 16 February where he pleaded, "Protect our police from daft Lefties". Vincent claimed that "since the death of Colin Roach all hell had been let loose. And the victims are the police. They face trial by pressure group". Outsiders, Vincent said, had stirred things up just as they had done around the Deptford fire in 1981: ".. . in no time at all the trouble-makers were whipping up the issue for political purposes. Private tragedy was turned into public stunt". This was happening now too, Vincent argued.

> It takes two to make good race relations and those who turn West Indians against the police create bad relations.

4.23 Apparently, the Professor did not consider the possibility that the motivation for the campaign had come from within the Black community. In addition, the suggestion that 'outsiders had stirred things up' implied that the community did not have legitimate criticisms or grievances against the police. In *The Daily Express* the background feature on the Colin Roach affair was not published until the morning of the first day of the inquest, (6 June 1983). In a story entitled "Death the Left has made into a cause", *The Express* printed photographs of three people (all white) whom it described as:

> Brynley Heaven — a former member of the Communist Party and now chairman of Hackney's self-styled police committee.
>
> Gareth Peirce—a well known Left-wing London lawyer.
>
> Ian Haig — Secretary of the Hackney Council for Racial Equality.

4.24   *The Daily Express* feature began by saying that the inquest would hear how Colin Roach had "killed himself". It continued its background to the story by describing say how the inquest was not likely to satisfy "a group of Left-wingers" who had "swung into action following Colin's death". The reader is told that the police on the first demonstration included his brother and his friends, who were genuinely baffled by his death, *but* (our emphasis) among them was "Ian Haig, a community worker". The story adds that Ian Haig "rushed out a report containing 45 allegations of police brutality against coloureds" and that "Councillor Brynley Heaven set the ball rolling" by calling for financial support for the campaign.

4.25   The article is worthy of some comment. First, in stating that Colin Roach had killed himself, just before the inquest began, the feature was deeply prejudical to any juror who might have read it. Second, in mentioning the demonstration of January, the story identified Ian Haig as being distinct from Colin's family and friends, whom it conceded were "genuinely baffled". This suggests that there was something not genuine about the HCRE allegations of "police brutality" which were "rushed out" subsequently. Third, when we are then told how Brynley Heaven "set the ball rolling" by calling for financial support from "the Labour dominated council" (of Hackney) it is clear that this story has explained the fact that a campaign developed and gained momentum purely in terms of the actions of individuals, the 'Left wingers'. Phrases like "swung into action" and "set the ball rolling" are employed to assist in this explanation.

4.26 Overall the personalisation of the campaign around these individuals and the mention made of their 'Left-wing' credentials as if these were a slur, attacked the credibility of the campaign. It also omitted the fact that the campaign arose from a Black community challenging the illogicality of the 'suicide' explanation of Colin Roach's death. These attacks, slurs and omissions combined to support the prejudical statement in the article that the inquest would be hearing how Colin Roach "killed himself" that day.

4.27 A few national newspapers produced articles prior to the inquest which redressed the balance (slightly) in favour of an even handed presentation of the different views on how Colin had died. In 9 national news stories which came out within 48 hours of the demonstration on 22 January, only 1 in *The Guardian* of 24 January, told the reader any background details about why Colin's family and friends were questioning the police explanation of his death. It also described the "angry" response to the death by the Black community as a result of a history of bad relations between that community and the police. This did not represent a 'feature' article (although *The Guardian* eventually published a feature in April entitled "Behind the rift between police and Blacks"). The first two national feature articles about Colin Roach presenting a 'balanced' picture were *The Daily Mirror* story of 26 January, mentioned earlier, and the lengthy article in *The Times* of 28 January, "Why Colin Roach's death left a legacy of unrest".

4.28 The presentation of the issues in these latter two stories was a rare example of an attempt to explain why there had been a genuine community reaction to the death of Colin Roach. In *The Times* article of 28 January a series of interviews with Colin's friends (mainly Jim Joseph and Keith Scully) trace his movements on the night of his death and we are told of the issues surrounding the police treatment of the Roach family following Colin's death.

4.29 The article also noted how Hackney Black Peoples Association (HBPA) has been calling for a full inquiry into policing for some time, a point ignored by almost all national daily newspapers, and indicated that the police explanations of Colin's death "are seen by Black leaders as an attempt to cover their own backs at the expense of the family's feelings".

4.30 In *The Daily Mirror* story of 26 January it was also pointed out that Colin's family and friends did not know him to be suicidal and that the family's version of events challenged that of the police. However, it is important to note that neither *The Times* nor *The Daily Mirror* was able to offer such a detailed examination of alternative views or interpretations throughout 1983, particularly in the period after the inquest into Colin's death.

4.31 In most cases, national daily newspapers continued to present news about the Colin Roach campaign which ignored the views of the campaign and the wider Black community on the questionable nature of Colin's death or the relevant policing history. Instead, the press focussed on the role played by local authorities in the affair.

4.32 On 8 February *The Daily Mail* attacked Hackney Council's decision not to pay the police precept, claiming that the action amounted to a "fine" and that it was illegal. The story carried no account of the discussions which led to the decision, nor any explanatory quotes from any of those involved in making the decision. Nor did the paper explain the background to the Council's decision, stating simply – and incorrectly — that the decision was "because of the death of a 21 year old coloured man". It was left to *The Guardian* of 9 February to explain the Council's decision by saying that the death of Colin Roach was "the latest focus for longstanding grievances against the police among the Black community".

The Inquest

4.33 The only newspapers to cover the issues surrounding the inquest with any consistency were *The Times, The Guardian* and *Daily Telegraph*, each of which on the whole presented straightforward accounts for the moves by the GLC to have the inquest moved from St. Pancras Coroner's Court. *The Daily Mail,* however, in its first report on the GLC moves, some days after these had begun, claimed that Labour GLC councillors were ignoring police warnings on the likelihood of disorder if the venue were changed (20 April 1983).

4.34 When the decision was made to hold the inquest in Clerkenwell County Court the change of venue was reported in *The Guardian*. The inquest itself and the six days on which it sat between 6-20 June was covered in fairly consistent detail by papers such as *The Guardian, The Times, The Daily Telegraph* and *The Morning Star.* However, most of the articles were cast as news pieces, mainly descriptive in nature, and none really questioned or highlighted particular aspects of the evidence given each day during the proceedings.

4.35 It remained the case, however, that selectivity and a difference in emphasis were present in the press reports of the inquest as it had been previously. First, in relation to the allegations that Colin had "heard" voices and spoken of "voodoo": these were not substantiated by Mr. Roach who in fact denied them on the first day of the inquest when it was alleged that he had made these comments in the statement taken from him by the police. However, articles such as:

Voodoo voices riddle *(The Sun 7 June 1983).*

Colin Roach was hearing voices before his death
(The Times 7 June 1983).

conveyed a particular impression which was heightened by articles which reflected the attempt by the police barrister to prove that Colin was the victim of 'cannabis induced psychosis':

Drugs clue to shooting *(Daily Mirror 7 June 1983).*

A totally opposite impression was conveyed by stories such as:

Roach showed no suicidal tendencies
(Morning Star 7 June 1983).
Suicide view challenged by Roach Inquest
(Guardian 7 June 1983).

These reflected the fact that Dr. Cox had been sure Colin was not suicidal and the police pathologists's view of Colin's death had been effectively challenged by Mr. Mansfield in cross-examination.

4.36 It was even more interesting that five national newspapers carried articles emphasising the fact that Dr. West, the pathologist engaged by the Roach family, had concluded that it was suicide:

It was suicide, Roach jury told
(Guardian 14 June 1983).

Roach not involved in struggle
(Times 14 June 1983).

Shot gun victim 'killed himself'
(Daily Mail 14 June 1983).

Suicide, says the Roach family's own pathologist
(Daily Express 14 June 1983).

Roach 'shot himself'
(Daily Mirror 14 June 1983).

However, the fact that Dr. West had conceded that Colin could have been shot by someone else was hardly reported by the national daily press at all, except in one newspaper:

Roach murder possible
(Morning Star 14 June 1983).

4.37 Other significant aspects of the inquest into Colin's death, like the inconsistencies in police evidence revealed by Mr. Mansfield's cross-examination, were largely ignored in the press. The day on which the Coroner adjourned the inquest after refusing to allow Mr. Mansfield to question D.C.S. Robertson on the prolonged detention of James Roach was described in articles such as:

Uproar hits Roach inquest
(The Sun 18 June 1983).

Roach inquest interrupted amid parents' shouts of 'lie' and 'bias'
(The Times 18 June 1983)

Mum's outburst halts Roach inquest
(The Daily Mirror 18 June 1983).

Apart from giving the general impression of chaos, these essentially descriptive stories did not indicate the importance of the contradiction in evidence between D.C.S. Robertson and Mr. Roach over the length of the period for which he had been detained at the police station before being told of his son's death.

4.38 The inquest verdict was treated almost unanimously by the press as a vindication of the views which they had themselves expressed earlier during the campaign. In both the 'quality' press and the tabloids a news story about the verdict was complemented by a feature or editorial which explained the campaign for a public inquiry in retrospect. Taking examples from both a 'tabloid' and a 'quality' newspaper, two news stories in *The Times* and *The Daily Mail* of 21 June were entitled "Colin Roach shot himself, decides inquest jury by 8-2 majority" *(The Times)* and "Anger at Suicide verdict on Roach" *(The Daily Mail)*. These were followed later in each newspaper by a feature entitled "Youth's death used to fuel mistrust of the police" *(The Times)* and by an editorial entitled "The real stench at Stoke Newington" (in *The Daily Mail)*.

4.39 *The Daily Mail,* in its news story, described the way the inquest ended and the jury's majority verdict without any particular comment. Then, in the editorial, it said that:

> Colin Roach, a disturbed young Black man, put the barrel of a sawn-off shot gun into his mouth and pulled the trigger... There has never been a shred of evidence to the contrary.

It then reminded its readers that "professional protestors" had "moved in" and "exploited . . . genuine emotion and whipped up anti-police feeling".

The article ended with the phrase:

> Yes, there should be an inquiry. Not into the suicide of Colin Roach . . . but into the anarchic and racist motivation of the martyr-makers. For that is the real stench emanating from Stoke Newington.

4.40 *The Times,* like *the Daily Mail,* confined its news story in reporting the inquest verdict without comment. However, *The Times'* feature article which explained how Colin's death had been "used to fuel mistrust of the police" was perhaps surprising considering that it appeared to contradict the open minded approach exemplified by the earlier *Times* article of 28 January. At that time it had outlined the questionable nature of Colin's death, something which we have argued in the previous chapter was compounded by the questions unanswered in the inquest. However, *The Times* now argued that:

> not a scrap of evidence has emerged to show that his death was anything other than a bizzare and tragic suicide.

4.41 *The Times* did concede that there was a history of tension and mistrust of the police in Hackney but believed that Colin's death had been:

> used by the Left to fuel that mistrust in the cause of seeking more police accountability, at the expense of police and community relations in an area where there are genuine difficulties to be tackled, not exacerbated.

4.42 The article further conceded that there did exist serious contradictions of evidence between the police and Mr. Roach, but asserted that "even if the police treatment of the family was callous, nothing alters the overwhelming medical and circumstantial evidence that Colin Roach killed himself".

The Times went to the extent of saying that the Roach family had been "less than honest" about Colin's state of mind:

> He was, they have said, a bit depressed. From the evidence to the inquest, it is clear that he was seriously disturbed.

4.43 The reasons why the evidence was "clear" that Colin was "seriously disturbed" are not stated. However, just as the daily inquest report of *The Times* gave hardly any indication that the evidence of the police and the two pathologists was shown to be inconsistent under cross-examination, this article in effect reinforced these omissions. In addition to this, the officer who 'found' Colin Roach was praised for having given an account which "had a ring of truth about it".

4.44 *The Guardian,* in an article entitled "why an open and shut case became an issue" (21 June 1983) expressed very similar sentiments. It also attempted to explain why the "open and shut case" of a depressed young man killing himself could become a "cause celebre".

4.45 The article suggests several reasons why it may have "seemed" to Black people that the police were not investigating the death, and smearing the man with mental illness. It also criticised the *Daily Mail* for wrongly describing Colin as a "young mugger", which made it seem that "the press were once again colluding with the police".

4.46 However, the upshot of the *Guardian's* story was that the campaign attracted (within days) the political lobbies which "want greater police accountability in London" and the story ended with the response of the two police officers from 'G' District; Chief Supt. Burgess pointed out that:

> The majority of people in Hackney have no complaints about the police.

While Commander Taylor explained the police reaction to Colin Roach's death by saying that:

> overtures to improve community relations met rebuffs.

4.47 Although the article did not ignore the views of the community in challenging the police account of Colin's death, it ended with authoritative police quotes, suggesting that it was the "political lobbies" who had rebuffed the police, while the "majority" in the community had no real grievances.

4.48 There were two 'postscripts' to the death of Colin Roach and the inquest as far as the national press was concerned, both of which occurred shortly afterwards. First, there was the inquest jurors' letter to the Home Secretary announced fairly modestly by small news bulletins such as:

> **Inquiry ordered into Roach case**
> *(The Times 29 June 1983).*
>
> **Rap for police in Roach letter**
> *(Daily Express 29 June 1983)*
>
> **New probe into Roach Case**
> *(Daily Mail 29 June 1983).*

These descriptive items merely indicated that there was to be an investigation of the Jury's concerns by the Police Complaints Board under Section 49 of the Police Act 1964.

4.49 However, the impact or effect of this reporting paled into insignificance compared with the massive coverage given the following day to Sir Kenneth Newman's (Metropolitan Police Commissioner) press conference at which he launched his first annual report, inspiring headlines such as:

> **Police chief attacks political extremists**
> *(The Times 30 June 1983).*
>
> **Police chief hits at enemy on left — political agitators are shielding criminals, says Newman**
> *(Daily Express 30 June 1983).*
>
> **Labour chief hits back at police chief's attack on Left**
> *(Daily Mail 30 June 1983).*

4.50 The point which was recognised by all the newspapers which carried the news of Newman's 'attacks' on his 'enemies' was that he specifically referred to the campaign for a public inquiry into the death of Colin Roach. He mentioned activist "groups" which "deliberately trawl for issues they can elevate to the status of cause celebres". When asked if this statement referrred to groups involved in the Colin Roach case, Newman was widely reported to have said "I think there are elements of that in the Colin Roach case". In the report itself, Newman had written generally about what he described as a "campaign of dedicated denigration of the police", without mentioning Colin Roach, adding that this campaign included "uneducated and unfair criticism of police performance against crime . . . and tendentious accounts of complaints against the police, all bolstered by a variety of hostile broadsheets and giveaway newspapers" (*Daily Mail* 30/6/83).

4.51 The impact of Newman's stance was picked up immediately by press editorials and features. However, what is more significant for our purposes is that any subsequent articles which examined the Colin Roach campaign did so from a perspective strengthened by Sir Kenneth Newman's remarks and therefore subsequently made reference to Newman in attempts to 'explain' how the campaign occurred. For example, the *Daily Express* produced a feature in the same issue which carried Newman's remarks and promised that:

> As police warn off 'the enemy within' (the article would provide) proof that activists are at work. (*Daily Express* 30/6/83).

The title of the feature "This Sinister Exploitation of Human Tragedy" echoed both Newman and the features produced earlier by the *Express* such as the one on 6 June 1983. This feature conducted an examination into a community centre in Hackney in which it was maintained:

> . . . a centre for the distribution of extremist literature, is a rallying point for Black and civil rights demonstrators, and the nerve centre of the Colin Roach Family Support Committee.

One part of this story with a familar ring was its claim that:

> law and order teeters on the brink of breakdown as immigrant families with no axe to grind and lives to lead are whipped into an anti-police fury.

4.52   One final example of the convergence between the press condemnation of the Colin Roach campaign following the inquest verdict and its tendency to feature Newman's views, as expressed in his annual report, was provided by the feature written by Roy Kerridge which appeared in several publications, including the *Daily Mail* on 1 July entitled "Myths that poison the minds of Britain's Blacks".

The story was introduced by the comment "here, an expert exposes the brainwashing of Britain's Blacks..." and related Newman's depiction of activists who are "constantly at work, persuading young Blacks that they are victims of deliberate police persecution" to the contents of the feature.

The feature told of "young men of West Indian parentage" (who) "often feel they are strangers in a bewildering country". What is revived in this story is the notion that when these young men, "trustingly look to white friends for advice (they) . . . become enveloped in a cloud of unreason".

In one sentence, this writer tied together the notion that Colin was mentally ill and associated this 'illness' with left-wing thought:

> Untold numbers of young men like Colin Roach leave school every year seeing unknown enemies everywhere. Feeling themselves to be the victim of unseen forces, they succumb easily to mental illness. Much of modern left wing thought seems itself inseparable from paranoia!

4.53   It is clear from this brief examination of the press treatment of the death of Colin Roach that a consistently racist current ran throughout much of it and reached its peak when the issue could be considered 'over' (after the inquest) and conclusions could be drawn about 'what it had all been about'. Both in the 'quality' press and in the tabloids, it was soon accepted that the Colin Roach campaign was associated with particular identifiable 'targets'. For example, crime and criminality were linked both to the Black presence on the demonstrations and to the biographical depiction of Colin Roach; Left wing 'extremists' and local authorities were discovered to have been involved and then accused of having 'whipped up' everything and the police were portrayed as the party who was under 'attack', not the protesters. In addition, doubts about Colin's mental state were given free reign by press stories both in the early days following his death and following the verdict of an inquest which had proved (as far as the media were concerned) that what they had first said about Colin Roach being mentally ill and having killed himself, was correct.

4.54 It is also clear that few national newspapers ever explained why Colin's family, friends and the Black community were questioning the police explanation of his death. Neither did they relate Colin Roach's death to the history of bad relations between the police and the public and, in particular, the history of well-documented cases of malpractice against Black people by police at Stoke Newington police station. In omitting to do this, the press failed completely to explain to its readers precisely why the death of Colin Roach had massive reverberations through the borough. Few national papers bothered to try and explore this history even though to have done so would have helped explain why people were demanding a public inquiry. For instance, when Hackney Council for Racial Equality published its dossier on its experience of policing, only three national newspapers covered the report: *The Times* in an end-piece to its report on Colin's funeral (19/2/83), *The Guardian* in a short news item (22/2/83) and the *Morning Star* (21/2/83). After the inquest verdict, the background feature which did appear (in *The Times* and *The Guardian*) not only failed to get to grips with the concerns of many people in Hackney but even retreated from the more open minded approach characteristic of their earlier features.

4.55 In our view, the inquest verdict of suicide and the certainty (against the evidence) of two pathologists and the Coroner that this was the case, ensured that *The Times* and *The Guardian* revised their position in line with these institutional and 'final' definitions of Colin's death as suicide. It was after all true that the pronouncements of the pathologists that they believed Colin killed himself were covered more widely than Mr. Mansfield's revelations (through his cross examination of witnesses) that the forensic evidence suggested that Colin could not have fired the gun. In a wider sense, the depth of press coverage given to Sir Kenneth Newman in his attack on the campaign is symptomatic of the willingness of the press to reproduce the definitions of the powerful.

4.56 However, we must also acknowledge that institutional status does not always ensure a relatively great amount of coverage. Ernie Roberts, M.P. received little press coverage in February 1983 for initiating a motion in Parliament demanding a public inquiry into the death of Colin Roach, yet *The Times* carried a substantial report on 18 March 1983 on how another Labour M.P. (Alex Lyon) had "attacked" the "Roach campaigners". Indeed, while it is clear that the RFSC's views were rarely reproduced in any national daily newspaper, it is equally clear that Ernie Roberts' warnings of a breakdown of police-community relations could only make the national press if labelled as fears of a "race riot".

4.57 Colin Roach's death was not reported objectively or impartially. It began with the police account of his death, which linked mental illness with an avowed but unexplained certainty that no one else had been involved. Instead of portraying an inexplicable death of a young man with "too much to live for" and the justifiable reaction of the family and community, the press gave the public a picture of a bizarre 'suicide' leading to 'voilent protests' motivated only by a wish to attack the police; while the police interpretation of Colin's death as suicide merged with the original facts of the case. The motivation for the protests was gradually relocated from the Black 'mob' of 22 January to the 'outside agitators' who were sometimes said to be 'Black militants' but more often described as white left wingers'. The minor involvement of the Greater London Council in the campaign was treated as if militant or left wing outsiders were in control. Meanwhile an expectation was developed in press features and editorials that all these 'unnecessary' protests would be answered by the inquest. The inquest verdict of suicide, itself partly an outcome of prejudical media attitudes that Colin Roach had committed suicide, was followed by more features and editorials saying effectively 'we told you so'.

Chapter 5

The Wider Political Context

5.1 A death occurs in circumstances which are by any standards unusual. It has been described already that Colin's family, his friends and the local community responded to the event in a way which reflected their awareness of a history of oppressive policing and their determination to challenge the official explanation of his death. It was then shown how unsatisfactorily the Coroner's inquest dealt with the unanswered questions arising from Colin Roach's death, even to the extent of multiplying these unanswered questions. The portrayal of Colin Roach and the case for a public inquiry into his death by the media was shown to have reinforced the notion that Colin committed suicide long before the inquest reached its verdict, in addition to providing a reason for the press to 'close the lid' on the campaign following the verdict and the remarks made about the whole affair by Sir Kenneth Newman at the launch of his annual report in July 1983. In this chapter we consider how and why it was possible for two Home Secretaries during 1983 to refuse requests to set up a public inquiry both before and after the inquest.

The Police Complaints Board Investigation

5.2 Two of the ten jurors in the Colin Roach inquest had evidently not agreed with the majority verdict of suicide, while the disquiet of all ten about the police's role in the affair had been expressed in their letter (reported in Chapter 3) to the Home Secretary. Their specific criticisms were that the Roach family had been "kept in the dark" over the death of their son, that the police had not been "sympathetic" and that "the case could have been investigated more professionally and extensively".

5.3   Leon Brittan, the Home Secretary of the newly elected Conservative Government of June 1983 said in reply to a Parliamentary Question on 28 June 1983 that:

> Now that the Jury has delivered its verdict on the death of Mr. Colin Roach, I have looked again at the requests for a public inquiry made to my predecessor before the inquest. I am not persuaded that such an inquiry is desirable or necessary. Members of the inquest jury have, however, sent me a letter in which they have said that they are satisfied that they reached a fair verdict, but have made certain criticisms of the police handling of the case and in particular of their treatment of the other members of the Roach family . . . The Commissioner of Police for the Metropolis has arranged for the criticisms to be investigated as a complaint under section 49 of the Police Act 1964.

5.4   The Police Complaints Board investigation was headed by Mr. J.S. Evans, an Assistant Chief Constable from the Greater Manchester Force. The PCB replied to the jurors on 9 April 1984. Although the *Mail on Sunday* (28 January 1984) had already leaked the information that the Director of Public Prosecutions would not be asked to prosecute any officers as a result of the investigation. The findings of the PCB were as follows:

(1)   Mr. Roach had said that he was questioned for over three hours despite repeatedly asking about his son.

The PCB said:

> While it is clear that Mr. Roach was questioned for several hours and asked to provide a statement at a time when he was clearly distresed . . . it was not improper for the police to have questioned Mr. Roach and the two men who were with Colin prior to his death.

(2) Mr. Roach had said that only after he refused to answer any more questions, having been in the police station nearly three hours, was he told (at 3am) of Colin's death. However, the police had claimed he was told by 12.45am.

> The PCB said:
>
> The contention of the police that Mr. Roach was informed of his son's death soon after his arrival at the police station... cannot be established beyond doubt but the Board are satisfied that the investigation has produced no evidence to the contrary.

(3) Mr. Roach had not been allowed to see Colin's body in order to identify that it was his son, despite repeated requests.

> The PCB said:
>
> Detective Chief Superintendent Robertson refused Mr. Roach's request to see his son's body... out of protective sympathy towards a man who was already distraught at the news he had been given and because he... was anxious to protect the scene until all the evidence had been obtained.

(4) Mrs. Roach had not been given any information about Colin or her husband despite repeatedly telephoning Stoke Newington Police Station. She did not hear what had happened until Mr. Roach returned home, hours later.

> The PCB said:
>
> The reasons why she was not informed of what had happened appear to have been well intentioned.

(5) Mrs. Roach had said that her husband was not brought home by the police until 5am.

> The PCB said:
>
> It was nearly 4am when Mr. Roach finally got home.

(6) Mr. and Mrs. Roach had said that two officers had searched Colin's room leaving it in complete disarray and had woken up his younger brother and that W.P.C. Maddison had assaulted Mrs. Roach gripping her by the throat.

The PCB said:

> The search was conducted as discreetly as possible with the permission of Mr. Roach. Its purpose was to ensure that evidence valuable to the inquiry or ammunition had not been left there.

(7) The conclusions of the PCB were that:

> There has now been a very full, impartial and probing investigation which has produced no evidence of wilful misconduct.

5.5 The findings of the PCB investigation highlighted the ineffectiveness of the police complaints procedure itself, a matter which is discussed in more depth in relation to the policing in Hackney, in Part II of this report. Following the inquest jury's request that the Home Secretary "look into the matter", the request could reasonably have been interpreted as a further reason to set up a public inquiry under section 32 of the 1964 Police Act. The legal grounds for such an inquiry being set up following the inquest are examined later in this Chapter.

However, it was Leon Brittan's decision instead to deal with the inquest under section 49 of the Act as a police complaint.

5.6 While it is clear that the jury believed they had "fairly reached a decision of suicide" (i.e. they had not challenged the police account of how the death had occurred), they had been "deeply distressed" about police conduct. However, the PCB investigation appears only to have underlined a further denial by the police of the substance of the jurors complaint. It could not even substantiate what they decided was improper. It found, for example, "no evidence" that Mr. Roach really had been "kept in the dark" for 2½ hours over Colin's death, and said nothing of significance about the complaint that the case could have been "investigated more professionally and extensively."

The result of the PCB investigation, then, shows that as an 'alternative' to a public inquiry into the death of Colin Roach and the surrounding circumstances, it failed even to examine a narrowly-defined range of those circumstances.

Clearly it is necessary to return to the theme of this Chapter. How and why was a public inquiry refused both before and after the inquest?

5.7   At first sight the answer may appear simple. Prior to the sitting of the inquest, the Government was able to argue that all the questions arising from Colin Roach's death would be answered by the inquest. Following the suicide verdict, it was even less likely that a newly re-elected Conservative government would respond to the kinds of outstanding questions which we have shown were raised by the death of Colin Roach. However, the 1964 Act has in the past been judged largely at the discretion of the Home Secretary in office at the time. As we argue below, it is clear that the position of William Whitelaw and his successor, Leon Brittan, in not responding to the call for a public inquiry, was influenced by a variety of groups and institutions having a greater or lesser significance in shaping the political climate at that time.

5.8   These 'groups' include the police, the media, the Black community, other community groups, the Courts, Parliament, the St. Pancras Coroner, the GLC and Hackney Borough Council. It was in the context of the position taken on the death of Colin Roach by these groups, positions which were increasingly polarised as time went on, that the Home Secretary responded negatively to the demands for a public inquiry. What we are seeking to explain is why the unanswered questions arising from the death were given no satisfactory response by London's police authority, the Home Secretary.

In order to do this it is necessary to examine:

(a)   The reasons given by William Whitelaw and Leon Brittan for refusing to set up a public inquiry in 1983.

(b) The statutory basis of a public inquiry under section 32 of the Police Act 1964 and the circumstances in which previous section 32 public inquiries have been set up.

(c) The response of other individuals, institutions and groups to the issues raised by the death of Colin Roach and how their responses may have affected the political climate in which William Whitelaw and Leon Brittan said 'no' to a public inquiry.

The Reasons Why a Public Inquiry Was Refused in 1983

5.9   There were numerous occasions during 1983 when the Home Secretary (William Whitelaw, before the June election, Leon Brittan afterwards) was asked specifically for a public inquiry into the death of Colin Roach, from the placards which appeared on the first spontaneous demonstration organised by Colin's friends on 14 January to the plethora of letters from organisations supporting the campaign and Parliamentary questions raised by a number of MPs, not to mention the four demonstrations led by the RFSC.

5.10   The official response to these demands has been mentioned earlier. Until May 1983 William Whitelaw (and other Home Office officials responding on his behalf) had argued that "a full independent and public inquiry" into Colin Roach's death was "precisely what the Coroner's inquest will provide". Following the pronouncements of both Dr. Chambers, the St. Pancras Coroner, and Mr. Justice Woolf (the High Court judge who in a ruling to settle the dispute over the venue of the inquest opined that an inquest was not a public inquiry), Mr. Whitelaw denied that he had considered the two to be identical. Finally, following the inquest verdict, his successor, Leon Brittan stated that an inquiry would neither be "desirable" or "necessary". This was echoed in further replies by the Home Office.

5.11   The reasons provided by the Home Office for refusing a public inquiry into either the death of Colin Roach or the wider question of policing in Hackney were curiously inconsistent during 1983. For example, in a reply to Clifton Robinson of the CRE on February 3, William Whitelaw asserted that an inquiry into the death of Colin Roach would "prejudice", "duplicate", or "anticipate" the inquest findings. This was evidently not thought to be the case in 1974 when a Section 32 public inquiry was held in addition to an inquest (as discussed later in this Chapter). Other replies did not give these reasons but merely said that the inquest would be a public inquiry, which, as discussed already, was not a view agreed with by the Coroner or by a High Court judge.

Following the inquest, it was argued by Leon Brittan, the new Home Secretary, in letters to Hackney Council (3 August 1983) and Ernie Roberts, M.P. (25 August 1983) that a public inquiry would "arouse expectations, not all of which could be fulfilled". This argument is apparently based on the assumption that a public inquiry is of no use unless it meets all 'expectations' everyone has of it.

5.12 It is even more interesting to note that every organisation or individual who wrote to the Home Secretary and asked for an inquiry to consider other aspects of policing in Hackney besides the death of Colin Roach, was given a reply which cited consultation between police and the community as being a better answer to the problems of policing in Hackney.

For example, letters by William Whitelaw to Clifton Robinson of the CRE (3 February 1983) and Ernie Roberts, M.P. for Hackney North and Stoke Newington (24 March 1983) both suggested that the arrival of a new Commander in 'G' district, with his policy of "trying to reduce local problems by contacts between the police and community representatives at local level" were valid reasons not to grant a public inquiry. In the letter to Ernie Roberts it was further argued that despite "genuine concern about past events" in Hackney, the personality of the Commander made it "a time to look forward rather than back". Mr. Whitelaw added on 19

May in a letter to Christopher Price, M.P. that he was "doubtful" whether such an inquiry would be in the best interests of police/community relations in Hackney, although he said he was" prepared to consider the matter again when the inquest has been concluded".

5.13   Leon Brittan, who had become Home Secretary by the time the inquest was concluded, refused a public inquiry (as mentioned earlier) in a Parliamentary reply of 28 June and continued the 'consultation' theme by adding:

> more generally, what is needed now, in the best interests of good relations between the police and the community in Hackney is for those concerned to sit down together and consider calmly and responsibly how the problem of the area can be tackled. I very much hope that it will soon be possible to establish a Hackney Police Community Consultative arrangement consistent with the guidelines issued by my predecessor .

5.14   These arguments were developed further in Leon Brittan's letter of 8 August 1983 to the leader of Hackney Council in response to the Council's repeated call for a public inquiry into policing in Hackney. While he acknowledged that "there is a widespread feeling that the actions of police officers in Hackney have not always been above reproach", his overriding concern appears to have been to "improve" police relationships between the Black community. He pointed out that the establishment of a public inquiry would do:

> positive harm to this relationship whereas consultative arrangements would have a vital role to play.

5.15   Not only were several reasons used for suggesting why a public inquiry would be harmful but each time the Home Office had refused an inquiry it offered a substitute. First, the forthcoming inquest itself, second, a police complaints investigation and third, the establishment of police/community consultative arrangements in Hackney. None of these options, however, were capable of redressing the issues for which an inquiry was being demanded: The 'unanswered questions' arising from Colin Roach's death and the history of police oppression of the Black community in Hackney.

Basis and Previous uses of Public Inquiries

5.16 Since the Police Act 1964, the Home Secretary, as police authority for London, has possessed powers directed to promoting the efficiency of the police. Section 32 of the 1964 Police Act states:

"1. That the Secretary of State may cause a local inquiry to be held by a person appointed by him into any matter connected with the policing of an area.
2. Any inquiry under this section shall be held in public or in private as the Secretary of State may direct".

However, since the Police Act 1964 there have only been two such 'Section 32' inquiries. Both these inquiries, the Red Lion Square Disorders of 15 June 1974 and the Brixton Disorders of 10-12 April 1981 were held by Lord Scarman.

5.17 The first of these inquiries was set up following the death of Kevin Gately, an anti-fascist protestor, in a demonstration against the National Front where the SPG had been deployed in circumstances considered by many to be controversial. The second inquiry was set up following the events in April 1981 which had followed a period of intense police activity in the Brixton area. In both cases the Home Secretary provided Lord Scarman with terms of reference which referred to 'disorder'. In 1974 these were "to review events to consider what lessons may be learned for the better maintenance of public order". While in 1981 they were: "To inquire urgently into the serious disorder in Brixton... and to report with the power to make recommendations".

While it is clear that both the Scarman inquiries focussed on 'disorders' these cannot be said to be the only possible subject of a 'Section 32' inquiry. 'Disorders' are only one of a range of the matters "connected with the policing of an area".

5.18 When it is considered that the purpose of the Home Secretary's powers under the Police Act is "to promote the efficiency of the Police" (section 28, Police Act 1964), it must then be asked whether a 'section 32' inquiry which investigated a history of police misconduct in an area of Hackney falls within that purpose. In July 1983 the RFSC requested a legal opinion on the prospects of judicial review of the Home Secretary's decision not to hold a public inquiry. Lord Gifford Q.C. who provided that opinion (reproduced as an appendix to this report) stated that:

> to promote the efficiency of the police certainly includes that the police are law abiding and enjoy public confidence, for a police force which misconducts itself could not reasonably be described as efficient.

5.19 Lord Gifford, however, also pointed out that it is solely within the discretion of the Home Secretary to decide what was best calculated to promote efficiency. Lord Gifford did not consider it was possible to challenge William Whitelaw's earlier refusal of a public inquiry as unlawful since "in turning down an inquiry because of the pending inquest", he was "taking into account a relevant matter". But Lord Gifford did think that in light of the inconsistencies in police evidence revealed in the inquest "it was certainly a case when an inquiry under section 32 could and should be established".

5.20 It is arguable then, that in 1983 the statutory basis for a Section 32 inquiry into the death of Colin Roach and the surrounding circumstances did exist. It is clear that an inquiry and an inquest cannot be regarded as mutually exclusive for two reasons: first, there had been an inquiry as well as an inquest in 1974 and second, it was the unanswered questions in the inquest which (in Lord Gifford's opinion) strengthened the case for a public inquiry. The fact that the previous 'Section 32' inquiries had been set up under both Labour and Conservative governments (in 1974 and 1981 respectively), suggests that Section 32 inquiries are not made impossible by the political orientation of any one government.

The Response of the Police

5.21 In a wider sense, the Metropolitan Police, like other police forces in recent decades, have come to respond to events 'politically' by using the public profile of their Chief Officers to argue for resources and changes in the law and key policy making decisions of government. One of the first Metropolitan Police Commissioners to exercise such a role was Sir Robert Mark. He commented in his autobiography about the role of the Metropolitan Police in relation to the decision of the Home Secretary to set up a 'Section 32' inquiry following the death of Kevin Gately, in 1974:

> Nothing could be more certain than that an inquiry will be held, if only to placate criticism and defuse the situation. The inquest will clearly not be sufficient because it will be confined to inquiring about the death. From a police point of view, nothing could appear worse than to appear to have an inquiry imposed upon the force. There remains only one sensible course of action, to get in first and demand an inquiry ... This is in fact is what we did and precisely what happened.

5.22 In examining the response of the Metropolitan Police as an institution under Commissioner Newman to the demand for a public inquiry into the death of Colin Roach, however, there were significant differences from the situation in 1974. First, there was no 'weak minority government' wishing to 'defuse the situation' by setting up a public inquiry. Therefore, the police did not have to face the certainty that an inquiry would be held. Second, Colin Roach had not died during a public 'disorder'. There was therefore no possibility of a public inquiry attributing his death to the 'disorder' itself while justifying as expedient the police tactics used against the protestors (this had been the result of the 1974 Scarman Inquiry). Third, any inquiry into the death and circumstances surrounding the death of Colin Roach which examined the policing background would also have had to consider previous questionable deaths of Black people in Stoke Newington Police Station. The combination of these factors suggests that the Metropolitan Police in 1983 were most unlikely to support an inquiry into the death of Colin Roach and/or policing in Hackney.

5.23 In addition to these factors it appears that as the Colin Roach Campaign developed during 1983, first 'G' district and then the Metropolitan Police as a whole, became increasingly more embroiled in responding to it. In the early stages of the campaign, Commander Taylor was often quoted in the media giving the police answer to the latest developments and he adopted a stance of saying at least to newspapers like the *Hackney Gazette* and the *London Standard* that he had held numerous 'briefings' for community leaders and the family. (In fact the Roach family have told us they were never contacted in any way by the police following the events of 12-13 January). And the first 'briefing' held by Commander Taylor three days after Colin's death totally backfired in its stated attempt to defuse the situation. it was not uncommon to see officers of lower ranks responding in the media to the issue also: for example the 'Newsnight' BBC television programme of 14 February 1983 featured Sgt. Robert Drew, and P.C. Paul Pacey who spoke at length about the 'myths' surrounding the police station (Stoke Newington) which existed, without foundation, in the community. Furthermore it is noticable that even following the 'suicide' verdict of the coroner's inquest (20 June 1983), Kenneth Newman himself found it necessary to mount an attack in the media against the supporters of the Colin Roach campaign at the launch of his first annual report on the policing of the Metropolis, 1982/83.

5.24 There were other ways in which the Metropolitan Police as an institution responded to the campaign for a public inquiry. The policing of the demonstration features here. An answer to a Parliamentary question by the Conservative M.P. Harvey Proctor, on 24 March 1983 revealed that 574 officers had been deployed to cover a demonstration of 180-275 people (a police estimate) on 12 March, which meant 2/3 police to one protestor. However, this seems insignificant compared to the number of police revealed by the Commissioner's report for 1983 to have been deployed on 22 January 1983 as a result of "events in 'G' district following the death of Mr. Colin Roach": 1,895 officers. Such an over-reaction to a few hundred protestors clearly required manpower from other districts. Another example of the reaction of the Metropolitan Police as an institution against the campaign for a public inquiry took place in the courts. Not only were there convictions (mostly in Magistrates Court) on the basis of the police evidence following arrests on the demonstrations, but in the High Court dispute over the inquest venue the Metropolitan Police became involved to the extent that they argued that disorder would occur if the inquest was held in Hackney Town Hall.

5.25 Therefore it is reasonable to say that opposition from the Metropolitan police to the *case* for a public inquiry into Colin Roach's death was closely associated with its opposition to the *campaign* which sought that inquiry. The latter opposition took place in the High Court, in the Magistrates Courts and on the streets of Hackney, where arrests were made in extensive numbers during the demonstrations. This in turn suggests that whatever had happened at Stoke Newington that night, the officers from there acted as if they had a vested interest in shutting down debate about it. For example, (a) by rapidly supplying a 'suicide' and 'mental illness' definition to the press and (b) by trying apparently to smash the demonstrations. The mounting effect of all this police opposition culminated in Sir Kenneth Newman attacking the campaign as an instance of "dedicated denigration" of the police in his first annual Report.

5.26 Indeed, Newman's outburst in June 1983 indicates that the Metropolitan Police response to the death of Colin Roach and the campaign for a public inquiry had become an explicitly political one. This revealed a high degree of opposition to the prospect of a public inquiry. It is worth noting that when Barnor Hesse from RFSC told a demonstration outside Stoke Newington police station on 12 March 1983 that the Police were "demonstrating against our demonstration" he was referring to over-policing as an obvious expression of opposition to a public inquiry. The relationship between the police and the media (particularly, the press) suggests that police were also 'demonstrating' or 'campaigning' in the realm of ideas, perceptions and public understanding.

5.27 While this does not mean there was a 'conspiracy' between newspapers and the police, it helps explain how Kenneth Newman's public attack on the Colin Roach campaign was interpreted favourably in newspaper editorials like that of *The Times* (28 June 1983) which praised him for "taking the bull by the horns". Chapter 4 showed how, for their own reasons, most national newspapers were hostile to the case for a public inquiry, particularly after the inquest.

Other Responses to the Campaign for a Public Inquiry

5.28 In examining the way that other groups and institutions reacted to the event which followed the death of Colin Roach in 1983 a few observations may be made. Chapter 2 showed how the policing of the demonstrations led to over 80 arrests. The legal 'attack' experienced by defendants which had led to a formal complaint being lodged about magistrate Johnstone is examined in more depth in Appendix 5 (the evidence of the Community Alliance for Police Accountability relating to the trials). This evidence calls into question the independence of magistrates from the police as well as questioning their 'political' role in criticising people for the mere fact that they were demonstrating for a public inquiry.

5.29 The independence of the judiciary from the police is also called into question by the Coroner's inquest. This point has been made in Chapter 3. However, it may be added that the independence of Coroner Douglas Chambers from the police was also made questionable by the dispute which arose over the inquest venue. Prior to the dispute being taken to the High Court during April 1983, Dr. Chambers had held an informal hearing of arguments about where the inquest should be, on the 18 April. According to a bulletin of the RFSC published at the time:

> The Council wanted the inquest moved to Hackney Town Hall. The police opposed this but refused to give any evidence ... They said they would only give their reasons in secret. They said they would produce affidavits later in the day. They are of value only in formal court proceedings, not in

the sort of informal hearing the Coroner was conducting. Later in the day the Coroner announced he was making an application to the High Court for a declaration that the inquest should not be moved. The police affidavits were going to be used to support his case. (NB: it will be recalled from Chapter 2 that these affidavits claimed there would be 'disorder' if the inquest was held in Hackney Town Hall). How did the police know that the Coroner was going to need the affidavits? Was this a deal cooked up by the Coroner and the police before the inquest started? If the Coroner colludes with the police can he be regarded as independent? . . .

5.30 It is also necessary to examine the role of Parliament in responding to the campaign for a public inquiry. Chapter 2 indicated that a number of MPs supporting the campaign had signed a motion initiated by Ernie Roberts (MP for Hackney North and Stoke Newington) demanding a public inquiry, in February 1983. Following the inquest verdict, Ernie Roberts made a substantial speech on "policing in London" during a Parliamentary debate (1 July 1983). Ernie Roberts told the House that the Colin Roach case is only the tip of the iceberg and went into "detail about the cases of the White family, Mrs. Knight and others" all of which he cited as reasons for "an inquiry into the activities of the police at the Stoke Newington police station as well as into the Colin Roach affair".

5.31 While Ernie Roberts was certainly able to highlight the need for a public inquiry in Parliament, the obstacles against building up the level of support necessary were considerable. In Parliamentary terms, it was perhaps a greater priority for Opposition M.Ps in 1983 to oppose the Police Bill. This did not mean that all M.Ps showed great interest in policing matters, however. At a time when the Police Bill had just been introduced and two controversial shootings (Colin Roach and Steven Waldorf) had occurred, between 6 December 1982 and 4 February 1983, only 18 of London's 92 M.Ps asked Parliamentary Questions on any aspect of policing. In fact, despite the two controversial shootings, there were only 58 questions asked altogether on the Metropolitan Police in this period (out of which nine were refused replies either due to "disproportionate cost" or the information being "not available" or "not in the public interest" . . .).

5.32   It must also be noted that Opposition M.P's were not, for various reasons, unanimous in their support for a public inquiry into the death of Colin Roach. It was mentioned in Chapter 2 that another Hackney M.P. (Stanley Clinton Davis, south Hackney) had initiated a motion which obtained a few more signatures than the Ernie Roberts motion. This motion deplored "allegations that Colin Roach had been murdered by the police which it believed might inflame passions dangerously in the Hackney area", while saving qualified support to the demand for a public inquiry being "sympathetically considered" after the inquest.

5.33.   But the most damaging Parliamentary attack on the case for a public inquiry came from a former Labour Home Office Minister, Alex Lyon. While speaking during the Committee Stage of the Police Bill on 17 March 1983 he said:

> All the evidence is that this young man killed himself. But a campaign has been mounted by people who are supposed to be in favour of justice for Blacks, suggesting somehow that police covered this up, when there is not a jot or little evidence that was so.

He also added that it was "a nonsense to say that the police had acted improperly".

5.34   Our examination of the parliamentary response to the campaign for public inquiry into the death of Colin Roach suggests that the issues involved did not command sufficient concern and attention amongst politicians to persuade them to pressure the government to set up an inquiry. While the General Election of June 1983 was one in which a strong emphasis on policing and more 'law and order' were particularly prominent in the Conservative electoral manifesto, the arguments on policing used by other parties in the electoral campaign did not for the most part extend beyond opposition to the Police Bill, the passage of which was in any case postponed because of the election. Following the inquest and the election of a Conservative government with a strong majority, the political conditions for a public inquiry were no more favourable and a good deal less so.

5.35 In conclusion then, the factors to be considered in explaining the refusal of the Home Secretary, Leon Brittan, to hold an inquiry were as follows. While his predecessor, William Whitelaw had not entirely ruled out the possibility of an inquiry, he had made it a possibility which could only be considered after the inquest verdict. The inquest verdict of 'suicide' suggested that the death had been explained as long as the Home Secretary was prepared to ignore the serious questions which it had left unanswered and provide a cosmetic answer to the complaint by the jury in the form of a PCB investigation. It was clearly within the Home Secretary's discretion to authorise an inquiry under section 32 of the Police Act once he received the jury's complaint. The view expressed by Metropolitan Police Commissioner, Sir Kenneth Newman in the national press was that the inquest had explained the death and that the campaign for an inquiry had been at the best unnecessary and at the worst an anti-police campaign. Against this background it is not surprising that public opinion may have been shaped to some extent against the prospect of a public inquiry in June 1983. Nevertheless, as highlighted by Lord Gifford and the views of our own recommendations (see below), the serious and unanswered questions raised by Colin Roach's death had only been compounded by the inquest. For this reason, the Home Secretary's refusal to set up an inquiry after the inquest must be challenged.

Recommendations to Part I Of The Report

Public Inquiries

We recommend:

(1) **That there should be an immediate public inquiry into the death of Colin Roach and the surrounding circumstances.** In our view the legal grounds for a judicial review of the then Home Secretary's refusal to hold such an Inquiry following the inquest verdict in 1983 have been demonstrated (see Appendix 3, Gifford's opinion) and we are certain that the additional evidence which we have heard regarding the circumstances surrounding the death of Colin Roach makes the case even more urgent. Such an inquiry should be held under section 32 of the Police Act 1964. We fully support the recommendation made in 1983 by the Roach Family Support Committee that any such inquiry must include Black people's representation.

(2) **That the Home Secretary, as police authority for London should make greater and more frequent use of 'section 32' public inquiries.** He should do so in cases where serious abuses in police power are widely believed to have occurred without any assumption or prejudice that such cases must arise from or be associated with serious public 'disorders' in order to merit a public inquiry of this kind.

(3) **That in consideration of future requests for local inquiries to be set up under section 32 of the Police Act 1964, the Home Secretary of the day should not attempt to suggest or argue that the purposes for which an inquiry is being demanded may be equally well served by any of the following:**

(a) **A coroner's inquest** (in cases where a public inquiry is being demanded into a death in police custody or any other death in which the police are suspected to have been involved).

(b) **A police complaints investigation under section 49 of the Police Act 1964.**

(c) **The establishment of successful police/community consultative arrangements** (in the locality for which a section 32 inquiry is being demanded).

We make this recommendation not only because each of these three measures were entirely inadequate remedies to the death and the issues surrounding the death of Colin Roach, but also because *these measures do not appear to us to be designed or intended to deal with cases in which the conduct of a police force arising from a history of suspected malpractices towards a particular community is seriously in question.*

The Coroner's Inquest

The following recommendations represent measures which this Inquiry believes are necessary to ensure that bereaved families are afforded adequate protection in coroner's inquests. All the recommendations have been made in the past by INQUEST. Recommendations 4 and 6 were in addition made by the House of Commons Select Committee on Home Affairs (1980); recommendation 6, was also recommended by the Brodrick Committee (1971); recommendations 5 and 6 were made by the Broadwater Farm Inquiry (1986). These recommendations do not attempt to cover all aspects of potential inquest reform, but are in our view relevant to the evidence we have considered within this Inquiry's terms of reference:

We further recommend:

(4) **That the police investigators' report on a death should be made available to legal representatives of the interested parties at the inquest.**

(5) **That legal representatives of interested parties at the inquest should have the right to address arguments to the jury.**

(6) **That interested parties at the inquest should be entitled to legal aid.**

(7) **That the right of inquest juries to add 'riders' to their verdicts should be restored.**

Arrests, Charges And Sentencing, Arising From Demonstrations

It is clear from the evidence we have seen that considerable injustices were experienced by those arrested on the Colin Roach demonstrations in 1983. Arrests were made mainly to break up peaceful demonstrations and charges were based quite often on flimsy evidence, particularly regarding the identification of those accused of criminal offences. Conviction rates for Magistrates Courts, comparatively low by national standards (52.7% compared to 82-85%), further questioned the legitimacy of many of the original charges being brought. We note and deplore the fact that the new Public Order Act (1986) has increased the discretion of the police to arrest peaceful protestors via the creation of new offences like 'disorderly conduct' and the extension of others like 'threatening, abusive or insulting words or behaviour'. Nevertheless we believe it is still worth making recommendations commenting within the scope of existing law. Recommendations 8 and 9 below have previously been made by the National Council for Civil Liberties, while recommendations 9, 10, 12 and 13 were made in the Report of the unofficial committee of Inquiry into Southall, 23 April 1979 (1980). In addition recommendation 11 was made by the Broadwater Farm Inquiry (1986).

We recommend that:

(8) **The offence of obstructing the Highway under the Highways Act 1981 should be amended to ensure that an arrest and prosecution can only take place when there is an actual obstruction caused which makes it impossible or very difficult for other users of the highway to go about their business.**

(9) The offence of 'obstructing a police officer in the execution of his or her duty' under the Police Act should be restricted to physical obstruction.

It is regrettable that a practice exists in which charges triable before a jury may be withdrawn and replaced by identical or lesser summary charges, triable only before a magistrate when the defendants have pleaded not guilty to the original charge. This practice suggested that the police knew that their evidence would not have been sufficient to obtain a conviction in a Crown Court and therefore relied upon the greater likelihood of magistrates to convict. We have seen nothing to suggest that the Crown prosecution service introduced in 1986 is sufficiently independent of the police to prevent this practice from taking place.

We therefore recommend that:

(10) Serious offences including the allegation of violence against police officers should carry a right to jury trial and that the Crown prosecution service does not continue the practice of substituting summary charges, in contested cases where evidence is likely to justify a Crown Court appearance based on the original charge.

The trials of the defendants arrested on Colin Roach demonstrations also indicated several features of questionable conduct by stipendiary and lay Magistrates. Such conduct was criticised in the official complaint made to the Lord Chancellor about Magistrate Johnstone of Highbury Magistrates Court. This conduct exacerbated injustices created by many unnecessary arrests and charges.

We endorse the recommendation made by the Broadwater Farm Inquiry:

(11) That magistrates should recognise that they are expected by the public to be impartial arbiters between the police and the accused, who appear before them as

innocent persons because they have not been proved guilty.

We have also identified three other areas to which magistrates need to pay particular attention:

Identification Evidence
We deplore the tendency of magistrates to attach greater weight to the evidence of police officers than that of defence witnesses and/or photographic evidence.

We therefore support the recommendation made by NCCL:

(12) **That 'magistrates sitting in demonstration cases ... should pay particular heed to the standard of proof required in matters of identification'.**

The readiness of certain magistrates to convict on insufficient evidence cannot be separated from the views expressed, particularly by Magistrate Johnstone, to imply that it was not legitimate to have been involved in the protests.

We therefore agree with NCCL:

(13) **That magistrates sitting in demonstration cases should take care to avoid charges of bias through injudicious comment.**

The fact that defendants receiving prison sentences were denied bail pending their appeals, making them serve their sentences first, represents an attack on the right to appeal.

We therefore recommend that:

(14) **Magistrates exercise their judgment to protect the right to appeal at all times.**

Police evidence was not only insufficiently capable of obtaining 'normal' conviction rates in magistrates courts, it was also shown by photographic evidence to be full of lies and half-truths.

We recommend that:

(15) Magistrates take action when it is clear that police witnesses have committed perjury.

The observations of the Broadwater Farm Inquiry are relevant here:

> If magistrates supinely acquiesce in whatever the police require, then the courts of Justice as well as the police become the objects of cynicism and disrepute.

Finally, in this section, while we accept that practices of individual magistrates across the country will inevitably show wide variation,

We nevertheless recommend:

(16) That the public exercise their right to complain to the Lord Chancellor and the Home Secretary when the conduct of a particular magistrate gives serious cause for concern.

Part II

Policing in Hackney

Chapter 6

The Metropolitan Police: A Contextual Introduction

6.1 In this section we aim to do two things. First, we give some basic information about the Metropolitan police force, its size, the area it covers and its organisation (and re-organisation) in recent years. Most of this information we have culled from sources other than the Metropolitan Police itself, and particularly from the work of the former Greater London Council Police Committee Support Unit and its magazine, *Policing London.* As we have already mentioned, the Metropolitan Police would not agree to submit evidence to the Inquiry.

6.2 Following this basic information, we then go on to discuss some of the key developments in the policing of London in the last decade and a half. The policing of London — indeed of all major urban areas — underwent a qualitative change in the 1970s. Although such a change cannot, and should not, be pinned down to exact dates, nor isolated from wider political, social and economic developments (nationally and in London), there are certain aspects to this change which we think it important to note, as they are of particular relevance to this Inquiry.

6.3 Ours is obviously not a comprehensive account: detailed discussions of developments in policing can be found elsewhere. (See for instance Tony Bunyan: *The Political Police in Britain* (1976) and Phil Scraton: *The State of Police* (1985).) We wish simply to draw attention to some of the more crucial developments and events of the last decade and a half, in order to place the policing of Hackney and particularly the policing of the Black community in Hackney, in its proper context.

Some Background

6.4   The Metropolitan Police ('The Met') force was set up in 1829. Rural police forces were established in 1856. The stated objective of the Met was first framed in 1833 and remains its basic aim. Primarily, this is:

> the prevention of crime: the next that of detection and punishment of offenders if crime is committed. To these ends all the efforts of police must be directed. The protection of life and property, the preservation of public tranquility, and the absence of crime will alone prove whether the objects for which the police were appointed have been attained.

6.5   The boundary of the Met area extends in a 15/16 mile radius from Charing Cross, and corresponds broadly to the other boundaries of the Greater London Council area, before its abolition in 1986.

6.6   The Met is a highly centralised force in terms of policy making with many specialist departments. However, it is fairly decentralised in terms of operational matters. Its structure has recently been radically re-organised. Until 1986 the Met was divided into 4 main areas, each with a Deputy Assistant Commissioner. Within those 4 main areas, it was divided into 24 smaller districts, each district corresponding to a letter of alphabet. Under the new structure, the Metropolitan Police Division ('MPD') is divided into 75 divisions, grouped into 8 areas. Each area (apart from Westminster which is an area of its own) stretches from Inner London to the outer edges of suburbia. Each represents a convenient administrative unit for policing purposes. However, as they no longer correspond to local authority boundaries, these new areas no longer have any geographical or administrative meaning to the public.

6.7   Under the old scheme, which was in operation at the time of Colin Roach's death and for much of the period discussed in this report, Hackney was designated 'G' District, which was coterminous with the Borough of Hackney boundaries. The district was divided into 2 divisions, the stations for which were Hackney, Stoke Newington and City Road (which was the headquarters). The Commander of 'G' District (as in any other) was in effective charge of policing strategy in the area, reaction to local events, initiatives, community relations policy, etc.

6.8 It is not entirely clear how policing policy for Hackney, or any other London borough, has changed under the new plan. The separation of responsibilities between the Met's headquarters at Scotland Yard, the newly created areas and the already existing divisions has yet to be clarified. It is clear that London boroughs are no longer dealing with a single commander responsible for the policing of a given borough. Local Councils now have to relate to two or more Chief Superintendents in charge of a division, and various area personnel, in charge of different area functions.

6.9 The Met is by far the largest police force in the country. It is, for example, three times the size of the Greater Manchester police force, the next largest police force in the country. In November 1985, the Met employed 26,844 police officers and over 13,000 full time civilian staff. Of its staff, 15,361 officers and civilians (36% of the total) work at headquarters: 3,000 work in specialist branches; the rest are employed on the administration of the force and the creation and production of policy. Concentration of police power on the streets, however, depends almost entirely on the area in question. Despite the progressive emigration of many Londoners to the suburbs of the City, shifting the pattern of population, the policing of Central and Inner London remains a priority of the Met. There are likely to be more police officers on the streets in these areas.

6.10 In 1985 the Met produced a rough estimate of the cost of policing each London borough. In all, the Met spent some £600 million, 65% of its total budget, on staffing local police stations. The figures show that generally the inner city boroughs have over double the policing resources allocated to outer London. The Outer London borough of Sutton, for example, has only 131 officers on its streets compared to Westminster with 2,566 officers, kept there at a cost of £73 million. Looked at in another way, Hackney (in common with other inner London boroughs like Camden, Islington, Tower Hamlets) has roughly 1 officer to every 200-300 members of the public, compared to Sutton or Bexley which have 1 officer per 700 members of the public. Policing strength (and style) also depends on police perception of an area: there is a crude division in their minds between 'good' places and 'bad' places. This is what Metropolitan Police Commissioner Sir Kenneth Newman meant by the term 'symbolic locations': places where a heavy police presence is needed to emphasise the rule of law and order. Historically, Hackney has been one such 'symbolic location'.

6.11 Theoretically, the basic system of police patrolling is the unit beat system which was introduced on an experimental basis in 1966, and covered the whole of London by 1968. Under this system the area covered by a police station is divided into a number of 'beats', that is smaller geographical areas. On each relief (a shift) an officer will be assigned to patrol a 'beat' either on foot or by car. There has been a lot of criticism of the unit beat system, and particularly the increasing reliance, and use, by police officers of cars to patrol their beat. The 1983 Policy Studies Institute report on the Metropolitan Police found that:

> Generally, officers will patrol on foot only if there is no vehicle for them to ride in, and where single officers are assigned to a vehicle they tend to pick up other officers (who are meant to be walking) during the course of a shift.

(Police and People in London, 1983, Vol. IV, pg 21-22).

6.12 Partly to offset these criticisms, and partly to improve police-community relations home beat officers are being used on a more permanent basis by the Met.

There are now 1,397 home beat officers in the Met, mainly in Inner London areas. Home beat officers are responsible for a larger geographical area than the unit beat system: they are expected to establish contacts and friendly relations with the people and organisations in their areas. They may be assigned to specific tasks related to community relations and juveniles, and have a role in the collection of information on incidents involving Black people. Obviously, racist attitudes and assumptions affect home beat officers as much as any other police officer, and the temptation to take gossip and rumour as fact are some of the problems of this work.

6.13 Home beat officers tend to have a low status within the force. They are often known as 'hobby bobbies' and career-ambitious police officers will not remain home beat officers for long. As their work is not taken very seriously, home beat officers are easily siphoned away from their own area if an emergency arises elsewhere or large numbers of officers are required to deal with a public order situation. Where an emergency arises in their own area, senior officers and policy makers will ignore the home beat officer and the knowledge that s/he may have built up of the local community. This failure of communication within the police force was noted by Lord Scarman in his report on the Brixton disorders of 1981 and was also the subject of a public row between the officer in charge of the home beat team on Broadwater Farm Estate, W.P.S. Meynell, and senior officers during the post-mortem on the cause of the 'riots' of October 1985. W.P.S. Meynell said that senior officers ignored her regular reports of rising tension on the estate.

Police Officers and Police Pay

6.14 The majority of police officers in the Met (and other area forces) are white and male. The number of women in the force is artificially depressed by over-rigorous recruitment procedures. Only 7% of the women who applied to join the police force in 1984 were successful in their applications. The Met has even fewer Black officers: 289, which is 1% of the total. The Met have made periodic attempts to recruit

Black officers: in 1975/76, a £25,000 advertising campaign to get more Black recruits was launched, but resulted in only 11 applicants, of whom 5 subsequently joined.

The small numbers of both Black and female officers in the force, reflects and reinforces the public sense that the Met is institutionally racist and sexist. This lack of heterogeneity within the police isolates them from the wider community, particularly in areas like Hackney where there is a large Black community. But police isolation is aggravated by other factors. For example, police officers tend to live away from the community, and have a separate social life. Many officers live in special police accommodation, provided as part of the job. Behind Hackney's Stoke Newington police station, for example, there is a five storey section house for single officers. One writer, who accompanied Hackney police officers for a short period as part of his research and who was not unsympathetic to the force, described Stoke Newington police station as follows:

> Even physically, the police seemed isolated and beleaguered. Stoke Newington nick is like a fortress. Only 5% of 'G' district officers live in the community they serve. Young recruits live in the tower block of flats overlooking the courtyard, the garage, the steaming stables. Married officers have their semis in the suburbs. From their centralized headquarters, the police sally forth like commandos, equipped with all the latest technology, into enemy-held territory.
>
> *(Paul Harrison, 'Inside the Inner City', Penguin, 1983).*

6.15 Age is another factor in the composition of the police force. Lord Scarman noted in his report that "young officers are an unavoidable feature of contemporary policing" and younger officers are bound to predominate in street policing: 36% of police officers in England and Wales are between 18 and a half and 25. Before 1956, only 20% of the police had been recruited before the age of 20, yet by 1973 the figure had risen to 52%. Officers also tend to be recruited from outside London — between 60-80% of the Met's recruits, many of them from the North, Scotland and Wales. There is a long tradition of recruiting from these areas, for which no explicit justification is now given apart from a general reference to high unemployment. The Met does not acknowledge a policy of deliberately excluding Londoners from its ranks, nor of ensuring that London's working class communities are not policed by their own members. However, this is the effect, and puts London in line with other European capital cities, where the police are also drawn from the provinces.

6.16 A final factor, separating the police from the wider community they serve, is police pay. Whereas all other public sector workers, without exception, have seen their pay decline in comparison with average pay changes since the beginning of the 1980s, the police have soared ahead. Police pay is regularly updated in accordance with the recommendations of the Edmund Davies pay review of 1979: 13.5% in September 1979, 21.3% in 1980, 13.2% in 1981, 10.3% in 1982, 8.4% in 1983, 5.2% in 1984 and 7.5% in 1985. The police are now leaders in the pay tables for public sector workers, earning more than teachers, nurses, town hall staff and other civil servants. They also earn more than private sector workers. In London, a constable's basic salary (including London Weighting) increased by 85% between March 1980 and December 1985.

Changes In Policing Strategy In The 1970s

6.17 A key change in Metropolitan police strategy in the last decade and a half has been the move away from preventative policing (theoretically the strategy of the post war period) to 'reactive' or 'fire brigade' policing. This new brand of policing was initiated by Sir Robert Mark, in the early 1970s. It is a strategy underpinned by increased police use of technology, in particular through computers, radios, cars and specially-equipped vans. This change in strategy has not only affected the way police organise themselves, but crucially their relationship with the public who they increasingly meet in abrasive, conflict situations. John Alderson, ex-Chief Constable for Devon and Cornwall, said in

1978 that this kind of policing was "more akin to that of an occupying army". From evidence submitted to us, this has certainly been the experience of Hackney residents who have been at the receiving end of heavy-handed 'fire brigade policing'.

6.18   One of the most significant elements in the development of this style of policing was the establishment of the Special Patrol Group. Originally set up in 1965 in the context of a preventative policing strategy, the SPG was supposed to be a mobile anti-crime unit which could aid local London divisions but it soon became clear that the SPG had important public order functions too. These assumed a new significance in the early 1970s when, in the wake of the 1972 miners' strike, the then Conservative government reviewed its public order preparations. One of the key questions of this period was whether or not to set up a paramilitary 'third force' to stand between the army and the police to deal with strikes, demonstrations and terrorism. The police, together with the Home Office, opposed the idea but in doing so they effectively committed themselves to fulfilling this role. The role of the SPG was crucial in this respect as was clearly illustrated in a series of incidents in the 1970s.

6.19   In 1973, the SPG shot and killed two young Pakistani workers who had entered the India High Commission in London and taken hostages 'armed' with toy pistols. In 1974, the SPG was present in Red Lion Square at an anti-fascist demonstration during which Kevin Gately, a student, was killed. In 1977, the SPG was used to clear pickets and demonstrators from the Grunwick factory during the long industrial dispute by Asian workers. In 1979, an unidentified member of the SPG killed anti-racist demonstrator, Blair Peach, during the 23 April demonstrations against the National Front in Southall.

6.20   When it was first set up, the SPG had 100 officers, organised in 4 units. Today there are 8 units with a total of 240 officers, although it is not clear how reorganisation under

Plan 7b will affect the units. The SPG has its own independent command structure — the A9 branch at Scotland Yard. Since its formation, SPG recruits have been drawn from volunteers from the 24 London police districts. Their average age is 30. The SPG have carried out local and London wide roles.

6.21 In the wake of the 1981 riots, local SPG style groups called Instant Response Units ('IRUs') were set up in each of London's 24 police districts. They were later renamed District Support Units ('DSUs').

6.22 The police have always denied that the SPG, or any of its successors, play a 'paramilitary' role. Yet a former Metropolitan Police Commissioner, Sir Robert Mark was explicit about the role that SPG units played. He described how the SPG "acted as a reserve at demonstrations at which militant elements were thought to cause disorder and in particular to assist police in protracted industrial disputes involving dockers and building workers". Training too is paramilitary: a Southern Television documentary in 1976 called "The Man in the Middle" showed SPG training exercises and equipment at its main training centre, in which the SPG was shown practising the 'wedge', to break up demonstrations (based on the army's experience in Ulster), unarmed combat, the use of riot shields and CS gas. Equipment carried by a fully-equipped SPG includes riot shields, rifles, sub-machine guns, smoke grenades, truncheons and visors.

6.23 But it is the continued deployment of the SPG in the community, on its anti-crime work, which has particularly led for calls for its disbandment. When the SPG is not required for special assignments, it goes into 'high crime' areas for periods for up to a month, using 'saturation policing' techniques. These high crime areas are mainly working class areas of the city, including those with large Black communities. Brixton, Lewisham, Hackney, Peckham and Notting Hill appear year after year on the list of areas to which the SPG has been sent.

6.24   Evidence submitted to us made reference to SPG operations in Hackney, particularly in recent years.

6.25   In February 1980, Commander David Mitchell, the newly arrived Commander of Hackney, drafted 5 units of the SPG into Hackney, apparently to quell the rise in street crime. According to a special Campaign Against Racism and Fascism Report on Hackney: "There was no consultation with the community. Indeed as resentment against Mitchell's aggressive tactics grew, the leaders of the community refused to consult with him. An outspoken Black councillor called for "total non co-operation" with the police whilst West Indian youth at Dalston's Cubies Club barred his entry when he came to address a meeting... (Mitchell's) policies played no small part in the eruptions of July." *(Searchlight,* March 1982).

6.26   In November 1983, the *Hackney Gazette* 'Police Beat' column reported on a row between Hackney Council and the police over the presence of the SPG in the borough. The SPG were drafted into the Borough in October, but the Council were not informed. According to Chief Superintendent Stapley of Hackney police, this was "because the Council never pay any attention" to correspondence with the police. Chief Superintendent Stapley was reported to have said that he was almost positive that 100% of the public were pro-SPG, and that the unit was brought in because the local force was undermanned whilst officers were undergoing a period of training for neighbourhood policing (23/11/83).

6.27   A few months later, in February 1984, the *Hackney Gazette* reported that the SPG were back in Hackney. According to Chief Superintendent Barr of Stoke Newington, this was due to an increase in burglaries. The paper reported that the Council were encouraging about the 'new role' of the SPG: they were going out in uniform and on directed foot patrols (10/2/84).

The PSI Report

6.28 In 1979, following persistent criticism about the state of relations between the police and Black people in London, the Metropolitan Police Commissioner, Sir David McNee commissioned an in depth study of the police. The Policy Studies Institute (PSI) were eventually given the brief to look at relationships between the wider community and the police, and to consider a range of attitudes within the police.

6.29 The study began in 1980 and was organised in four separate sections: a survey of over 2,000 Londoners; an in-depth observation study of a group of young Black people; a survey of 1,770 police officers; and in-depth observation and interview study of police work throughout the two years.

6.30 The PSI report presented a highly critical portrait of the Metropolitan police force at work. It showed that institutional racism is embedded in the force. The researchers endorsed the findings of previous critical reports. They found that: Black people are more likely to be stopped; the pervasive imagery in the force unquestioningly links Black people to crime; there is a poor response to racist attacks; demonstrations by Black people are more aggressively policed; in some cases racism may be the main cause of police aggression towards Black people.

6.31 The report showed that racism is part of the culture of white masculinity which exists within the force. This cult of masculinity, as the PSI described it, is constructed around heavy drinking and stories of fighting, violence and sexual conquest of women. Police women are purposefully excluded, humiliated and sexually harassed and are rejected "as full members of the group or colleagues on an equal basis".

6.32 The report also showed that the police perceive communities and neighbourhoods on the basis of respectability or non-respectability. They have a view of 'slag' and 'filth' which is:

> A special concept of social class, mixed with an idea of proper behaviour . . . just as important to police officers as racial or ethnic groups. In this scale, the 'respectable' working class and the suburban middle class stand highest, while the 'underclass' of the poor and rootless, together with groups regarded as deviant, such as homosexuals or hippies, stand lowest.

Police Powers

6.33   Up until its abolition in 1981, the 'Sus' law — the clause covering suspected persons, under the 1824 Vagrancy Act — was the legislation under which many young people, particularly Black youths, were apprehended by the police. There was widespread resentment against the police because of their frequent use of this Act. We look in more detail at the police use of this Act in Hackney in Chapter 8. Broad-based campaigns against the 'Sus' laws eventually succeeded in leading to their abolition.

6.34   However, the powers of the police have been considerably widened by the introduction of the Police and Criminal Evidence Act 1984. This followed the deliberations of the Royal Commission on Criminal Procedure (RCCP), held between 1977 and 1981 to consider the pros and cons of legislation to give the police more power. In his evidence to the RCCP, Metropolitan Police Commissioner, Sir David McNee stated that because of the restrictions on certain of their powers, the police had learned to use "stealth and force illegally". He also stated that because people were becoming more aware of their civil rights, it was becoming increasingly difficult for the police "to bluff their way into obtaining consent to take body samples, or enter premises legally". His proposal to the RCCP, therefore, was an extension of many of the police powers, to legitimise many of the procedures they were already using regarding arrest, detention of suspects, searching of premises and so on.

6.35   The 1984 Act eventually incorporated the majority of the police's most significant proposals to the RCCP, although theoretically balancing this with non-statutory safeguards for the rights of suspects. It is generally recognised as a piece of legislation which considerably increases already formidable police powers.

Chapter 7

Policing History in Hackney

7.1 It was not possible for the Inquiry to research and write a complete history of the policing of Hackney in the post-war period, although we have no doubt about the value of such a history.

7.2 This Chapter examines policing in Hackney mainly between the years 1945-1970. Two major areas are considered briefly: public order and race relations.

Policing and Fascism

7.3 One particularly controversial aspect of policing in Hackney after the 1939-45 war was the police response to the activities of the fascist organisations, active in the area and responsible for the harassment of and assaults on Hackney's large Jewish population.

Jewish people had begun to settle in Hackney from the early 1900s; their numbers increased when many Jewish refugees came to Britain to escape the fascist persecution.

7.4 It seems clear that Hackney was regarded as a strategic target by fascist groups who were attempting to forge a stronghold in the London boroughs. The London Life and Labour Survey of 1881 had labelled Hackney as "one of the worst parts of London". Oswald Moseley, a former Labour M.P concentrated his political campaigning efforts in Hackney in an attempt to rally popular fascist support. Colin Sparks in his book "Never Again" suggests that support for fascists nationally had decreased in the early to mid 1930s. In the following Sparks describes Moseley's attempts to re-

Photograph: David Hoffman

'Cable Street Riots'

Aftermath of a facist march led by Sir Donald Mosely in the East End of London (4, October 1986).

establish the political credibility of his party, i.e. the British Union of Fascists:

> From 1935 onwards it (British Union of Fascists) developed a new perspective which can only have been designed to hold the organisation together until the predicted worsening of the social and economic climate led to the renewed possibility of mass recruitment. This strategy was to concentrate considerable effort in the East End of London in an attempt to build a firm base among the local population.

7.6 The Union Movement organised several marches in the East End of London, particularly in 1936, where there was a reported sixty fascist meetings a month. These meetings, which met with strong opposition from the local population, the Jewish people were said to have gained particular support from the Communist party. The clashes between fascists and anti-fascists inevitably provoked scrutiny of the police action in response to this conflict, as the following indicates:

> All their (fascist) marches had been attacked and the familiar story of systematic police support for the fascists, had been seen on numerous occasions. The battle in the East End was a long protracted campaign . . .

The 'Battle of Cable Street' 1936

7.7 The celebrated battle of Cable Street, contributed significantly to the passage of the Public Order Act of the same year (1936). The 'battle' was the most telling example of effective mass organisation against fascism, in which 30,000 people physically prevented a Moseley march taking place:

> There was a mass mobilisation of the East London population who fought a long and bitter battle with the police. Against this the police proved too weak to force a passage for the fascists.

By 1945 there was a rapidly increasing Jewish settlement in the East End. This rate of increase continued until the 1950s.

7.8 The end of the Second War unfortunately did not herald the decline of fascist organisations or the cessation of anti-Semitic activity. Far from this anti-Semitism gained a revival immediately following the end of the War. Certainly the local newspaper (the *Hackney Gazette)* carried stories almost every week from 1945-1950 about fascist activity in the area with startling front page headlines. The *Hackney Gazette* leaders of the 23 January and the 20 February 1946 gave some indication of the tension of the times, e.g. "Remnants of the fascist gang", "The revivals of anti-Semitism".

7.9   Headlines like these tended to describe incidents of gratuitous attacks on the person or property of Jewish people. One of the most serious and offensive was the attempted destruction (by fire) of a Clapton Synagogue on 10 December 1946. The perpetrators, the National Guard, a fascist organisation, who readily claimed responsibility for the attack, were never (it seems) brought to book.

7.10   Almost from the start of this spate of attacks, concern was expressed over the level of police protection of Jews and their property. After the December incident questions were put to the Home Secretary, Mr. Oliver, by the M.P. for Central Hackney, Mr. Hynd. Hynd queried the action the Government intended to take in order to place a curb on such dangerous activity.

7.11   Despite efforts like this to reduce or eliminate the problems of fascism, fascist activity merely seemed to escalate and the succeeding years saw an increase in the number of meetings and processions which, given the level of violence at those meetings, were uncomfortably reminiscent of the war years.

7.12   The first signs of serious confrontation became evident on 4 March 1949, when the Stamford Hill Association of Jewish Ex-Service Men and Women (AJEX) organised a meeting to 'combat the fascist menace'. The meeting held in Finsbury Park, north London, invited several speakers. David Weitzman, then M.P. for Hackney north and Stoke Newington, was amongst them. It was at this meeting that public dissatisfaction was voiced concerning the protection of Jewish people and their property. It has been argued that:

> the rise and fall of AJEX could be measured with the rise and fall of fascism and anti-Semitic activity in the country... who else could Jewish men and women call upon to defend their interests...

This was by no means the only implied criticism of the State's failure to act in the interests of Jewish victims.

7.13   Mr. Cecil Hyams who was a prominent member of the association, spoke of a "dangerous philosophy of leaving fascists alone and if the police would not protect the public, the ex-serviceman's association were ready to take action".

7.14   Organisations like AJEX, although gaining much support, also attracted considerable detractors. These were mainly people who viewed fascist activity as an exercise of the democratic right of free speech. The phrase "I may (hate) what you are saying but I will defend (to the ends of the earth) your right to say it" was a popular one of the day.

7.15   If the Jewish stance is viewed as extreme or inadvisable, it should be noted that collective political activity directed against them was not their only headache of the time. Fears were growing over the increasing number of attacks upon Jews.

7.16   During one incident a boy of fifteen was attacked by two men with sticks and bottles and so badly injured that he was forced to stay in hospital for three weeks. (*Hackney Gazette*, 11 July 1949). Much of the persistent and everyday individual incidents were conveniently forgotten in the violence and fascist/anti-fascist clashes at public meetings.

7.17   The meeting of AJEX of the 4 March in fact preceded a Moseley march planned for the 18 March, scheduled to move from Dalston to Tottenham.

7.18 Various efforts were made to ban the march. This culminated in a deputation to the Home Secretary led by the Mayor of Hackney (Alderman), urging him to ban the procession.

7.19 Since 1936 and the passing of the Public Order Act, the Commissioner of the Metropolitan Police has had the power to ban specific marches if he is satisfied that such a march is likely to lead to a breach of the peace.

7.20 Local Councillors contended that the planned march would lead to a breach of the peace and drew attention to the "shoals" of letters and telegrams received by the M.P. for Central Hackney, protesting against the proposed march. A telegraph from the Town Clerk to the Home Secretary read as follows:

> Having regard to the fact that the selected route lies within an area which contains a substantial Jewish population, the march is condemned as being deliberately provocative in its purpose ... we forsee a breach of the peace involving damage to property and injury to persons ...

7.21 As an alternative to his power to ban a march under the 1936 Act, the Commissioner is empowered, with the permission of the Home Secretary, to make an area out of bounds to processions for a specified period. The Commissioner of the day, Sir Harold Scott, refused to make an order. However, shortly after the procession took place and as a direct result of the procession, a ban was imposed which lasted for three months. This illustrated a tendency for Commissioners to operate 'a wait and see' policy in respect of meetings 'likely to cause a breach of the peace'. This became more evident in later years and is a significant observation on the style of pre-emptive policing.

7.22 The Moseley meetings (the events of which were reported in the 23 March edition of the *Hackney Gazette)* is significant not only because of the level of violence at that meeting, but also because it followed criticism of police/government response to such activity and illustrated how the

Jewish community had to take a stand to defend themselves. Thus it was a testing ground for both.

7.23 The fears of the local community about the march on the 18th were not misplaced. The following is an extract of the *Hackney Gazette's* account of the events:

> Several police officers were injured during violent disturbances when supporters of the Union Movement held a meeting in Ridley Road, Dalston. Hundreds of mounted and foot police were on duty. A motor coach and fifteen CWT truck were used as a barricade in Kingsland High Street. Marchers (numbering about two hundred) were flanked by columns of policemen. More police reinforcements followed in lorries at the rear of the procession . . . hundreds of people swarmed around booing, jeering and shouting: 'down with fascism'. Police horses reared as leaflets were thrown in the air.
>
> Hordes of screaming men and women were pushed back into Kingsland High Street by police officers.
>
> Several times the route of the procession was changed in order to avoid an ambush.
>
> Several times the situation looked extremely ugly, but the police managed to keep the crowd under control.

7.24 It was becoming increasingly apparent that the confidence of the Jewish community in the willingness or ability of the police to protect them from such attacks was waning. A front page leader in the October edition of the *Hackney Gazette* ('Pro-fascist charges against the police') accused the police of being supportive of the fascist 'cause'. This certainly did not help to alleviate the growing fears of the Jewish community.

7.25 The article, parts of which were reported in most leading newspapers of the day, was written by a journalist for the **New Statesman** and **Nation,** under the nom-de-plume 'John Hadlow'. Hadlow's article described a disturbing incident which occurred during a Union Movement march one Sunday, some time in September or October 1949 (specific dates were never revealed).

7.26   The following is an extract from Hadlow's letter as published by the **New Statesman** and **Nation**. The description of events was taken from Hadlow's own observation of scenes of confrontation between members of the Union Movement and anti-fascists in Dalston Lane:

> A youth appeared running for his life, pursued by about twenty men. One of his pursuers was swinging a car starting handle and two more had knuckle dusters. There were thirty-two policemen with a senior local policeman standing within thirty feet. They watched the youth being tripped, beaten with the starting handle and kicked in the ribs. His glasses were smashed, one eye closed and his forehead cut. Those who attacked him ran off down the street without one police hand raised to stop him.

7.27   It was against this background that the first major call for an inquiry into the political disturbances in the Hackney area was made. These disturbances were referred to as 'political hooliganism'.

7.28   A general inquiry into the policing of these disturbances was not specifically called for. However, according to a *Times* report (23 November 1949), the Home Secretary promised a Judicial Inquiry into the incident described by Mr. Hadlow, provided his allegations could be substantiated.

7.29   But although political concern quickly rose once the alleged incident was first made known, it swiftly died down again once it became clear that the true identity of the writer would not be revealed.

7.30   The reluctance of the writer to identify himself can be explained, at least in part, by events which followed the incident in Dalston Lane. This was made known in the House of Commons by Mr. Platts-Mills, M.P. in a supplementary question to the Home Secretary. Platts-Mills argued that the police knew of the identity of Hadlow, that they had 'visited' his employers and as a direct result of that 'visit' he had been sacked by his employers.

7.31 Hadlow had feared further victimization and had apparently expressed the feeling that if he came forward with his identity it would be "difficult if not impossible to earn (his) livelihood".

7.32 This was all vigorously denied by the police while the editors of the **New Statesman** and the **Nation** were unable to confirm the rumours of police victimization.

7.33 In the absence of specific information relating to time, place, names, etc., in respect of the Dalston incident, the Government argued they could not justify initiating an inquiry into Hadlow's allegations. However, a further development was reported to the House of Commons. An independent witness (a member of the public) had also observed the incident observed by Hadlow.

7.34 But again the Government of the day were saved from setting up a Judicial Inquiry, because that witness was reluctant to come forward without support from the journalist (Hadlow) or other members of the public who had witnessed the scene.

7.35 That was the end of any realistic hope for a Judicial Inquiry. However, as questions were still being asked, the Home Secretary responded by making a number of limited inquiries. The sum total of this was that the Home Secretary obtained reports from the local police relating to all incidents in Dalston taking place around the time of the incident in Dalston Lane. From these, he was able to completely vindicate the police.

7.36 Despite his publicly expressed confidence in the conduct of the police, the Home Secretary was nonetheless moved to make the following statement to the House of Commons:

> The sitation in east London at this time is a particularly delicate one, requiring my constant personal attention. My conference with the principal police officials concerned have left them in no doubt as to the insistence of the Government

on the maintenance of law and order without consideration for the political, religious or racial affiliation of any individual citizen who may be the subject of attention either as in need of protection or for breach of the law.

7.37 There was a tendency by the police, and to a lesser extent, the media to categorise such incidents as wholly criminal. This allowed the police to respond merely to individual incidents without tackling the question of organised and systematic violence. The policing effect of such a categorisation was simple — attacks were reduced to the normal routine of policing, they were not prioritised or seen as systematic and thus, there was little hope of reducing their incidence. The consequence of this also produced its own pattern of response. The victims of fascist attacks ceased to rely as much on police protection. Instead there was an increasing degree of internal organisation and autonomous self-policing of affected groups.

7.38 In evaluating any change in the situation over this period of time, the most significant is the developing awareness amongst the Jewish community that positive action on their part was the most realistic solution to their predicament.

7.39 The activities of fascists and fascist organisations declined briefly during the 1950s but increased again towards the end of the decade. This led local Jews to organise patrols at night to defend individuals and their property from attack. For example, in January 1960, AJEX led a silent protest march against the resurgence of fascism in the area and at the dismissal of the dangers of this by the police. The march was followed by two other events. On 19 January 1960, a 'no Nazis' march was held in the Stoke Newington area. This attracted a large number of North and East London councillors, as well as M.P. David Weitzman. On the 26 January, a meeting of the Association of Victims of Fascism, led by Max Oppenheimer, was held and was 'packed to capacity'.

7.40   Between 1960 and 1964, and in particular the two year period 1962 — 1964, a number of meetings produced many violent situations leading to renewed demands to the Government to pass legislation which would outlaw much of the activities indulged in by Moseley's movement and other fascist organisations. This led to the passing of the Race Relations Act in 1965. However, before this was achieved there was to be many a bitter exchange between local government officials and Central government concerning the police.

7.41   After one meeting of the Union Movement held on 31 July 1962 and which, according to the report of the *Hackney Gazette* (23 August 1962) ended in 'five minutes fiasco after turbulent scenes', the then leader of Hackney Council, Martin Ottolangui, called a special meeting of the Council where he voiced a strong protest against the 'mishandling' by the police of the meeting and their 'needless' action against demonstrators. He made his accusations against the police in an amendment moved at the special meeting which was requisitioned by fourteen members of the Council to prepare a resolution "requesting the Government to take immediate steps to ban all organisations that preach the doctrine of racial discrimination and hatred".

7.42   The Council leader alleged that the mounted police, used to disperse the crowds, "drove the people around like cattle". He went on: "I strongly move this amendment that this Council protests to the Home Secretary and the Commissioner of Police about the mishandling of the situation by the police at the Ridley Road meeting and in particular to the needless action used against the crowd before the meeting started".

7.43   A Hackney councillor, Stanley Clinton-Davis, criticised the police's failure to take action to prevent the meeting during which Alderman L. Sherman (a former mayor of Hackney) was struck in the face with an iron bar. Clinton-Davis stated that the presence of Moseley, not merely his words, was enough to provoke the "violent, inevitable consequences". He emphasised that the police already had the necessary powers to avert such clashes as occurred in Ridley Road.

7.44   Councillor Mrs. Sally Sherman, who was also injured at the meeting, described what she claimed to be unnecessary police action:

> Having managed to get rid of Moseley and his supporters in something like six minutes, it was up to the police to know that the crowd would then disperse happily by itself, but the police ran amok and started shoving everybody.

7.45   Accusations like these were illustrative of a growing feeling that the police failed to adequately handle such situations and an emerging awareness that they often provoked confrontation by their very presence.

From Fascism to Racism

7.46   Conflicts between Hackney's Jewish population and fascists on the one hand and the anti-fascists and the police on the other, soon gave way to increasing conflicts between the police and the growing numbers of Black people who came to live in Hackney in the 1950s and 1960s. Almost from the beginning of the Black settlement in Hackney, Black people alleged and complained of hostile police behaviour towards them.

7.47   In August 1970, the Community Relations Officer from Hackney Council for Racial Equality wrote to the Home Secretary of the day calling for a public inquiry into the serious racial disturbances between the police and the Black Power Movement. This was reported in the August 27 edition of the *Evening Standard,* as was the Home Secretary's eventual refusal.

7.48   The immediate circumstances surrounding H.C.R.E's call for a public inquiry thus remained unclear. What is certain, however, is that the demand came amidst increasing concern over the treatment of the Black community at the hands of the police.

7.49   As far as Black people were concerned, the most obvious areas of concern ranged from claims by Black people that they had been racially abused and attacked by police officers, often in enclosed situations; (e.g. at police stations and within their own homes), to claims of serious invasion of privacy as a result of police raids on privately owned property.

7.50   Dudley Dryden, MBE, in giving evidence to this Inquiry cited the following as marking almost the beginning of what appeared to be a series of concerted campaigns by the police against the Black community: "The days of the late night parties . . . when police would raid parties given by Black people . . . ostensibly to search for drugs".

7.51   Local newspapers carried several reports of such raids, particularly in the 1960s. For example: February 20 1962 "police raid West Indian party"; November 4 1962, "police raids in Alvington Crescent and Cecilia Road, Dalston". There appeared to be a clear feeling from the Black community that the police were motivated much more by the fact that such activities were regarded as alien to the British way of life, than any justified fear that a breach of the law was in progress. A frequent protest was that 'it is the custom in West Indians to throw parties'.

7.52   Still more worrying were the number of complaints of assaults by police, and instances of racial abuse. Just over a year before H.C.R.E's call for a public inquiry, a group of young Black men staged a demonstration outside one of London's Magistrates courts in protest against such police activities:

> Banner Waving Youths Allege Police Brutality (*Hackney Gazette* August 18 1960). The demonstration followed an incident in Ridley Road, Dalston where three Black men, Neville Kelly and Arthur Ramsey, both aged eighteen and Gerald Calliste, aged twenty-eight, alleged that a police officer, named Chapman, had assaulted Kelly and had subjected Calliste to a barrage of racial abuse.

Ironically enough, the threemen were themselves arrested and charged with using insulting behaviour and obstructing a police officer in the execution of his duty. During the hearing of the case against the threemen, two independent witnesses gave evidence which tended to support the allegations made by the three men. Sonia Cheung of Stoke Newington said she saw the police officer try to 'choke' Kelly, and the other witness, one George Joseph, claimed that the officer went 'beserk' and started pushing Kelly with his shoulder. The fact that the three men, who were not the original aggressors, were arrested, marks a familiar practice of the police which became increasingly evident in later years, i.e. the attempt to cover up their activities by bringing charges against people who claimed to have been the victims of some kind of police malpractice. On rare occassions this led to successful civil actions against the Metropolitan Police for false imprisonment and malicious prosecution (see the section below on Stoke Newington Police Station).

7.53 This practice was *sometimes* the subject of adverse comment by the Magistrates. For instance, in a case where a man was arrested and charged with using insulting behaviour, the Magistrate Evelyn Russell, in dismissing the case, accused an officer based at Stoke Newington police station of having charged the defendant in order "simply to cover up your mistake in arresting the defendant".

7.54 In general, however, Magistrates tended to be less condemnatory of the police. There was little recognition that the police could ever put a foot wrong. Indeed one Magistrate was moved to make a strong statement concerning alleged attacks on the police, *(Hackney Gazette,* 6 February 1962):

> Police officers are not there to be kicked and abused. There is too much of it. Day after day I hear of police officers being set about by thugs for no other reason than that they are doing their jobs.

7.55 That Magistrates tend to be prosecution minded is a general observation which obviously has an adverse effect on any person charged with a summary offence. However, this particular tendency causes even greater problems where prosecution evidence is tainted with stereotypical notions of a particular class of defendant. There is some indication that many complaints made by Black defendants, often in court, were virtually dismissed without further investigation. An important reason for this seems to have been a view taken by the police and courts that Black people were inherently unreliable and excitable. Noisiness, excitability and general excess of emotion figured very frequently in police description of events leading up to the arrest and appearance in court of Black people, usually on charges of assault and obstruction. For example, on 24 June 1960, the *Hackney Gazette* in their section 'Reports from the Courts' gave details of a case in which allegations were made against the police following 'scenes' outside Dalston police station. One of the accused officers described the people outside the police station (there were five) as being "all rather excitable and noisy". This description may well have influenced the Magistrate in deciding that the evidence of the defendants was "unreliable".

7.56 In another case reported on 23 September 1960, this same tendency (to accept police evidence almost without question) led the Magistrate, Geriant-Ross to make the rather curious statement that he was "quite satisfied that evidence had been given to the best of the witnesses' (a Black man and woman) recollection and belief", but that nevertheless their story was "confused and unreliable". The facts of the case were as follows: The police were called to premises occupied by a Mrs. Buffong as a result of a dispute between her and her landlord. According to the defendants (the police) had allegedly told Mrs. Buffong to 'get out' of the house and she and her two young children had been 'forced to leave' in the middle of the night. It was further alleged that one of the police officers (by the name of Burtenshaw) 'hustled' Mrs. Buffong along the passage of the house and in the course of the dispute, another officer (by the name of Clark) had seized Mrs. Buffong by her dressing gown "near her chest".

7.57   One of the most telling examples of this kind of stereotyping is illustrated through a case reported on 23 January 1962. A summons had been brought against a police officer (John Graham) attached to Stoke Newington police station (at that time, 'N' Division). The summons was later withdrawn and the person who brought the summons, Desmond Petinaud, later pleaded guilty to assaulting an officer. The Magistrate stated that he would deal lightly with the defendant (on the assault charge) because "he got excited, as perhaps people from his country did more readily than people born here".

7.58   That the defendant in this case was perhaps dealt with more leniently than would usually be the case, as a result of this warped perspective, was the exception rather than the rule. There is much evidence that the allegations made in court against police officers of misconduct were met with little sympathy or belief as the following two cases indicate:

In a report of a case on 1 April 1962, the Magistrate, when commenting on an allegation of police misconduct, said that it was a pity the defendant should dissipate the goodwill of people in England towards Black people by making such allegations and concluded: "I don't believe those things for a single moment".

In the second case reported on 5 February 1954, the Magistrate, Blake Odgers, stated in response to an allegation that a defendant was racially abused by a police officer: "I am not going to listen to a lot of ranting stuff about British people treating coloured (sic) people like beasts".

7.59   It is unfortunate that so many of the records of these cases exist only in newspaper reports, which do little justice to the seriousness of some of the allegations in the way in which they are reported. Allegations made by individual members of the public, usually with no witnesses and often with few sensational features attached to the allegation (i.e.

no obvious cuts and bruises) tend to be tucked away in the back columns of the newspapers. Even where it appears that the newspaper has taken up the case and it becomes front page headlines, the interest is hardly sustained.

7.60   So it was that on the 31 January 1964, the *Hackney Gazette* carried a story with the headline 'P.C's denial'. The report went on to describe an alleged incident whereby a 'West Indian' claimed to have been punched and struck with a truncheon by a police constable (George Deeming) attached to Stoke Newington police station. This allegation, it seems, went the way of the rest, attracting little attention.

7.61   Less than three months later, on 10 March 1964, the same paper carried a front page story headed "Serious allegations against police". It continued: "Some serious allegations against the police said Counsel, would be made in a case in which a Jamaican, Clinton Soutar, appearing on remand at a north London Magistrates' Court, was accused of using insulting behaviour and assaulting an officer". The defendant who, according to the newspaper report, walked into the court with the aid of a stick, alleged that he was assaulted and kicked by police at Dalston police station. Despite evidence of his injury (although we accept there was no actual evidence of the cause of the injury), Soutar's story was not accepted and the newspaper report ended with a record of the defence solicitor stating that they would appeal (presumably against Soutar's conviction for assault).

7.62   A few weeks later, on 24 March, the *Hackney Gazette* reported that a 'West Indian' was found lying unconscious on the floor of the detention room at Stoke Newington police station. He alleged that he was punched and stamped upon by the arresting officers, P.C.s David Jenkins and George Deeming.

7.63   There exists little information which would help to determine just how many of these allegations against police conduct were pursued through the police complaints machinery. There appeared to be little faith in this method of airing grievances against police. David Weitzman, M.P. for Stoke Newington and Hackney North, perhaps reflected much of the feeling about the inadequacy of the system, when in 1973 he called for an independent inquiry into the system of complaints against the police. Speaking about the injustice of police investigating complaints against themselves he stated:

> Almost invariably, I have received the reply that the matter is being investigated, and then that there is insufficient evidence that the officer concerned acted improperly.

Chapter 8

Police and the Community: The Black Experience in Hackney

8.1 The Inquiry received a considerable amount of evidence alleging a number of malpractices by the police and expressing concern at various aspects of policing in Hackney. Most of this evidence concerned police behaviour towards Black people and members of other ethnic minority communities. In this Chapter we look at the most common areas of complaint, using examples of cases made known to us: alleged malpractices by individual police officers such as wrongful arrest; unlawful use of force; racial abuse; the conduct of police raids on people's homes and the use of stop and search powers; police treatment of young people; police involvement in immigration control; and police responses to racial violence.

Wrongful Arrest

8.2 A frequent complaint of Black people in Hackney is that they have been wrongfully arrested by the police:

> In March 1977, G. was driving in Hackney. When he stopped at a junction, a police car stopped and a police officer said something to him which he did not hear. G. stopped and the police car reversed into him, damaging the wing of his car. One of the officers then asked for his documents. He said that he did not have the documents with him, at which point the officer accused him of stealing the car and called him a 'Black bastard'. G later sued the police for negligent driving, assault and false imprisonment. Before the case came to court, the police settled, paying G's legal costs and giving him a written apology. *(Hackney Law Centre).*

In April 1977, O, an Afro-Caribbean man, was grabbed outside his house by two police officers. He was assaulted and thrown into a police van. At Stoke Newington police station he was refused access to a solicitor and was later charged with obstructing a police officer in the execution of his duty. The charge was dismissed by the magistrates and O put in a written complaint, but this was dismissed. O then sued the police for assault and false imprisonment. He was awarded £500 damages and legal costs against the police. *(Hackney Law Centre)*

In September 1976, David and Lucille White, an elderly Black couple who lived in Stoke Newington, were arrested after a raid on their home. They were charged with assaulting the police, were cleared and were later awarded substantial damages. The case is dealt with in more detail in the section on Stoke Newington police station.

In September 1980, police raided a number of Hackney homes and arrested 18 Black youths. They were held in custody overnight but were released the next day without being charged. *(Searchlight,* November 1980).

In April 1981, several van and car loads of police responded to a reported robbery in Chatsworth Market, Hackney. They indiscriminately arrested several Black youths, detaining them for 12 to 18 hours. In contravention of the Judges' Rules, their parents were not informed. Only one of those arrested was actually charged with an offence — possession of cannabis. *(The Times,* 2/5/81).

In 1981, Newton Rose was arrested by Hackney police and later charged with the murder of a white youth connected with the National Front. The police latched onto the idea that the murder was a 'crime of passion' since the dead youth, Tony Donnelly, had been in the company of a woman who was Rose's ex-girlfriend. They ignored strong evidence that Rose had not been anywhere near the scene of the murder. Rose was convicted of murder in December 1981, but after a long campaign by relatives, friends and supporters, the Appeal Court quashed the conviction and Newton Rose went free

Campaign leaflet issued by the Newton Rose Action Committee in 1982 to protest against Newton Rose's wrongful conviction for murder.

In September 1982, a man was walking home from football training when a police van passed by slowly. An officer said to him: "What are you looking at, you Black bastard?" A few moments later the van turned round and came back towards the man. Three police officers got out, grabbed the man pushed him against the wall, and kneed him in the groin. The man was then taken to Stoke Newington police station where he was later charged with using 'insulting words'. The case was dismissed by magistrates and £100 costs awarded against the police. *(Hackney CRE)*.

In August 1984, Vincent Bailey and his son Arthur were walking in Hackney. They passed a police van and one officer grabbed Arthur Bailey. Vincent Bailey shouted at them to free his son, at which point he was grabbed, handcuffed and thrown onto the floor of the police van. At Stoke Newington police station he was told he had been arrested for obstruction. He was held for six hours and then released without charge. The following day, a police officer called at Bailey's home to apologise. *(Caribbean Times 7/9/84)*.

Unlawful Use of Force

8.3 In theory, the police may only use 'reasonable force' in making an arrest. In practice, allegations are frequently made that quite unjustified and unnecessary force is used, sometimes even in cases where no arrest is made:

A man in his late 40s, was driving along a main road in June 1979 when the door of his van swung open. He stopped to close it. Two police officers passing asked him to get out. When he did so, he was forced up against the parked car and one of the officers trampled on his feet. The complainant suffered considerable pain as he suffered from back trouble. *(Hackney CRE)*.

B went to the police station in September 1981 where his son was being held. When he protested at a police officer's statement that his son had committed a theft, he was grabbed round the neck, held to the floor and his head banged on the ground. He was then thrown down the steps of the police station. *(Hackney CRE)*.

In November 1981, a man was waiting for a bus in Dalston. When the bus arrived, the woman conductor allowed only two women on and barred C from getting on. When she moved inside the bus, however, C got on, and took a seat just vacated by another passenger. The conductor nevertheless demanded that he get off the bus. Two police officers arrived and pushed C off the bus, held him on the ground, one knee in his back, and handcuffed his hands behind him. *(Hackney CRE).*

In November 1981, Nellie Knight and her daughter Jennifer were severaly assaulted at Stoke Newington police station. Mrs. Knight had to have hospital treatment and her arm was put in a sling. *(Hackney CRE)* (We deal with this case in more detail in the section on Stoke Newington police station).

In 1983, two teenage brothers were walking from their home to meet their mother at the end of her work. They were about 300 yards from their home when they were stopped by three police officers who asked them where they were going. The boys said that they were going to St. Leonard's Hospital to meet their mother. They said that the officers then started to assault them. One of the boys suffered a sprained ankle, the other a broken foot. No charges were brought against the boys and although their father wanted to pursue a claim against the police, he later decided against it. *(Hackney Legal Defence Campaign Final Report).*

Racial Abuse

8.4 Many Black people who came into contact with the police in Hackney also complain that they have been subjected to racial abuse:

G, the man whose car was damaged by a police vehicle (see above), was called a "Black bastard" *(Hackney Law Centre).*

Two teenage girls walking across a road in Dalston in January 1981 ignored a police officer who shouted at them: "Hey, you girls". The officer then rushed over to them calling them "stupid Black gits" and "Black bastards". *(Hackney Law Centre).*

A, the man who was arrested when he was walking home from football training in September 1982 (see above) was not only called a "Black bastard". In the police van on the way to the police station, the officers addressed him as "coon" and the driver said; "All you coons go walking down the streets as though you own it". *(Hackney CRE).*

F, an Asian man, who had been arrested in July 1985 in connection with an alleged driving offence, was taken to the police station. There he was repeatedly called names such as "Paki bastard". When he pointed out that he was from Sri Lanka, he was then called "Sri Lankan bastard". *(Hackney Law Centre).*

8.5 Black women who come into contact with the police may be subjected to abuse which is not only racist but also sexist:

A Black man taken to Stoke Newington police station noticed some Black women there, whom he later learned were canteen staff. He heard on officer say: "Who's them Black whores looking at?" *(Hackney CRE).*

In October 1983, Mrs. J. reported to the police that she had been raped by a White man near Stoke Newington Common. Police, she said, told her to "leave it out" because it was impossible for a Black woman to be raped by a white man. When she insisted she had been raped she was met with further abuse and was told that it was "wishful thinking" on her part. *(Hackney Legal Defence Campaign Final Report).*

Stop and Search

8.6 As in many other areas of London and other major cities, the police use of their powers to stop and search appears to be a major issue among Black people, especially the young in Hackney. The following cases illustrate how the police have used their powers:

In April 1979, X, a man in his early 20s, got off a bus near Mare Street and was stopped by a police officer who pushed him and asked him what he had in his pockets. When asked why he wanted to know, the police officer said that he suspected him of stealing something. When asked what he was supposed to have stolen, X was told by the officer: "We'll see about that". He then radioed for more police. A panda car arrived and X was then taken to Hackney police station, where he was searched and held for an hour before being released without charge. *(Hackney CRE).*

Y, a man in his 50s, was walking along a road in Homerton in the heavy rain in March 1980. Three men got out from a car and asked him where he was going. He said that he was going to the shops. He was then seized, pushed up against some railings and roughly searched. The man was abused before being released. Although the man made a formal complaint, he was later persuaded to withdraw this because it would be a long, drawn out affair. *(Hackney CRE).*

Z, a man in his 20s, went into a record shop in June 1980, but did not buy anything. In the shop he was approached by a man in plain clothes who identified himself as a police officer who said Z was walking "too close to the tills". Z was then asked to go outside, where there was another plain clothes officer. Z was searched and gave his name and address. He said to the police officers that the reason there was trouble between police and Black people was because the police treated them as though they were all alike. One of the officers said that the reason was that "Blacks commit so many crimes". In response to a formal complaint, the Police Complaints Board said that the officers had been making proper use of their stop and search powers. *(Hackney CRE).*

In October 1983, two youths, one Black and one white, were walking towards Downs Park when they were stopped by two plain clothes police officers in an unmarked van. They were questioned about a speaker which they were carrying and taken to Stoke Newington police station. They were held there for three hours until another friend came to confirm their ownership of the speakers. *(Hackney Legal Defence Campaign Final Report).*

8.7 The police in Hackney also made extensive use of the notorious 'sus' law (repealed in 1981), which made it an offence to be a 'suspected person' loitering with intent to commit a criminal offence. The 1978 Runnymede Trust study of the use of the law showed that the police in Hackney used the law less than many other police divisions, but used it disproportionately against Black people. Thus, in 1977, the police in 'G' District arrested and brought charges against 81 people for 'sus'. But 61 per cent of these were Black. This put the Hackney police behind only Lambeth and Wandsworth police in their use of 'sus' against Black people. In Hackney too, it seems 'sus' was used as a means of keeping Black people, particularly Black youth, off the streets as the 'crime' could be proved in court solely on the evidence of two police officers. (Clare Demuth: *'Sus': a report on the Vagrancy Act 1824,* Runnymede Trust, 1978).

8.8 'Sus' was eventually repealed following a widespread campaign by Black community groups and others, but their efforts were attacked by the head of Hackney's Police, Commander David Mitchell, who said that those who complained about the use of 'sus' were usually "the ones responsible for committing the crimes". (*Searchlight,* March 1982).

Police Raids

8.9 Considerable disquiet has also been expressed at the conduct of police raids on Black people's homes and other premises used by Black people:

> On 16 July 1975, police with dogs raided the Four Aces club in Dalston. They claimed to be searching for four youths who had stolen a purse. Streets were cordoned off whilst a full-scale search got under way. In the ensuing melee, 18 youths were arrested. *(Institute of Race Relations: Police Against Black People,* 1979).

> In 1976, the Stoke Newington home of David and Lucille White was entered by officers from Stoke Newington police station, looking for stereo equipment which they suspected their sons might have. The couple, still in their nightclothes, were assaulted by the police, arrested and taken to the police station. Both Mr. and Mrs. White required hospital treatment, but it was they who were charged with police assault. They were both acquitted and were later awarded £51,000 damages for what a judge described as a 'catalogue of violence and inhuman treatment'. He added that the police had been guilty of 'monstrous, wicked and shameful conduct in the name of justice'. *(Daily Telegraph* 24/4/82).

At about 5 in the morning in 1977, officers arrived with a warrant to search Mrs. C's home in Dalston. They had Mrs. C's son at the police station and claimed that he had a bag of jewels on him when he was arrested and that they were searching for more jewels which he had stolen from Hatton Garden. They found nothing and it later transpired that the whole story of the jewels was a complete fabrication. *(IRR: Police Against Black People, IRR, 1979).*

Mr. and Mrs. A, a couple living in the Clapton area, were awoken one morning in October 1981 by a knock on the front door. Mrs. A opened the door to find eight police officers demanding to see their 18 year old son. They then pushed their way into the house, saying they had come to make a search. Mr. A asked whether they had a search warrant and was told that they didn't need one and that they had a lot of trouble from "people like him" in the borough. Mr. A noticed that the front door was open and tried to shut it. He was then arrested for obstruction. *(Hackney CRE).*

Mr. and Mrs. B, a couple in Clapton, were awoken at 7.30 in the morning in January 1982. From her bedroom window, Mrs. B saw a lot of men in plain clothes standing outside with pick axe handles and iron bars. One of the officers shouted that if she did not open the door he would "kick it off". The police officers said they had come to see her son about a robbery but refused to show any warrant. One of the officers went outside and made a large snowball and threw it into the passage of the house. Another officer used his pick axe handle to smash the glass in the back and front doors. *(Hackney CRE).*

In July 1983, Mrs. X opened her front door in Clapton to find police there looking for her brother. She was pushed out of the doorway and the police entered her home without showing any warrant. The house was searched throughout until the police were satisfied that her brother was not there. Mrs. X also alleged that she was racially insulted before the police left. *(Hackney Legal Defence Campaign Final Report).*

Armed police entered a house in Holly Street, pushed a gun at the occupant and asked him where the money was. The man in question had been in trouble with the law before, but this had been 10 years previously and involved a robbery in which only a replica gun had been used. This incident was brought to mind after armed police shot and paralysed Mrs. Cherry Groce in Brixton in 1985, *(Hackney CRE, oral submission)*.

In February 1986, a young Black couple living in Dalston were woken by a dozen police officers, four carrying guns. The police claimed that they were looking for firearms and ammunition, but after a search which caused extensive damage, none was found. A man was arrested and charged with possessing a stolen credit card. *(Caribbean Times 14/3/86).*

Police over-responding to incidents

8.10   Much of the evidence to the inquiry also alleged that the police in Hackney frequently over-responded to reported incidents:

In June 1980, Ras Elroy Bailey, a bass player with the reggae band, Black Slate, was walking through Downs Park where he joined in a game of football with some friends who were playing there. After about 10 minutes he noticed a police car drive into the park, then a van and another car. The next thing he knew the police had cleared everyone from him and a police officer from the van was pointing a gun at him, telling him to put his hands up. Bailey was then taken to Stoke Newington police station, where he was questioned about possession of a gun. After being questioned for three hours, Bailey was released without charge. *(West Indian World 20/6/80).*

In January 1981, a police officer was patrolling his home beat on Woodberry Down estate when he decided to arrest a youth for swearing at him. The youth fled to his home and locked himself out on the balcony. Within minutes, more than 30 officers and a dog van had been called to the estate and at one stage more than 10 officers were crowded into the flat and 5 people were arrested and charged. Four of those arrested were later cleared of obstruction or assault and only the youth who was originally to be arrested was convicted of using insulting language. *(Guardian 28/3/81).*

In October 1984, a police helicopter was called out when a police officer on patrol in Lower Clapton Road spotted a youth on the roof of a warehouse. A considerable number of officers also appeared on the scene. When an officer trying to reach the youth fell through a roof, other officers according to an eye-witness, became visibly aggressive and were heard to shout "Jump nigger". *(Hackney Gazette,* 19/10/84).

Conclusion

8.11   It is obviously not possible for the Inquiry to investigate these cases or to comment on their truth or accuracy and, no doubt, many will respond to this part of the report by dismissing it as 'anti-police propaganda'. We believe that this would be a serious mistake for a number of reasons. First, just as it is known that relatively few people report offences to the police, so it seems clear that few people report alleged malpractices by the police to independent agencies. It is reasonable to conclude that the cases presented to us, along with those reported in newspapers, represent only a fraction of the incidents which leave members of the public feeling aggrieved.

8.12   Second, the cases span a considerable period of time. This consistency, together with the fact that cases relate to the same issues over and over again, indicate that there is a consistency to police behaviour. Furthermore, the pattern and nature of the complaints is quite consistent with those reported over the years in other areas with substantial Black populations, such as Liverpool 8, Moss Side in Manchester, Handsworth in Birmingham or Brixton in south London.

8.13   Third, the Inquiry is not the first body to have raised these issues. In 1979, for instance, the Hackney Black People's Defence Organisation marched through the borough, demanding an end to police harassment. In 1980, Hackney CRE complained that the police commander was a "real danger to community relations" and in 1983 joined the growing demand for an independent public inquiry into the policing of the borough.

8.14   The Inquiry is convinced that the police in Hackney have, over a period of years, been guilty of serious abuses of their powers and their position and that the failure by the police and the Home Office to recognise this and to take the necessary remedial action has contributed to a serious deterioration in relations between the police and sections of the community in Hackney.

Police and Young People

8.15 Many of the complaints about the behaviour of the police towards Black people concern young people as the following cases show:

> In August 1976, N, an Afro-Caribbean youth, returned from a run with some friends to find a police officer sitting in his mother's car. The officer refused to say what he was doing and when N and his friends protested, three police officers got out of a nearby car. N and one of his friends were assaulted and all the youths were subjected to racial abuse. They were then arrested and charged with obstructing a police officer. The charges were dismissed at Highbury Corner magistrates' court the following month. After a formal complaint against the officers had been rejected, N sued the police and was awarded £50 damages for assault, but was ordered to pay police costs in relation to complaints of false imprisonment and malicious prosecution. *(Hackney Law Centre).*
>
> In July 1979, a mother and her teenage son complained to Hackney CRE that the youth had been fingerprinted and photographed and that they had been 'persuaded' to withdraw a complaint on the grounds that fingerprints and photos were taken all the time *(Hackney CRE).*
>
> A, a teenage male, was walking with a friend down a main street in Dalston when they were grabbed from behind. At first they thought they were being attacked by racists. They were then shown police ID cards. A, was grabbed by a trouser pocket and hurled against a wall. His college pass was taken from him and his name noted by one of the officers. A, asked for his pass back, but was ignored. A's parents then went to Dalston police station to make a complaint, but were told that there were no complaint forms there and that they would have to go to Hackney police station. The next day they were visited by an officer, who said that the police officer involved in the incident had admitted that he had acted wrongly. *(Hackney CRE).*

In November 1979, three boys, all under 17, were chased by a man in the Clapton area. They ran to the house of an aunt of one of them who called the police. When the police arrived, they accused the youths of stealing cars and taking wing mirrors from cars. The youths were all taken to the police station, but the police did not notify their parents, nor did they say which station they were taking the youths to. The mother of one boy said that she rang all the police stations in Hackney, but was told that her son was not there. Her son alleged that he had been assaulted while in police custody. *(Hackney CRE).*

A, a teenage boy, was arrested at about 1.00pm in January 1980 and accused with three others of having attacked an old lady. His school, however, when contacted by the police, indicated that all the boys probably had alibis. About an hour later, the school confirmed alibis for all the boys, but they were not released until 7.15pm. The police Complaints Board dismissed a formal complaint on behalf of one of the boys. *(Hackney CRE).*

B, a teenage male, was walking in the Clapton area with his mother, two sisters and three friends, when they heard a screech of brakes. A police car had pulled up beside B and his friends who were bending over a key they had found on the pavement. A police officer told B to get in the van and told his friends that if they did not push off, they would be put in the van also. B was pushed into the van, driven a bit further away and searched. B was then released from the van and rejoined his family who had witnessed the whole incident. *(Hackney CRE).*

C, a 15 year old male complained that he had been watching a fight in the street along with some other youths, when he heard a police siren and, with the rest of the group, ran away. A police officer caught up with him, took hold of him and pushed him against a wall, saying he was 'nicked'. A second officer then took him and punched him in the stomach and threatened to break his nose. He was then put in a police van and taken to Hackney police station. *(Hackney CRE).*

8.16 In addition to such cases of police harassment on the streets, concern has also been expressed about the relationship between the police and schools in Hackney. In its pamphlet *Police Out of Schools* (1985), Hackney Teachers' Association (HTA) cited the following cases:

> A teacher from Hackney Downs School witnessed 12 and 13 year old boys in their lunch hour being stopped, spread-eagled and searched by a squad of Special Patrol Group officers.
>
> At Edith Cavell School a boy was accused of theft of a wallet and the police were involved in the investigation without the child's mother (his only parent) being informed. He was cleared of any involvement, but during the investigation the head teacher told his mother that they could not give her any details of the police investigation, as the police had instructed them not to. His mother then spent a long time trying to establish that there was no reference to the allegation of theft on her son's school record.
>
> At another school, a teacher had intervened when he saw some boys from the school being questioned and frisked just outside the school premises. The police became abusive towards him, arrested him and charged him with assault. He was later acquitted in court.

8.17 The Hackney Teachers' Association pamphlet also contained the following account by a Hackney teacher:

> X is a 16 year old Black person who has spent all his life in Hackney, and he is unimpressed with any claim to the effect that the local police force is not racist.
>
> His first confrontation with the Hackney police occurred when he was eleven. He had left his home to return to school, when he was stopped and questioned by two police officers. They wanted to know where he had been, what he had been doing, and where he was going. He remembers their sarcastic and patronising manner: 'as if they are putting me in the wrong'. It is an approach that X has come to expect, as he has been stopped and searched approximately 15 times in the 5 years since the first incident. Quite understandably, the first experience frightened him! It led him to become very aware of the police, and his experiences have told him that his ordinary behaviour — for example, walking and standing — could be seen by the police as questionable and suspicious. This is not

the case with white people who do not face the same risk of being stopped and searched simply for being on a street.

I have worked with and spoken to countless young Blacks in Hackney who have experienced the same problem as 'X' in their dealings with the local police. The incidents do not have to be extreme to make the young Black people feel that they are being treated unfairly by the police; that they are being attacked by an openly hostile organisation. Therefore there seems to be obvious justification in the accusation that the Hackney police force *is* racist. It declares itself to be so every time it harasses somebody like X and there are plenty young people in the local schools like him.

8.18 Cases such as these, HTA said, raised "issues of grave concern to parents and teachers, and to the Black community in particular because they are most often the victims of police malpractice and racism". HTA went on to identify four particular matters of concern arising from the presence of police in schools:

(a) Despite the ILEA Guidelines, parents are not always informed when the police are called in or given access to school files.

(b) The lack of information available to parents about those occasions when the police are routinely in schools. This now extends to disco dancing, five a side football, the showing of police films and free lectures on 'child development' and 'animal appreciation'.

(c) The freedom with which the police enter school premises, staff rarely know when or why they are there and, unfortunately, few staff feel free to challenge their presence.

(d) The intimidating atmosphere that police can produce in a school, both for children and staff. One example is police getting in touch with the parents of children who expressed hostile attitudes during the police presentation in school.

8.19 It was issues and cases such as these, along with the killing of east London teacher, Blair Peach, at an anti-racist demonstration in Southall, which led Hackney Teachers'

Association to adopt in 1979 a policy of non-co-operation with the police. As HTA put it in *Police Out of Schools:*

> This policy of not co-operating with the police in schools... came into being because of what teachers learned about the police in Hackney and, most importantly, what they learned about the police from the everyday experience of their pupils.

8.20 Such a policy, HTA argued, was essential if teachers were to have the confidence of Black pupils and their parents. In any case, HTA argued, there was nothing that especially qualified the police more than any other group in society to teach five-a-side football, road safety, law or even not to go with strangers. Alternative non-racist agencies existed in all these areas, it said, if schools wanted outsiders to develop these and other areas of the curriculum.

8.21 This Inquiry also considers that strict guidelines are required to regulate the presence of the police on school premises at other times. In general, the Inquiry believes the police should be brought onto school premises only in the most serious circumstances, for example, to investigate a serious assault. In all cases, schools should have a duty immediately to inform parents of any pupil whom the police may wish to question. No pupil should be interviewed by police unless her or his parent is present.

Policing Immigration Controls

8.22 Since the Immigration Act 1971 came into effect in January 1973, the police have played an increasingly important role in enforcing immigration controls *within* Britain. The act effectively ended Black and Asian immigration for settlement and, in general, only permitted the immigration of white people (patrials — those with an ancestral connection with Britain) or of people defined as the 'dependents' of people already settled here, mainly wives and children. But the law was not only concerned with preventing people from entering the country. It also provided extensive controls on those already living in Britain. In particular, it extended the power of the Home Secretary to deport people or to order their removal if they were thought to have entered the country illegally. It also gave the police wide powers of arrest without warrant in cases of suspected illegal entry, breach of conditions, harbouring an illegal entrant or overstayer and obstruction of an immigration officer or anyone else carrying out an immigration function.

8.23 Even before the Act came into force, the Metropolitan Police had created a new, national unit concerned with immigration. The Illegal Immigration Intelligence Unit (IIIU) was set up in September 1972 and became fully operational in March 1973. Its function was to 'receive, collate, evaluate and disseminate information on known or suspected offenders'. In its first year of operation, the IIIU carried out over 200 enquiries and made over 70 arrests. These included raids on 13 addreses in East London and the questioning of all those present about their immigration status. A number of people were taken to Leman Street police station, including one man who had lived in Britain for six years.

8.24 Similar raids have taken place since, both in London and other parts of the country, and have been well documented. One of the problems, however, is that there appears to have been no centralised recording of immigration raids until 1980 and, even then, only raids regarded as 'major' were recorded by the Home Office. In addition, it is known that neither those subjected to raids nor those whose premises or businesses are the sites of raids are particularly keen on publicity. There is, therefore, a gap in our knowledge about the precise extent of such raids, both generally and as they relate to Hackney. It seems safe to assume, however, that there have been unreported passport raids in Hackney if only because of the large numbers of 'rag trade' premises in the area employing substantial numbers of Black and other ethnic minority workers and because it is known that such premises are known to have been major targets elsewhere.

8.25 In any case, considerable concern was expressed to us about a recent raid in Hackney:

> In April 1985, the Directorate clothing factory in Richmond Road was raided by six police officers and four immigration officials, ostensibly to apprehend two individuals. Neither of the two people named in the search warrant was present, but the police took away a number of other people, mainly Turkish Cypriots. The police said the number was six, but others claimed that the number was at least ten. Those detained were held overnight without any access to legal advice. Action by the Hackney Anti-Deportation Campaign ensured that the detainees were allowed to see a lawyer the following day, but several of the workers were never accounted for. According to the HADC, they left the country 'voluntarily' under police pressure. *(Hackney Anti-Deportation Campaign).*

8.26 Representatives from Hackney Anti-Deportation Campaign (HADC) told the Inquiry that the Directorate raid was "only one of many" which had come to its attention (a point also made by Councillor Brynley Heaven, Chair of the Police Committee just after the raid itself), although they emphasised that they had heard of this raid only by chance, because one of the workers at the factory knew one of the members of the Campaign. They also said that although raids were now generally carried out with a search warrant, following protests about previous raids where no warrants were used, frequently the individuals named in the warrant were not known in the workplace. HADC also said that raids appeared to be more common in the spring and that there was some evidence to suggest collusion between the police, immigration service and factory owners who wished to rid themselves of some workers before the end of the financial year.

8.27 Whatever the precise extent of passport raids in Hackney, their impact is clear. As HADC told the Inquiry "The overall effect of this behaviour by the police and immigration authorities is to create a climate of **fear and suspicion** . . .".

8.28 The Immigration Act also gave the police the power to demand to see the passport of anyone 'reasonably suspected' of a breach of immigration law, for example of being an illegal entrant or having overstayed leave to remain in Britain. Where there was no 'reasonable suspicion', however, the police were not supposed to demand to see passports. So, for example, they were not supposed to demand the passport of someone simply because s/he was Black. This had been made clear in 1973 by the Home Office which issued a circular to all police forces, asking them to avoid actions which could be construed as harassment of Black people, for example: "a request to inspect the passport of someone who comes to ... notice in connection with a minor offence, but whom there is no reason to suspect of being in the country illegally". In 1974, an instruction to the same effect was written into the Metropolitan police rule book. Such advice and rules appear to have little effect on the police in Hackney, in the same way that they had little effect in other parts of the country where the police came into contact with Black people, as the following cases show:

> In 1978, a Black school child born in this country, was stopped on his way to school in Hackney and asked for his passport. Since he did not carry it with him, he was taken to the police station and detained for one and a half hours. His mother subsequently received an apology from a senior officer who told her: "Some of the younger officers are a little over-enthusiastic". *(Hackney CRE,* quoted in IRR: *Police Against Black People,* 1979).

> A young man in his 20s was stopped in the Dalston area by two officers in a panda car and told that they were looking for someone who fitted his description. On telling the police his name, he was told: "You people tell a lot of lies. Have you anything to prove who you are?" He produced his London Transport bus pass and photocard. He was then asked where he had got it and was then asked where he worked. The man replied that he was a student. The police then asked to see his passport, but the man said it was with the Home Office. The police then asked for a Home Office receipt, but the man said that he had a letter at home. The police then said that he would have to go with them. The matter was only resolved by

the intervention of Dudley Dryden, a shop-owner in the nearby Ridley Road market. *(Hackney CRE).*

In March 1980, a police officer called at a flat in the Homerton area. He asked the man who answered whether he was the occupier and was told no. He then asked the man for his name and date of birth and these were given. The officer then used his radio to call the police station to check this information. He then asked to see the man's passport, but the complainant refused. The police officer then told the man that he would have to go to the police station. The man then decided to show his passport, hoping that this would get rid of the police officer. The officer noted the details and returned the passport *(Hackney CRE).*

In October 1980, a man was walking up a main road and stopped to look in a shop window. A police officer, accompanied by a police cadet, came up to him and asked if he was Nigerian. The man replied that he was not and asked why they wanted to know. The officer then asked for his name and address, whether he was a student, where his place of work was, and how long he had been in the country. The man again asked why they wanted to know all this and was told: "There are a lot of illegal immigrants in this country. Are you settled here?" The man refused to answer these questions and the officer then radioed for assistance. An inspector arrived with another officer, appeared satisfied with the man's response and then left. The police officer, however, persisted in his questioning and eventually the man gave him his name and address. The Police Complaints Board said that the officer thought the man was behaving suspiciously but said that his line of questioning was against Force policy and that he would be advised of this. The Board did not consider, however, that his action warranted disciplinary proceedings. *(Hackney CRE).*

8.29   The police may also question Black people about their immigration status when they come into contact with the police for another reason:

In June 1982, after the death of an Asian man, over 20 of his friends and relatives were taken to Stoke Newington police station and held for questioning, some for up to 30 hours.

They were not informed of their rights, were denied access to a solicitor and were racially abused. In addition, many were wrongly accused of being in the country illegally. They were only released after pressure on the police from the Hackney Asian Association. *(Hackney Asian Association).*

8.30 But police involvement in enforcing immigration controls within Britain has not been confined to carrying out raids on workplaces and homes, or to demanding passports or questioning individuals about their immigration status. They have, on occasion, taken a much more extensive and direct role as is illustrated by the case of the Hasbudak family:

Polat and Kebire Hasbudak came to Britain from Turkey in 1976. They overstayed their initial leave to enter and two children were born here, Zeynep in 1977 and Fatih in 1979. The Hasbudaks lived all the time in Hackney and Fatih and Zeynep attended William Patten School in Stoke Newington, In 1983, Polat and Zeynep were ordered to leave Britain because of their overstaying several years before. The children could not, however, be ordered out as they were born here and were therefore British citizens. An appeal against deportation was rejected in November 1983 and the family went into hiding. The campaign against the deportation was supported by a wide range of organisations and individuals in Hackney and London, including the pupils and staff at William Patten School. According to Hackney Teachers' Association, when the family went into hiding the school was subjected to harassment by the police, including surveillance by phone tapping, interfering with mail, police observation of the school and even observation of the school by police helicopter. According to the HTA, even children of only nursery school age were questioned by the police about the possible whereabouts of the family. In March 1984, Polat Hasbudak was lured out of hiding by a message informing him that a registered letter was waiting for him at the post office. When he went with a friend to collect this letter, he was pounced on by a group of police officers and taken to Ashford Remand Centre to await deportation. After his deportation, his wife and children gave themselves up and left the country in April.

(It is worth noting that, as was pointed out to us by the Hackney Anti-Deportation Campaign, that the police must have had the co-operation of at least one post office worker for their ruse to have been successful).

8.31 The involvement of the police in enforcing immigration controls has created a situation where Black and Asian people, as well as people of Turkish or Cypriot origin, fear any contact with the police in case this should mean that they are questioned and challenged about their immigration status. This means, for instance, that many people will not even report incidents in which they have been the victims of criminal activity. In general, it is clear that police involvement in enforcing immigration controls has been a significant source of tension between the police and sections of the community in Hackney. This is a point which was made at a more general level by the Institute of Race Relations (IRR) and the joint Council for the Welfare of Immigrants (JCWI), Britain's principal independent immigration advice agency, in evidence to the Royal Commission on Criminal Procedure in 1979. The IRR, recommending the repeal of the penal and criminal provisions of the Immigration Act 1971 said that:

> These provisions make every Black person in this country a potential suspect in the eyes of the police and the harassment and suffering they create for many people is not justified by the end of 'real' illegal entrants detained. Also we believe that these provisions help create an attitude towards Black people which is incompatible with the police's functions of protecting all sections of the community.

8.32 The JCWI argued that:

> A major cause of the suspicion and mistrust with which the police are viewed by many within the immigrant community is the role given to the police in the enforcement of immigration control.

Racial Violence and the Police Response

8.33 Black communities in Britain have been subject to racial attacks and harassment ever since they have lived here. Yet the nature and extent of the problem has rarely been recognised by the police and others in authority. This much is clear from the extensive literature on the subject which has shown a clear pattern of police response to reports of racial attack. This has included the denial of racial motive, unwillingness and refusal to prosecute attackers, misleading and misguided advice to victims, hostility towards victims, and delay in responding to calls for help.

8.34 It was only in 1981, after a Home Office study of the issue, that the government began to admit that there was a serious problem, estimating that in any one year there would be about 7,000 incidents reported to the police in England and Wales. Despite this report and the belated official recognition of the seriousness of the problem, racial violence has continued and, many would argue, has increased dramatically, both in terms of the number of attacks and in the seriousness of the attacks. Thus, a report by the Greater London Council Police Committee based on evidence received from over 100 organisations, concluded that racial harassment was an "increasingly serious problem", while a survey by the Policy Studies Institute (PSI) concluded that the scale of racial violence and harassment might be as much as 10 times that estimated by the 1981 Home Office study. This, the PSI study said, had been based only on incidents reported to the police. While its own survey had found that the vast majority of incidents were not reported to the police. (Colin Brown: *Black and White Britain: the third PSI survey*, Heinemann, 1984).

8.35 Within this general context, the Black residents of Hackney have also been subjected to racial violence and harassment, although the extent of the problem does appear to have been considerably less than that found in the neighbouring borough of Tower Hamlets. Nevertheless, this does not detract from the seriousness of the problem, nor does it lessen the impact of such violence on its individual victims and their families and communities. The violence has resulted in at least two deaths:

In June 1978, Ishaque Ali died from a heart attack following an attack near his home in Coopersale Road. Charges of murder were changed to manslaughter, but even these were reduced. Those responsible eventually only faced charges of assault with intent to rob and assault occasioning actual bodily harm.

In December 1978, Michael Ferreira was brutally stabbed by known fascists. He was then taken by friends to Stoke Newington police station where, it was claimed, he was allowed to bleed unattended for 20 minutes while police were more concerned to question his friends as to what they were doing at that time of the night.

8.36 A large protest demonstration was organised by HCRE and various local Black groups in Hackney, passing both Stoke Newington and Dalston police stations to protest at the inactivity of the police. Local groups claimed that the police "had not been able to show that they had either the ability or the willingness to protect people from the racist violence being promoted by the National Front and other racist organisations". Organisations and individuals began to discuss how best to protect themselves from such attacks. HCRE requested a special line to local police headquarters at City Road.

8.37 Other incidents include arson, assault and racist graffiti as the following cases show:

In June 1977, Centerprise, the Hackney community centre, was daubed with racist graffiti and its doors' locks filled with glass fibre compound which made access to the Centre impossible. *(Morning Star* 27/6/77).

An Asian family were terrorised by white youths from the day they moved into their home. Although they were finally rehoused, for six weeks they had been forced to live in one back room while their home was bombarded with missiles and abuse. All incidents were reported to the police, who said that they had called three times to investigate allegations of criminal damage "and two other occasions to intervene in neighbours' dispute". Apparently, however, they were powerless to prevent the total wrecking of the family's home or the death threats they received. *(Institute of Race Relations: Police Against Black People,* IRR, 1979).

In June 1979, an attempt was made to burn the flat of a Black family on the Jack Dunning Estate. The family said that the arson attack was the culmination of various racist activities against them, including the daubing of their front door with the letters 'NF'. A fire officer who helped get the blaze under control said that it was fortunate that none of the family had been in at the time. *(West Indian World* 28/6/79).

Also in June 1979, a mystery blaze gutted a West Indian owned shop in Ridley Road market, causing £4,000 worth of damage. The shopowner blamed the fire on local racists. *(Afro-Caribbean Post* 28/6/79).

During 1980, shops and stalls owned by Black people in Ridley Road were vandalised and daubed with the initials of fascist groups. Traders said they were victims of a racist campaign of damage and harassment *(Hackney Gazette:* 12/12/80).

In January 1981, the home of the Singh family near London Fields was so badly damaged by a firebomb that the family had to move into one room in their flat. The attack followed months of telephone threats on the lives of the family *(East London and Hackney Advertiser:* 13/2/81).

In March 1981, an attempt was made to burn down the premises of the Pan African Organisation in Dalston. About £1,000 worth of damage was caused. The day after the fire, the premises of Hackney CRE were also damaged: a window was smashed, doors were smeared with excrement and National Front slogans were daubed on the wall. *(Hackney Gazette:* 24/3/81).

In May 1985, Centerprise was extensively vandalised. Tomato ketchup and mayonnaise were poured over books in the Black and Women's sections of the bookshop and a total of £10,000 worth of damage was done. A note saying that the British National Party had visited was left behind and the initials of the National Front and the British Movement were scrawled over the walls *(City Limits:* 24/5/85).

8.38 Cases reported, both to the Inquiry and elsewhere, illustrate the persistent failure of the police to respond properly and effectively to calls for assistance:

> In October 1974, a Black man called the police when 12 people turned up at his door one night. He and his wife then made no fewer than 10 calls to the police during the next 20 minutes when no police officers arrived. When the police did attend, they did not appear to be interested in the family's predicament. *(Hackney Asian Association).*

> In September 1980, police called to an Asian family's home following a complaint of racial harassment by neighbours, simply warned the Asian family that they should not make any noise which would antagonise their neighbours. *(Hackney Asian Association).*

> In October 1981, a Black householder who called the police after he had been attacked by a white tenant was warned by a police officer that if he caused trouble he would end up behind bars. *(Hackney Asian Association).*

8.39 Reports also show that the police frequently deny that there is any racial motivation behind an attack or play down any evidence of such motivation:

> In 1982, Norma Richards and her two young daughters were found murdered in their home. Mrs. Richards had been stabbed and one of her daughters drowned. Even though they were the only Black family living on the estate, and despite the fact that Nazi insignia and racist slogans were found on the walls, the police appeared to ignore the possibility that there was a racial motive behind the murder. *(Searchlight:* September 1982).

> In January 1983, Black footballer, Laurie Cunningham's brother-in-law said police had removed some wallpaper in the house saying: "This is what we're going to do with all niggers". He also said that the police had asked him not to talk about this. *(Hackney CRE).*

8.40 Similarly, the police often seem reluctant or unwilling to prosecute racist attackers, even where there is clear evidence of their involvement:

In August 1985, C, an Afro-Caribbean, was assaulted outside his home by a number of youths. He gave the police the names and addresses of one of his attackers. The police refused to arrest the attacker and only did so when ordered by the Magistrate when C tried to take out a private prosecution *(Hackney Law Centre)*.

Representatives from Hackney CRE described to us a recent incident in which a Black man had been badly beaten up in a pub. It was described as a 'racial attack of the most violent kind', which resulted in the man receiving hospital treatment. Despite this, and despite the fact that it was clear who the assailant was, no charges were brought by the police *(Hackney CRE)*.

8.41 It is clear from the evidence submitted to us, and from the other material available that racial violence and harassment are serious problems for sections of Hackney's Black community. The fact that the police may actually record few reported instances is of significance only because it illustrates that most victims of harassment do not consider it worth their while making a report to the police, a point emphasised to us by a representative from Hackney Asian Association. It is clear, too, that the police have singularly failed to deal with the problem, and indeed, have contributed to it through their persistent refusal to take the issue seriously and to recognise the racist nature of many of the attacks suffered by Black people in Hackney.

Stoke Newington Police Station

8.42 Under the terms of reference of the Inquiry, we were asked to examine in particular Stoke Newington police station, the police station in which Colin Roach died. The death of Colin Roach was not, however, the only reason for a closer examination of the history and reputation of Stoke Newington police station which has for some years been a continuous source, focus and therefore a symbol of many of the general complaints made against the Hackney police force.

8.43 By the time of Colin Roach's death in 1983, Stoke Newington already had the reputation, particularly among the Black community, of being a place where people thought the worse was likely to happen, and often did. Even those who could not by any stretch of the imagination be called unsympathetic to the police recognised the contribution that this reputation made to the station's isolation from the community. Around the time of Colin Roach's death, a cartoon appeared in the Police Federation magazine, *Police*, showing Stoke Newington under siege from the community, while Paul Harrison, a freelance writer who spent some time with Stoke Newington officers before Colin Roach's death, and who admired the work of Hackney police, wrote of the station: "Even physically the police seemed isolated and beleagured. Stoke Newington nick is like a fortress". *(Inside the Inner City,* page 367, Penguin 1983).

8.44 Here we look at some of the reasons why. We begin with an account of two deaths that occurred in, or in relation, to Stoke Newington police station. We then look at the catalogue of incidents alleged to have occurred in the station, or as a result of action by Stoke Newington officers, from the 1960s to the present day. Finally, we look at the attempts that the Hackney police have made since Colin Roach's death, to change the image of the station.

8.45 Although we are focussing here on Stoke Newington police station, this does not mean that we believe that all problems concerning Hackney police stem from that station. Nor does it mean that other Hackney police stations have never received a single public comment or criticism. As the evidence presented to the Inquiry makes clear, the problem of policing in Hackney goes right across the force in the borough.

Deaths in Stoke Newington Police Station

8.46 Colin Roach was not the first person to die in Stoke Newington police station. Nor was he the first Black person to die there. During the 1970s there were two deaths in the station about which we received written and oral evidence, and which we describe below. While these deaths can only be understood in the context of policing practices in general and in the particular history of the policing of Hackney, they must also be examined within another context: the sharp rise in deaths in police custody (and other forms of custody) in the last decade and a half.

8.47   The issue of deaths in custody initially came to press and public attention after a sequence of highly publicised deaths in custody, or at the hands of the police. In one of the most famous incidents, Blair Peach, a white teacher, was killed after a single blow to the head from a member of the SPG at an anti-National Front protest demonstration in Southall in April 1979. In another case that year, Jimmy Kelly died on Liverpool waste ground after a violent arrest by several police officers. It was such highly publicised and seemingly violent deaths that led M.Ps like Michael Meacher and Stan Newens to investigate and publicise the dramatic dramatic increase in the number of deaths in police custody since 1970. The figures also showed that an unaccountably high percentage of these deaths, nearly half, occurred in the Metropolitan Police force area.

8.48   Most people in police custody die of drink or drug related problems: police stations are not the place to take a person suffering from an alcohol-related condition, nor are police officers the best qualified people to deal with them, or spot the difference between injury and intoxication. But this categorisation is not as unproblematic as it sounds: some drink-related deaths in custody have been aggravated by police failure to act (James Sullivan, James Hall, Robert Pratt, Wilma Lucas). Some people are driven, through depression and fear, or uncertainty about the future, to commit suicide in police custody (Matthew Paul and Oliver Clairmonte). Others, like Colin Roach, die in ambiguous circumstances where an inquest has not, or cannot, bring out the full facts. As in the death of Colin Roach, the police version or interpretation of a death will often sharply conflict with that of the family or friends of the deceased.

8.49 Deaths in custody became an issue that focussed sharply, for the public, the unease they were beginning to feel about policing methods and strategy, particularly in urban areas. For there is no doubt that the increasing forceful style of policing and the hardening of attitudes within the force as a result of economic crisis has contributed to the dramatic rise of deaths in custody, although such generalisations are difficult to pinpoint in individual cases. Similarly, well documented incidents of racist behaviour by officers in the Met is clearly connected to the number of Black people who die in police custody. Although there are no overall figures for the number of Black people who have died in police custody, either nationally or in London, even a preliminary review of research into the known cases in the most recent years reveals a disproportionate number of deaths among Black people.

8.50 In 1980 the House of Commons Home Affairs Committee inquired into deaths in custody between 1970 and 1979 and prepared a report which remains the most thorough examination of all the issues. (For a more recent account of deaths in custody, and other police related deaths in London, see Melissa Benn and Ken Worpole: *Death in the City,* Canary Press, 1986.)

8.51 On 13 May 1971, Aseta Simms died whilst in Stoke Newington police station. The police alleged that she had been drinking and brought about her own death whilst at the station. However, police doctors and relatives reported that there was swelling and bruising over her right eye and bruising over her head consistent with having been beaten. Some witnesses disputed the account given of her extreme drunkeness, which was the police view. A police doctor, who gave evidence at the inquest said:

> It is arguable that some people might die with this level of alcohol in their blood stream: but we have people with much higher levels who are still alive today. The bruising was consistent with someone falling about or with someone who had been beaten. There was very little evidence that she had inhaled vomit, but this was not the cause of death. I cannot truthfully say what was the cause of her death.

8.52 A verdict of death by misadventure was returned at the inquest. *(Who killed Aseta Simms?,* Black Unity and Freedom Party, 1971).

8.53 On Sunday, 10 December 1978, Michael Ferreira of Rushmore Road, Hackney, was attacked and stabbed by three white youths as he waited for friends to return from a fish and chip shop in Stoke Newington High Street. Michael and his friends had been on their way home from a party. His friends helped him into Stoke Newington police station where, according to the Hackney Council for Racial Equality:

> The police were more interested in questioning him, instead of getting him to hospital immediately, although they said later they called an ambulance straight away. His friends saw that he was rapidly weakening but could not get the police to accept that the most urgent action was needed. When the ambulance eventually came, it was too late. He died in the ambulance on the way to hospital.(Hackney CRE: *Policing in Hackney: a Record of HCRE's Experience 1978-82).*

8.54 There was widespread anger in the Black community in general, and particularly in Hackney, at the manner of Michael Ferreira's death. According to one account "the funeral became an occasion for a dignified and very large procession through Hackney, an event which specifically focussed a strong sense of hostility on Stoke Newington police station": (Melissa Benn and Ken Warpole: *Death in the City,* Canary Press, 1985, page 41.) As we noted earlier, a protest march arranged by HCRE and local Black groups was held on Saturday, 20 January 1979; it passed Stoke Newington and Dalston police stations, as a sign of protest at the inactivity of local police in the area.

Other incidents

8.55 We have limited information concerning Stoke Newington police station prior to 1970. What reports we have managed to unearth, mainly from the *Hackney Gazette,* show that the station attracted adverse publicity as early as the 1950s. On 20 January 1950, the *Hackney Gazette* reported that three constables attached to Stoke Newington police

Funeral march for Michael Farmer.

station appeared at north London Magistrates Court on charges of theft and handling stolen goods. On 2 November 1953, the *Gazette* reported that "statements said to have been put to an arrested man by Detective Sergeant Donald Adams of Stoke Newington police station were strongly criticised by (a defence lawyer) at a north London magistrates court". The charges against the defendants were subsequently dropped on the grounds that police procedure had not been properly followed. On 18 August 1969, in an article headlined "Banner waving Youths Allege Police Brutality", it was reported that 14 Black youths had demonstrated outside a London magistrates court after an incident in Ridley Road (near Stoke Newington station) on the previous Saturday. Although 3 youths had been charged with wilful obstruction, the point of their demonstration was that it had been local officers who were responsible for the aggression that flared up.

8.56 Documentation concerning the station and the activities of those attached to it is, however, overwhelming in the mid-to-late 1970s. It was during this period that local agencies began to keep dossiers of complaints against, and incidents, involving officers. Two such dossiers were submitted to us as written evidence, and they make chilling reading. We have already quoted at some length from the HCRE's *Policing in Hackney: A Record of HCRE's experience, 1978-82*. At least ten of the incidents related in that document concern Stoke Newington police station. The following are three examples:

> The complainants a man and a woman, went to a pub in Stoke Newington in September 1978 but were barred from entry. The woman went inside to ask the publican why they were barred. She was then thrown out very violently on her head and back. Two police officers came, they advised the man to take out a summons against the publican and left. The man and woman then went to Stoke Newington police station to report the matter. At the police station the police did not appear to be interested. They grabbed the woman, arrested and punched her and said she would be charged with being drunk and disorderly. (She was later acquitted). The man was

told to leave the station. He returned with his mother and smaller son to ask about his friend. The man was then arrested and charged with being drunk and disorderly. He refused to sign forms the police put infront of him. Both complained of being abused, unlawfully arrested and assaulted by the police, after seeking their help.

The complainant, a young man, was with his girlfriend in his car outside a club in north Hackney in the early hours of one morning in July 1979. A policeman who approached him produced a joint of cannabis which he alleged was the complainant's. The complainant was then asked to come to the station but when he queried how his girlfriend would get home (she could not drive) an assault followed and large numbers of police reinforcements arrived. There was a lot of racial abuse and the police seemed excited. He was violently and tightly handcuffed. His wrists bled and he was in great pain. He was taken to Stoke Newington police station. He asked for the handcuffs to be eased off but received another blow. At Stoke Newington police station there were a great deal of jokes and laughter among the police about the injury to his wrist. He was held overnight, but made no complaint as he felt it wasn't worth it.

8.57   The following incident was witnessed by the Chairman and Secretary of the HCRE during the disturbances in Stoke Newington in July 1981:

Late in the evening, a stone was thrown from near a small group of 2 or 3 girls at a group of 20 to 30 police. The police charged across the street and chased a youth past where the two HCRE observers were standing while a small number fell on one of the girls and beat her to the ground where she lay bruised and bleeding. It was only after repeated requests from the HCRE observers to the police that they used their radio to call an ambulance.

8.58   Equally disturbing was Hackney Law Centre's submission to us. This consisted of a detailed analysis of 47 cases dealt with by the Law Centre from 1977 to October 1985. Of these 47 complaints, 34 were by Afro-Caribbeans, 2 from Asians, 1 from a Moroccan and 1 from a white person, with 9 unknown. A breakdown of complaints by police station show that 16 of the total complaints (that is 43.2%) concerned officers from Stoke Newington police station, while 14 (37.8%) concerned officers from Hackney police station. 12 of the complaints were of harassment, 11 of assault. Here are 3 examples of the documented complaints:

> In November 1977, B, 11 years old, male, white, was taken from his school one afternoon to Stoke Newington police station without his parents or other responsible persons being informed. At the station he was questioned about an offence for a couple of hours without his parents or any other responsible person being present. No written complaint to the police was made.
>
> One afternoon in July 1977, Mr. D, 42, Afro-Caribbean, was driving to the dry cleaners where he was flagged down by two police officers in a police car. Some seven more officers arrived on the scene. Mr. D was dragged from his car, assaulted and searched. At Stoke Newington police station, he was assaulted, held in a cell for 4 hours, finger-printed without his consent, and vigorously questioned. He was eventually released without being charged. As a result of his treatment he suffered back pains and sleeplessness for some two months, and was unable to attend work during this time. A written complaint was made, but the Police Complaints Board decided that no disciplinary proceedings should be taken.
>
> In March 1984, the boyfriend of M, female, age unknown, Afro-Caribbean, was arrested for possession of cannabis. 3 weeks later, 3 police officers from Stoke Newington police station visited M, asking for a person she did not know. 3 months later she received a further visit from 3 police officers looking for the same person. 3 weeks later she received a third visit, this time from 5 officers at 9 in the morning, looking for the same person. This time she refused to give access to her flat and was pushed aside: the premises was searched without a warrant. She made a written complaint and received a verbal statement sufficient for her to decide not to proceed with her complaint.

The White and Knight cases

8.59 Perhaps the most well known of all the incidents involving police officers from Stoke Newington police station involved two Black families, the Whites and the Knights. Both cases received a great deal of press attention and were crucial in the formation of negative public perceptions of Stoke Newington police station.

8.60 David and Lucille White, an elderly Black couple, were awarded £51,000 damages against the Metropolitan Police in April 1982 for what the judge called a 'catalogue of violent and inhuman treatment' by Stoke Newington police officers. The treatment began in September 1976 when 17 police officers turned up at the White's Stoke Newington home on the pretext of looking for stolen goods. Although a search warrant had apparently been issued, nothing was found and the search warrant was never produced. Once inside the house the police officers seized upon the White's son, Dennis, and started beating him with a truncheon. When his parents came down to see what was going on, they too were set upon by the police. The Whites were then dragged barefoot to a police car with their son, who was now unconscious, and taken to Stoke Newington police station. There they were charged with 11 offences, including assault. Mr. and Mrs. White were acquitted of all charges although Dennis was convicted of attempting to wound a police officer and of damaging his tunic.

8.61 During the investigation into Dennis White's case, on one occasion the police turned up at the White's home in the middle of the night. Mrs. White was so frightened that she could not open the door. The police officer then jammed the door-bell with a twig, so that it would not stop ringing.

8.62 When the White's claim for damages against the police came to court in 1982, Judge Mars-Jones said that the police, in trying to cover up their behaviour at the White's home had been guilty of 'monstrous, wicked and shameful conduct in the name of justice'. Despite this statement and

Knight Defence Campaign

Support the Knight Family
and
PROTEST AGAINST POLICE VIOLENCE AGAINST BLACK PEOPLE.

JOIN THE PROTEST MARCH THROUGH HACKNEY ON

SATURDAY 21st AUGUST

Assemble outside Hackney Town Hall at 12.00 Noon
March via Stoke Newington Police Station to Rally Stoke Newington Common.

the extent of the damages awarded against the police, no police officer involved in the case has ever been disciplined.

8.63   In November 1981, police were called to a dispute with a neighbour by Nelly Knight. She and her daughter, Jennifer, ended up by being arrested, severely beaten up and racially abused at Stoke Newington police station. In fact, so bad was the beating given to Mrs. Knight that she had to have hospital treatment and her arm put in a sling. The Knights were then charged with a ring of serious offences, including grevious bodily harm and assault on police officers. Following a sustained public campaign and two Crown Court trials, both were acquitted of most charges at the first Crown Court trial, while the remainder were dropped after the jury at the second trial could not reach a verdict. According to HCRE, this case generated enormous depth of feeling in the community and contributed a great deal to the community's angry view of the police in the Stoke Newington area.

Changing Image
8.64   Stoke Newington police station is on a busy part of Stoke Newington High Road, surrounded by shops. It is a station like so many police stations, a structure of the late Victoria era. About half-way through the Inquiry, members of the committee went to see the station — although we were not invited in — in order to examine the lobby where Colin Roach died, and to get an idea of where the station is sited in relation to the local community, where the demonstrations happened and so on.

8.65   Stoke Newington station was not opened up to us on that occasion. However, the police are making attempts to appear more open to the public in general. The station itself is to be re-designed: initial plans indicated that a glass lobby was to be constructed to give a more accessible feel, although the risks of so much plate glass were obvious. And during May 1984, both the *Hackney Gazette* and *Islington Gazette* reported that "a huge public relations exercise attracted 3,500 people to a two day opening of Stoke Newington police station". Caribbean music was played, there was a disco and aerobics classes for children, and lessons in self defence (for women). The SPG was also present, explaining its new role in combatting burglarly. A Scotland Yard press officer said; "The atmosphere among some sections of the community 12 months ago was one of fear and trepidation. That is all water under the bridge now. We have opened our hearts and our police station to the public and no-one can accuse us of being a secret police with para-military functions".

8.66 We did not receive evidence from any individual or organisation who attended this open day at Stoke Newington.

Conclusions

8.67 The evidence presented to us on the issues discussed above leaves us in no doubt that the policing of Hackney over the years has been racist, whether it is considered in terms of the attitudes and behaviour of individual police officers or in terms of the overall police strategy. Black people in Hackney, especially (although by no means exclusively) young Black people have been seen by the police as constituting a problem of 'law and order' and have effectively been criminalised. At the same time, the police have clearly failed to provide adequate protection to Black people against racial violence and harassment. The police in Hackney have not policed on behalf of the Black community in Hackney, but against it.

8.68 In this context it is not surprising that the 'uprisings' or urban 'rebellions' of 1981 found expression in Hackney. In July 1981, as in so many other areas of the country, the anger of young Black (and some white) people were turned on the police as a result, at least in part, of the history of policing which we have tried to sketch above. Stones and firebombs were thrown in Hackney after police raided a cafe used by young Blacks in Sandringham Road. Hundreds of police were brought in and over 100 people were arrested in the whole of 'G' District, the highest number of arrests in any area of London at this time, apart from Brixton and accounting for 10% of all the arrests in London in connection with the 'serious public disorder' of July 1981.

8.69 What should also not be surprising is the considerable lack of any confidence in the ability of the police to investigate complaints against themselves. It was clear from the evidence presented to the Inquiry that few people who experience difficulties with the police have any serious confidence in the formal complaints system. Many of the complaints made, for example, to Hackney CRE and cited in its 1983 dossier were made also as formal complaints against the police. Yet, in not one case, did the complaints system uphold a complaint. Of course, it will be argued that this simply shows that the complaint was without foundation and that the police acted properly. But it can equally be argued that this shows, as has been argued by Hackney CRE, that the complaints system is not independent at all. As Hackney CRE showed in its 1983 dossier, complaints against police officers in Hackney were investigated by a Chief Inspector from another sub-division but from within 'G' District. Given the relatively small number of police officers serving in 'G' District and that the police are known to be a tightly knit and internally closed organisation, many police officers will be known to one another and to the investigating Chief Inspector, especially if the Chief Inspector has been moved around before becoming responsible for investigating complaints. While the complaints procedure did provide for investigators to be appointed from other divisions, this only appeared to happen where the complaint was made against a senior officer or was of a very serious nature. Even in such cases, HCRE concluded: "the police still investigate the police and share essentially the same group loyalty and the same perceptions".

8.70 On the basis of its own experience, Hackney CRE have also shown how, at an initial stage, the police will convert a complaint into their own terms, often putting or suggesting formulations of the complaint as it is recorded which can subtly change and sometimes soften the original complaint. This, Hackney CRE said, has led to tussles between HCRE representatives sitting in on an interview and the investigating officer. From then on, the complainant is "completely in the hands of the system" since there is no opportunity for the testing of conflicting views of the complainant and the officer complained against. In addition, the reports of investigating officers are always confidential, so there is no way of knowing what kind of report was made and whether it is detached and fair as they always claimed to be. The complaints system, Hackney CRE concluded, is "fundamentally unsatisfactory".

8.71 It is little wonder, HCRE told the Inquiry, that the police complaints machinery commands so little confidence amongst the public, hence the lack of interest in going through "a dreary, long-winded process which is so stacked in favour of the police". This, HCRE added was well known by the police who could be fairly confident that whatever they did, they stood little chance of being brought to book for excesses and wrong-doing. "The result of this is that there is no effective control over what police may say or do and they can in a real sense do whatever they like and fabricate charges to cover themselves. They are, in fact, unaccountable".

8.72 Whatever the truth of the individual cases, what is clear is that people in Hackney have no confidence in the police complaints system and that the system is not regarded in any way as a satisfactory means of controlling the behaviour of individual officers or of bringing them to account after the event.

8.73 The cases presented to us, the fact of the 1981 disorder, the absence of confidence in the complaints system — all these point to a major lack of public confidence in the police and in the policing of Hackney. Once again, we must express our regret that we were unable to discuss these (and other) issues with the police and to hear their side of the story. In the next Chapter we consider some of the ways in which the police have tried and are trying to deal with this decline in public confidence.

Chapter 9

Community Relations, Community Policing, Consultation and Accountability

9.1 In this Chapter we look at some of the ways in which the police in Hackney (as nationally) have tried to deal with a perceived lack of confidence amongst sections of the public. In particular, we look at the concept and practice of 'community relations', at strategies of 'community policing' and at moves to establish means of consulting with the community or its representatives. Finally, we look at how the Council has responded to what it has perceived as the policing problem in the borough. One of the problems facing any discussion of this kind is the terms which are used. Community relations, community policing, consultation, accountability are all terms which are frequently used in discussions on policing, but seem to mean different things to different people. We have tried, in the discussion which follows, to be clear about our own usage.

Community Relations

9.2 Like other police divisions in the Metropolitan Police and like the police outside London, the police in Hackney have devoted considerable efforts towards 'community relations' work, that is activities aimed at fostering good relations between police and sections of the community. The idea of 'community relations' as a distinct branch of police work is relatively recent. According to the current head of community relations in the Metropolitan Police, Lawrence Roach, until the 1950s, "every policeman was a community relations officer, seeking... to retain and reinforce the goodwill" of the public towards the police. What caused the police to start developing a new branch of community relations was changing attitudes towards authority ("something to be questioned rather than respected") and increased social mobility within society. But, in addition, Roach remarks, increased mobility "between cultures", that is mass immigration, changed the nature of the community to the extent that the police were no longer able to clearly identify with the people they sought to serve. In 1968, therefore, the Metropolitan Police appointed a chief superintendent with responsibility for the co-ordination and development of police activity in the field of 'race relations' and, in 1968, created a new Community Relations Branch to co-ordinate the work of the Community Liaison Officers (CLO) at divisional level. These officers were given a range of functions including co-ordinating and encouraging, police/community activities of all officers in relation to work with Black people and Black groups. (Lawrence Roach: 'The Metropolitan Police Community Relations Branch' in *Police Studies*. Vol. 1, No. 3, September 1978).

9.3 Since the Metropolitan Police refused to submit evidence to the Inquiry it is impossible for us to say much about the work of the CLO in Hackney, except that the CLO did attend meetings of Hackney CRE as an observer until 1983. In addition, it seems fair to conclude, on the basis of the evidence submitted to us, that the work of the CLO has had little impact on the general policing of the borough. Complaints about racial abuse by police officers, their abuse of these powers and their failure to protect Black people from racial harassment have been made, despite the existence of the CLO and despite whatever s/he was doing with regards to 'community relations'. In other words, it seems that Hackney is no different from other London boroughs where community relations work and community relations or liaison officers have been completely marginal in policing terms.

9.4 Some evidence for this can be found in Hackney CRE's experience with the police from the mid-1970s onwards. In conjunction with the police, Hackney CRE established a 'help on arrest' scheme in the mid-1970s. The idea was that people arrested would be informed by the police that they could have advice from an individual, on a list of designated people drawn up by Hackney CRE. By July 1977, however, HCRE chairman, Patrick Kodikara, was complaining that on several occasions people in custody had been denied access to HCRE representatives. Mr. Kodikara said that he was "beginning to doubt whether the police have the will to make the scheme work" *(East London Advertiser* 8/7/77). Indeed, the scheme was effectively finished within a year.

9.5 Hackney CRE had also had occasional meetings with the district commanders to raise matters of concern. In September 1980, however it announced that such meetings were to end as they appeared of no useful function. It explained:

> The experience in Hackney has shown how little effect these commitments can have. In Hackney it has been made clear time and time again that while HCRE can raise issues, the police reserve the right to be complete masters of their policing policy and that a liaison committee has only the function of raising issues. The basic issue in this debate is whether police liaison committees have any real value while there is no effective democratic accountability of the police. If liaison committees are to be more than talking shops, where decisions have some binding force on both parties, then the committee needs to be founded in a more formal link backed up by a change in the law. *(Hackney Gazette* 2/9/80).

9.6 Representatives of HCRE expanded on their experience of the liaison committee in evidence to the Inquiry. One of them told us:

> We have met with the Commanders and we have gone along with our particular complaints but our experience is that, however much we complain or hammer the table about what's been going on, we get the reaction like "That's terrible" or "That's wrong" and "We'll do something about this". We have found that if we go back there six months later to make the same point all over again, in a sense what really happens is that they listen, they make the comment that this isn't a matter upon which we can comment at this specific moment or . . . it could be deemed to be an operational matter and ruled out for any comment. We have come to feel that it is a pretty fruitless exercise.

9.7   Another HCRE representative said:

> It was one thing to meet with senior officers around the table, discuss what we assumed or knew then, to be the problems... but at the end of the day whatever their views were then, it did not appear to be filtering down to the grass roots level of the man on the beat.

9.8   Police community relations work has had the effect of absolving the police in general of their obligations to understand and be responsible to the Black community, and has relegated this to the work of specialist officers whose effect, in practical terms, is marginal.

9.9   It is worth noting that this observation has been made by the police themselves. A report on Hackney by some senior police officers on a training course remarked that: "The centralisation of the role of the Community Liaison Officer tends to create the attitude that community problems and liaison are his domain alone and not of every officer in the force. This apparent abrogation of responsibility does not bode well for community relations". *(The Urban Future: Inner City Conference, 12 July 1982,* Police Staff College, 1982).

9.10   The very concept of community relations, in other words, denies that the police are, or ought to be, accountable to the Black community.

Community Policing

9.11 Defining 'community policing' is not at all simple and the idea appears to mean different things to different people. In general, however, it can encompass a range of policing activities and strategies, including putting more police officers back on the beat, setting up neighbourhood watch schemes and the development of a 'multi-agency' approach to crime in which police work closely with other bodies such as local authorities, social services, schools and so on. What these all have in common is that they are attempts by the police to close the gap between the police and the public, or sections of it.

9.12 In Hackney, a variety of community policing activities have been tried by the police: 'neighbourhood policing' was introduced in the borough in 1983, neighbourhood watch schemes have been set up, and the police have tried to establish closer links with other agencies such as schools and youth clubs. In addition, the police have tried to present a more 'open' image to the public: a newsletter, 'The Neighbourhood', was published in October 1983 and distributed throughout the borough, and police stations (including Stoke Newington) have held 'open days' for the public.

9.13 The problems with 'community policing' are several. Community policing can be seen as an attempt by the police at greater control and surveillance over sections of the community, in which other agencies, supposedly independent, are brought under the effective direction of the police. (Police accounts of 'community policing' initiatives make clear the importance of using these to gather information). Equally important is the fact that community policing does nothing to deal with the real reasons for people's distrust of, and antagonism towards the police. Indeed, many would see community policing as a cynical public relations exercise by the police.

9.14 In any case, community policing, however it is defined, does nothing to give the public a greater say in what the police do and how they do it. Indeed, such policing has come to the force at precisely the same time as there have been growing demands for effective public accountability and control of the police. Control of community policing remains firmly in the hands of the police.

9.15 Finally, it should be noted, community policing does not, as some suggest, mean an end to 'fire brigade' or para-military policing strategies. The police themselves, including the pioneers of community policing, have made this very clear. The Metropolitan Police Commissioner, Sir Kenneth Newman for example, has put the people of London 'on notice' that the police will not hesitate to use the full range of riot control equipment and techniques if he considers this necessary. And at the same time as he implements programmes of community policing, he has created local District Support Units along the lines of the Special Patrol Group. At a national level, community policing has gone hand in hand with the extensive new powers given to the police by the Police and Criminal Evidence Act 1984 and further powers to control public demonstrations in the 1986 Public Order Act.

9.16 The Inquiry believes that community policing strategies are dangerous in ways which have not been sufficiently realised. Many critics of 'hard' policing have, for instance, advocated community policing as an 'alternative'. They are not alternatives to para-military styles of policing, but complements to it. They do not increase public say in policing and do not deal with the real problems of policing which we have described in this report.

9.17 We are in no doubt that many people welcome 'community policing' schemes as a sign that the police are interested in their problems and prepared to take their wishes into account in planning their priorities. Such schemes are not, however, the only ones to take people's fears about crimes and offences seriously and to try and do something about them. The 'community improvement' schemes developed by the Safe Neighbourhood Units of NACRO (National Association for the Care and Resettlement of Offenders), for instance, have brought together a range of people (residents, councillors, council officers, police, etc,) on certain estates to develop a comprehensive improvement project which reflects the wishes of the residents. In such schemes, crime and the fear of crime are taken out of the context of 'law and order' and placed in a context of community action. The residents play a major role in such schemes, while the role of the police is to provide information and respond to suggestions of the project management committee. Such schemes, however, face two important constraints. The first is that the local authorities are not able to offer such schemes the financial support which their activities might need. Second, residents in 'community improvement' schemes can only suggest to the police what the policing policy in the area might be. They have no way of ensuring that such suggestions are followed.

9.18 Despite these limitations, the 'community improvement' schemes show the potential for independent community action and responsiblity, particularly if they are backed up with adequate resources and finance and have some way of ensuring that their wishes on policing are implemented.

Consultation

9.19 The police, together with the Home Office, have also been pressing the idea of consultation with the public as a means of closing the gap which exists between the police and the community.

9.20 Following a recommendation by Lord Scarman in his report on the 1981 Brixton disorders, the Police and Criminal Evidence Act 1984 provides that arrangements are to be made by the Metropolitan Police Commissioner to obtain the views of the community about matters concerning the policing of their area. (Outside London, this obligation falls on the police authority). Although a number of London boroughs have established consultative committees, attempts by the police to establish one in Hackney have been unsuccessful, largely because of their opposition to the proposals made by Hackney Council.

9.21   Hackney Council did set up a Police Liaison Group in June 1977, comprising of police, councillors and council officers. This met periodically to discuss matters of mutual interest and concern. Those involved from the Council side reported that they had generally experienced difficulties obtaining a satisfactory response from the police on issues regarded as 'sensitive', for instance the use of the Special Patrol Group or the 'sus' law in the borough.

9.22   In July 1982, the Council's Police Committee set up a police liaison sub-committee to which the police would be invited, although they would have no voting rights, to discuss policing issues. The sub-committee was to be composed of councillors (all members of the police committee) and a number of co-optees representing local community groups. Its meetings were to be open to the public. The invitation was extended to the police and in November 1982, the chair and vice chair of the police committee met with a senior Home Office official to discuss the proposed liaison arrangements. It took almost one year, however, for the Home Office to respond formally to the Council's proposed plan. In July 1983, Home Office mininster, Douglas Hurd, told the Council that liaison should be conducted, not through a committee or sub-committee of the Council, but through a 'free standing' committee in which neither the police nor the Council predominated. The Home Office response was rejected by a meeting of the full Council in December 1983, which described it as 'unworkable and unrealistic' and which reaffirmed the Council's proposal.

9.23   In February 1984, the Home Office told the leader of the Council, Anthony Kendall, that the Council's proposals remained unacceptable and that the Metropolitan Police Commissioner would be authorised to proceed with consultation arrangements in Hackney without the involvement of the Council. The police did attempt to establish a consultative group without the Council and arranged a meeting to this end for early in October 1985. This meeting was abandoned after the uprising in Broadwater Farm, Tottenham.

9.24 After this abortive attempt, discussions between the police and the Council about establishing a consultative committee began again. In a draft memorandum of agreement, Councillor Brynley Heaven proposed abandoning the stance that any consultation had to take place in the context of a Council sub-committee and accepting the principle of a 'free standing' body as required by the Home Office. The draft memorandum, however, emphasised that the 'centre of gravity' of the new group would reflect the 'centre of gravity' of elected and organised representative opinion as expressed through local elections, representative local organisations and umbrella groups (including especially Black organisations). Voting members of the group would, therefore, be representatives of local organisations at all times. The group would also be serviced by the Council. This draft memorandum was agreed by the police and accepted by the Council's police committe. By the end of 1986, with the installation of Councillor Tommy Shepherd as the new chair of the Council's police committee, discussions had moved on but had not been resolved. In a letter to the Home Office (23/10/86), the Council made representations and stated that: "disagreement at this stage centres around the method of appointment of the chair of any consultative committee established in the borough". At the time of writing, there has been no further progress and no consultative committee has been established.

9.25 We have gone into this question of consultation/liaison in some detail both because it is important in terms of police/community relations in Hackney and, because the Council's position has frequently been misrepresented. It should be clear from the above account that Hackney Council has never been against consultation with the police. Indeed, the police sub-committee was set up precisely because such consultation was desired and because the police committee understood the situation of the local police, who could not be seen to be compromising their constitutional position by attending meetings of the full police committee. The Council's position was that it was prepared to accept the existing legal framework until such time as it could be changed, but that consultation had to have a clear representative base and be based on the broadest range of community interests. What it objected to was not consultation as such, but the form of consultation proposed by the Home Office. As noted above, the Home Office opposed the 'dominance' of either the police or Council in any consultative arrangement and guidelines had made it clear that the number of local councillors on committees should be limited to five.

9.26 Nor were Hackney Council the only people opposed to the form of consultation being proposed. Hackney CRE told the Inquiry that it was clear from discussions with colleagues in other community relations councils in London that the whole process of consultation did not work when a serious issue was at stake. They pointed out to the Inquiry, for instance, that the shooting of Mrs. Cherry Groce in October 1985 by a police officer was not made known to the local senior community relations officer, George Greaves, until three hours after it had occurred, even though Mr. Greaves is a member of the Lambeth Police/Community Consultative Group. Even when Mr. Greaves was told about the shooting, it was not the police who told him, but a journalist. Hackney CRE also made it clear that their opposition to a consultative committee stemmed in large part from their own experience with the police, which we discussed above.

Accountability

9.27 For its part, Hackney Council has made a commitment to the concept of police accountability and, in particular, has supported the idea of an elected police authority for London to which the police would be answerable.

9.28 It is now well known that London is the only area of the country to have no system of local police accountability. In every other part of the country the police are normally accountable to an elected police authority, on which local councillors are represented. The Met, from 1829 onwards, came specifically under direct control of the Home Secretary, who was (and remains) accountable to Parliament. There was some justification for this arrangement prior to the setting up of a proper local government structure for London, but since the inauguration of London local government, and particularly the creation of the GLC in 1965 (whose boundaries were virtually coterminous with the Metropolitan Police District), this geographically based argument has collapsed. By 1980, 94 per cent of the 7.3 million people living within the MPD were represented by the GLC.

9.29 Yet despite repeated representations to the Home Secretary from both Conservative and Labour GLC administrations, the position remains unchanged. London's police are still not accountable to London's population. The actual, practical effect of this absence of public control is felt most keenly in boroughs like Hackney.

9.30 One forceful argument for police accountability concerns money. Londoners contribute a significant amount towards the maintenance of the police in the capital. In 1986/87, the estimated total costs of the Met will be £852 million, of which £258 million is to be met by rates revenue, paid by Londoners. This is a big rise on the 1985/86 figures, when Londoners paid £227 million in rates. Part of this rise is accounted for by large annual pay awards to the police and the increasing cost of police equipment. Londoners pay this rate for the police (known as the police precept) through their local authority. The blatant contradiction between the considerable financial contribution which London ratepayers make to the running of the police and the absence of any say in how that money is spent or how the police decide their priorities has fuelled calls for a London wide police authority.

9.31 The call for a properly elected democratic police authority for London was made with renewed vigour after the election of a radical GLC after 1981. The GLC set up a Police Committee, whose aim was in part to put the case for police accountability in London, but also to do some of the monitoring and campaigning on police issues in the absence of any structure of accountability, and through grant funding, to aid other organisations to do the same. Other local authorities followed suit after the 1982 borough elections, and also set up police committees. Hackney's Police Committee met for the first time in July 1982.

9.32 We received written and oral evidence from several individuals (involved in some way with the Hackney Police Committee) on the campaigning and strategic aims of the Committee, and on the relationship between the police and the Council since 1982.

9.33 The Committee's key policies for change have revolved around basic issues of accountability, race and the 'separateness' of the police from the wider community they serve. But it is inevitable, given the very lack of accountability, that the Committee has often had to respond rather than initiate actions that further these aims. Hackney's Police Committee has responded to the community's feelings and demands in two distinct ways. Firstly, the Committee has clearly been open to the concerns of local organisations and campaigns, and particularly those of Black groups. The most obvious example was the Committee's response to Colin Roach's death and subsequent events. In the words of then Committee chair, Brynley Heaven, Hackney Council were "all the time responding to the wishes of the campaign (RFSC) rather than being a policy initiator; despite media attempts to suggest otherwise". We have discussed the relationship between the Council and the campaign in more detail in Chapter 2, but it is clear that the Committee did give the campaign a great deal of help on issues such as the re-siting of the inquest, calls for a public inquiry and the proposal that the Council refuse to pay the police precept for the borough, although this was never in fact carried out. Hackney Police Committee has also been, and remains, responsive to the public on an individual level. Members of the community are encouraged to come to the town hall to discuss, comment or complain about their experience of the police. Hackney Town Hall in Mare Street is relatively accessible, both geographically and in terms of atmosphere. Barbara Roche, Head of the Police Committee Support Unit (PCSU) told us that the PCSU keep monitoring forms for members of the public to fill in. Although the PCSU does not act as a casework agency, Barbara Roche told us that cases with any legal, or potential legal implications, are passed on to relevant bodies, like the local Law Centre.

9.34 Because of its' wide range of Council functions and services, the Council obviously has contact with the police at a number of different levels. Brynley Heaven, chair of the Committee, pointed out that the Council had not supported the 'break links' (with the police) resolution proposed by RFSC, despite media reports implying that they had. The Council were, he said, prepared to "engage in dialogue with the police in certain contexts, on certain conditions over certain substantive issues". However, he did point out that many of the voluntary sector in Hackney and groups like the teachers had cut themselves off completely from the police.

9.35 One of the earliest acts of the Police Committee was a review, through a survey/questionnaire, of the actual existing links between Council officials at all levels, but particularly middle ranking officers, and the police. On the basis of that survey, they drew up new guidelines. Barbara Roche told us that this survey was greeted with some relief by many Council officers who had not been clear about the ways in which they were to deal with the police. On the basis of that survey, the Committee drew up new guidelines on contact with the police. She said that the council allowed the police to use its premises for certain operations, for example, surveillance relating to hard drugs, but only after certain strict criteria had been met.

9.36 The Police Committee also liaise with other Council departments, for example, the Housing Department, when they receive complaints from members of the public about domestic violence or racist attacks which have been ignored by the police or other relevant agencies. The Committee has also worked directly with the police on such community-based schemes as the Crime Prevention Working Party, whose main aim is to improve security on housing estates, and the Victim Support Scheme.

9.37 The key issue facing the Committee since it began has been that of police consultation, and the structure in which that consultation takes place. The Council has consistently stated that it will meet and liaise with the police, but that this can only take place within a democratic framework. The police have a standing invitation to the Council liaison group (a sub-committee of the Police Committee), which was set up in 1982. However, except to have 'talks about talks', they have never attended. We discuss this issue in more detail below.

9.38 This information gathering capacity of the Police Committee (with its small staff, administrative back-up and resources) and the links and influences it inevitably has borough-wide, has established it as an important local counterpoint to the police. Groups like HCRE pointed out in evidence to us the difference that the existence of the Police Committee made to their work. Alan Badman from HCRE told us:

> The thing is, with limited information, people like myself who are prepared to get involved are not doing the job which we could do if we had more consultation and support. I think that things have improved in recent years with the Police Committee... I think we need an even better one. Before that it was mostly what we were doing and we were not doing nearly enough.

9.39 In his evidence to us, Brynley Heaven pointed out a number of interesting things about the local police and how they worked, which we think it worth quoting in the report. He said he thought that the police found it frustrating to no longer have automatic access to a local council which they regarded as 'moderate' or 'reasonable'. For a long time the local police have been used to dealing with a more conservative local establishment. Councillor Heaven and others pointed out the failure of the police, locally, to recognise what elements of opinion within Hackney might be sympathetic to them. While they have made spasmodic approaches to 'moderate' white councillors and other community leaders, police racism has led them to ignore, and even deride, Black leaders who might be willing to talk to them. We heard a great deal about one particular meeting, called after the Broadwater Farm disorders in autumn in 1985, by former mayor, Councillor Ken Hanson. Broadwater Farm is very near to Hackney, and the events there had an obvious resonance in the borough. The meeting was held in the Council chamber and attracted over 200 people, including many political, business and church leaders in Hackney. The police response to this meeting was reflected in a letter from Chief Inspector Terence Walter, the local community liaison officer, who dismissed the meeting as "completely unrepresentative" of even a section of opinion in the borough. People giving evidence to us put this down explicitly to the fascism of force thinking.

9.40   Councillor Heaven also made some interesting comments about the ways in which policing in the borough has changed in the past few years. These changes are not necessarily linked to the existence of the Police committee, although from his vantage point as chair of that Committee, he had gleaned a great deal about the workings of the police in the borough:

> A lot has changed ... The people who police 'G' District now are by and large a completely different bunch from those here a few years ago. We've been through several Commanders and Chief Superintendents in a short time. The new people are qualitatively different in that they know what they're doing, how they're doing it and why they're doing it ... they're intelligent, sophisticated, motivated and clear as to what their priorities are. They now have some measure of control over the ranks, some idea of what's going on in the station, which of course means that they're all the more complicit in things when they do happen. It's interesting to see how now, as a matter of policy, they now work with the Police Federation as a way of maintaining extra control and information over what goes on in the station ... What

happened before was the manager sat behind the desk and transmitted instructions from Scotland Yard and got involved in glamorous operations, but didn't appreciate the culture and priorities that were developing in the vans and the canteens and on the street. But Sir Kenneth Newman and his managerial revolution has brought about an element of actual control within the police force and the lower ranks. The organisation is acting more corporately, the management has more control over the ranks. But there has been a price to pay for this and one of the prices to pay, internally, is they've had to give some power and access to the Police Federation. They've had to let them into at least some of the formalities of decision making. They've had to co-opt some of the natural leadership of the locker room in order to get that control over the ranks. What has not changed is the racism in the police force... the basic question about race has not even began to be addressed, by this Met 'management'.

Conclusion

9.41 Having considered all the evidence, the Inquiry considers that more consultation between the police and community representatives is not the way forward for better relations between the police and the public and that those who have opposed the creation of consultation mechanisms with no real powers have taken the correct decision. It is clear from all the evidence that such consultation is not, as some people appear to believe, a step towards greater accountability of the police to the public, nor was it ever intended to be so. As a discussion paper by the Greater London Council Police Committee put it:

> The Act will result in the establishment of large, voluntary non-statutory committees within each borough with no power, no clear lines or accountability to the community and no clear relationship with the police. Their function will be no more than, at best, an exchange of views, on terms solely dependent upon the police. *(The Police Act 1984: a critical guide,* GLC, 1985).

9.42 Not only will the committees be little more than talking shops, but it is clear, both from Lord Scarman's discussions of the issue and from the present government's stated position, that the creation of consultative mechanisms is intended to divert growing demands for the police to be made properly and effectively accountable to elected representatives and in particular, to undermine those councils, such as Hackney, which have established their own Police Committees as a means of working towards such accountability.

9.43 Nor do we see programmes of 'community relations' or 'commuity policing' as making a significant or meaningful contribution to the improvement of police/public relations. While presenting a 'human face' to the public and appearing to address real problems, such programmes are, in practice, quite marginal and have little effect on the general pattern and direction of policing strategies. In the next, concluding chapter we set out a minimal programme for real change.

Conclusions and Recommendations to Part II Of The Report

When the Black people of Hackney responded in January 1983 to the news of the death of Colin Roach in Stoke Newington police station, they were not just responding to the death of a young Black man on police premises. They were responding to the death of *yet another* Black person in Stoke Newington police station and to a long history of what they perceived as racist and oppressive policing. It was for this reason that so many people at the time demanded a public inquiry, not just into the death of Colin Roach, but into the death and its context the policing of Hackney. And it was to examine these connected issues that this Inquiry itself was appointed.

It is clear that to the Inquiry, from the evidence we received from our own research, that there was good reason for the anger and concern expressed and felt by so many people following Colin Roach's death. The behaviour of the police in the immediate aftermath of Colin's death was nothing short of appalling and, with regard to Colin's parents, lacking in even basic humanity. (To this day, not one representative of the Metropolitan Police has offered one word of sympathy to the Roach family). In the longer term, we consider that the police have been guilty of serious malpractices and abuses of their power over a number of years. In particular, we consider that the policing of Hackney has been racist, both in terms of the behaviour of individual officers and in terms of the impact of the overall policing strategy. Black people in Hackney, especially Black youths, have been seen by the police as constituting a problem of 'law and order' and the police have failed to provide adequate protection to Black people against racial violence and harassment.

Such racist policing has been aggravated by moves towards heavy-handed, para-military styles of policing which have done little except contribute to a breakdown in relations between the police and substantial sections of the population. Of course, Hackney is not alone in this respect and policing in the borough is similar to that in many areas, both in London and elsewhere, and reflects policing developments both at the level of the Metropolitan Police and nationally.

The Way Ahead

What then do we see as the way ahead, the way forward to improve relations between the police and the public? First, the Inquiry considers that the history of police/community relations in London and elsewhere shows that there can be no fundamental change in police behaviour and therefore no lasting change in relations between the police and public, unless the police are brought under effective external control. As HCRE put it to us:

> The police so far remain unaccountable in any way to the community they purport to serve. As long as this is resisted by the police, the community will feel they are an alien and oppressive force. The tragic death of Colin Roach shows these feelings only too clearly. The response needed is a radical change in the policing in Hackney and of London to a force accountable to the community's local representatives.

The police, it should be remembered, are supposed to be a form of *service* to the public. They are paid for by the public and are supposed to be its servants. Yet, in reality, they stand above society, uncontrolled by it and not accountable to it. This situation must change.

(1) **The Inquiry believes that the proposals put forward by the Greater London Council before its abolition, on democratic control of the police in London provide a good framework for change.** These envisaged a London-wide police committee and police committees in all the London boroughs. These would all be normal committees of their councils and would together comprise a separate

Police Authority for London. This Authority would have control over policing in London, although the Home Secretary would continue to have responsibility for standards and efficiency. The borough council police committees would have control over policing policies in their areas and over policing operations. They would be assisted in this by general guidelines from the London-wide police committee which would also be responsible for London-wide policing matters and for administration.

These proposals obviously require legislation. Until such time as this legislation is passed, the Inquiry considers that local authority police committees, such as that set up by Hackney Council, have an important role to play in monitoring policing in their areas. They also have an important role in bringing matters of public concern to the attention of the police and in raising policing issues with the public.

(2). **The Inquiry also believes that any external control of the police must be accompanied by a machinery for investigating complaints against the police, which is completely independent either of the police or any new police authority and which has adequate resources to carry out its functions.** Like the new police authority, the new police complaints body should be required by law to publish a full account of its work at the end of each year.

Even with such external controls on the police, the Inquiry considers that there will be a need for independent monitoring of how these bodies function. We, therefore, consider that local independent police monitoring groups, such as the Community Alliance for Police Accountability in Tower Hamlets or the Newham Monitoring Project, will continue to have an important role, not least in providing support to victims of police malpractice. Such groups should be funded by the local authority or by the London-wide police committee, but should be independent of them, accountable to locally-representative management committees.

In addition to such external controls, there has to be a fundamental shift in styles of policing. As we noted above, policing in Britain has become increasingly para-military, squads and tactics have proliferated. The result has been, as many of our cases show, that minor incidents escalate into major ones because of over-policing and a generally aggressive police response. Although such developments have gone far, we do not believe that it is too late to start to reverse them.

(3) **We believe that specialist squads such as District Support Units and Territorial Support Groups (which superceded the SPG in 1986) should be disbanded and not replaced. We believe too that the 'fire brigade' style of policing should be abandoned and that stricter controls be placed on the issue of firearms to police officers.** There should be no question of police issuing plastic or rubber bullets, CS gas or water cannon, and police forces should be prohibited, at a national level, from holding stocks of such weaponry.

At the same time, there is a need to curtail the extensive powers of the police. This will require the repeal of certain legislation, for instance, the Police and Criminal Evidence Act, 1984. But it will also require the introduction of sanctions to ensure that police officers do not stray beyond their powers. There should, for instance, be a strict 'exclusionary rule' to prevent the use of unlawfully-obtained evidence and 'confessions'.

There is also a need for change within the police force. As we noted above, independent research has shown the extent to which police culture, at least within the Metropolitan Police, is based on values of violence, aggression, sexism and racism. Unless this culture changes, policing itself is unlikely to change.

(4) **The Inquiry believes that the police, as an organisation should make a firm, public commitment to tackling these values. Officers at all ranks should be made to understand that sexist, racist or violent behaviour is not acceptable and could result in dismissal from the**

force. At the same time, police practices which affirm these values have to be changed. Strict controls should be enforced on practices which can encourage violence or lead to the escalation of minor incidents. These include the use of high speed car chases, the issuing of guns or the formation of para-military special squads

Training of new recruits also has a part to play in changing the police culture. We are aware of the changes made in recent years to the training of Metropolitan Police recruits, but we are not convinced that these address themselves to the main issues. Racism awareness training, for instance, does not address itself to racism and a racist society, but to the prejudiced attitudes of individuals. Training, properly devised and emphasising the ideas of the police as a public service, responsible to all regardless of class, colour or sex, can help to inculcate the right values in the new police officer. The problem is, however, that research has shown that any beneficial effects which training may have, do not survive in the hostile world of the police culture. This underlines the need for fundamental change in that culture.

(5) In addition, the Inquiry believes that much more can be done and needs to be done by way of support for community initiatives in crime prevention. Tenants working to improve their estates and reduce opportunities for crime, women trying to reduce the risk of sexual violence and Black people challenging racial violence, these and other groups should be fully supported by local authorities and other agencies in their efforts to improve the life changes of members of the community.

Finally the Inquiry considers that the above general recommendations can provide a framework for altering the nature of policing in London today and for ensuring, not only that police abuses and malpractices are curbed, but that policing can be made more responsive to the needs and wishes of the people whom the force is meant to serve. We are in no doubt of the opposition which will exist towards such proposals and we do not believe that implementation will be easy. The alternative, however, is to allow a police force which is increasingly out of control and accountable to no one but itself.

Appendices

Appendix 1

Independent Committee Of Inquiry

Members

Reverend David Moore (Chairperson). Formerly Team Vicar at St. Werburgh's Vicarage, Bristol. Taught at Tulse Hill School 1974-1982. Ordained as an Anglican Priest (Church of England) 1982. Served title at St. Matthews, Brixton.

Councillor Merle Amory: Leader of Brent Council.

Ms. Melissa Benn: Freelance journalist and writer. Has written various articles on prisons, the police and the inquest system.

Ms. Fara Brown: Barrister specialising in criminal law.

Mr. Paul Gordon: Research and Information Officer at the Runnymede Trust. Author of a number of books, pamphlets and articles on racism, the police and immigration.

Mr. A.B. Ngcobo: Education Liaison Officer at the Inner London Education Authority.

Adviser to the Inquiry:
Professor Stuart Hall

Researchers:
Mr. Michael Medas
Ms. Patricia Tuitt

Administrator:
Ms. Maureen Pascal

Appendix 2

Individuals and Organizations who submitted oral or written evidence to the Inquiry:

Mr. Alan Badman, Hackney Council For Racial Equality
Mr. Banerjee, Hackney Asian Association
Mr. Ivan Beavis, Hackney NALGO
Mr. Dudley Dryden MBE, Hackney Council for Racial Equality
Ms. Elaine Graham, Hackney Legal Action Group
Hackney Anti-Deportation Campaign
Hackney Community Action
Hackney Law Centre
Hackney Teachers' Association
Harambee Project
Cllr. Ken Hanson, London Borough of Hackney
Cllr. Brynley Heaven, London Borough of Hackney
Mr. Barnor Hesse, Roach Family Support Committee
Mr. Maurice Hesse, Roach Family Support Committee
Mr. Chas Holmes, Roach Family Support Committee
Mr. Jim Joseph
Mr. Joe Joseph
Mr. Isaac Julien
Mr. Ace Kelly, Stoke Newington & Hackney Defence Campaign
Mr. Buddy Larrier
Mr. Dave Leadbetter, INQUEST
Mr. Mike Mansfield
Ms. Gareth Peirce
Ms. Barbara Powis, Community Alliance for Police Accountability

Mr. and Mrs. Roach
Ms. Pauline Roach
Mr. Ernie Roberts M.P.
Cllr. Denise Robson, London Borough of Hackney
Ms. Barbara Roche, Head, Hackney Police Committee Support Unit
Saxon Youth Club
Cllr. Shuja Shaikh, London Borough of Hackney
Mrs. G. Sullivan
Mr. Sylverius Thomas, Saxon Youth Club
Mr. Dennis Twomey, Community Alliance for Police Accountability
Mr. Tony Ward, INQUEST

Appendix 3
Lord Gifford's Advice

1. I have been asked to advise the Roach Family Support Committee as to the prospects of challenging in the Courts the refusal of the Home Secretary to order a public inquiry to be held into the death of Colin Roach and the circumstances surrounding it.

2. The Committee asked for such an inquiry by letter dated 3rd February 1983. They drew attention to the fact that Colin Roach died in a police station, and that the police had concluded, after the minimum of investigation, that he had committed suicide. They said that an inquest was not sufficient. In reference to the circumstances surrounding the death, they mentioned the treatment of the Roach Family, and the treatment of those who demonstrated in the days following the death. The police, they said, had exhibited "the entire panoply of racist actions and attitudes".

3. On 2nd March 1983 the Home Secretary replied. He agreed that it was necessary to have a full, independent and public inquiry into the matter. But, he said, "this is precisely what the inquest is intended to provide". While the death was still the subject of a coroner's investigation, it would not be appropriate to consider establishing a separate inquiry.

4. The inquest ended in a verdict of suicide. However the Coroner's jury wrote a letter in which they said that they were satisfied that they had reached a fair verdict, but made criticisms of the police handling of the case, and in particular the treatment of members of the Roach family. In a parliamentary answer on 28th June 1983, the new Home Secretary

said that he had looked again at the requests for a public inquiry, but was not persuaded that such an inquiry was desirable or necessary. He had referred the jury's criticisms for investigation as a complaint under section 49 of the Police Act 1964.

5. Section 32 of the Police Act states that:

> The Secretary of State may cause a local inquiry to be held by a person appointed by him into any matter connected with the policing of any area.

The Secretary of State for this purpose is the Home Secretary.

6. This power, like any other ministerial power, must be exercised lawfully and may be subject to legal challenge if exercised unlawfully. What does 'lawfully' mean in this context?

7. First, the Home Secretary must examine and as far as possible inform himself about any matter which is brought to his attention as being appropriate for a public inquiry.

This would include examining any new facts relating to a matter which he had already considered. In other words the Home Secretary may not ignore matters brought to his attention, at least unless they are frivolous.

8. Secondly, he must exercise his powers in accordance with the purposes for which the Police Act was passed. In this Act the purpose of the Home Secretary's powers is spelled out in section 28:

> The Secretary of State shall exercise his powers under this Act in such manner and to such extent as appears to him be best calculated to promote the efficiency of the police.

"To promote the efficiency of the police" certainly includes ensuring that the police are law-abiding and enjoy public confidence; for a police force which misconducts itself could not reasonably be described as efficient. But this section shows how far the law defines the Home Secretary's duties as a matter of judgment and opinion. He alone is the judge of what "appears to him" to be best calculated to promote efficiency. This does not mean that the possibility of judicial review of a decision under section 32 is ousted: it does however mean that a court may be less ready to intervene than in a case where the statutory language is less subjective or discretionary.

9. Thirdly, the Home Secretary must take all relevant matters into account and exclude from his mind all irrelevant matters. What is relevant, or irrelevant? That can only be answered by reference to the terms of the Act: a matter which could not reasonably be thought to relate to the promotion of efficiency in the police, would be an irrelevant matter.

10. Fourthly, the Home Secretary must correctly interpret any legal provisions which are applicable. Since in this case the law is expressed in such general terms, it will be difficult to establish any breach of this requirement.

11. Fifthly, a decision may be challenged if it is so unreasonable that no Home Secretary could have reached it. This legal principle has on exceptional cases allowed judges to overturn decisions which they consider to be perverse. The difficulty in applying it to the Police Act section 32 is that such a wide scope for different opinion is provided for. One Home Secretary could think that frequent local inquiries were desirable. Another could think that only in exceptional cases of widespread disorder should an inquiry be ordered (apparently the prevailing view for many years). Both views would be permitted by the Court, as views which could "reasonably" be held.

12. Against these principles I see no basis for challenging the Home Secretary on the history of the Colin Roach tragedy so far. *In turning down an inquiry because of the pending inquest, he was taking into account a relevant matter.* The fact that there was to be a public hearing of evidence relevant to Colin Roach's death was one of the facts

for the Home Secretary to consider, and it was lawful for him to decide not to hold an immediate inquiry pending the outcome of the inquest.

13. The Home Secretary's description of an inquest as a public inquiry was not in my view a mistake of law. He was saying that the inquest would be a public investigation of a relevant question, namely how Colin Roach came by his death. It is significant that Mr. Justice Woolf said:

> Although an inquest is therefore an inquiry which is to be held in public, it is not a public inquiry using that phrase as referring to the type of inquiry that the Home Secretary has been asked to set up.

But the Home Secretary has denied that he considered the two to be identical, and it is impossible to show that he was in fact under a misapprehension as to the law.

14. However the matter is not yet closed. I have seen the text of a memorandum about the Colin Roach inquest which is to be submitted to the Home Secretary. It points out the various reasons why a public inquiry remains necessary, in the light of the inquest experience. A number of powerful points are raised:

i) that the extraordinary failure of the police for 2½ hours to tell Mr. Roach of his son's death raises the suspicion, which in my view is a reasonable suspicion, that time may have been needed to concoct a story.

ii) that this suspicion is heightened by the lies (as the jury found them to be) told by the police about the length of this period, which the police claimed to be 15 minutes;

iii) that there was a remarkable absence of forensic evidence to show any connection between Colin Roach and the gun which killed him;

iv) that the gun could not be contained inside Colin Roach's bag without the end sticking out; yet Colin Roach's companion that evening saw the bag, but saw no gun;

v) that there was conflicting evidence as to who took two unused cartridges from Colin Roach's pocket;

vi) that no sensible explanation could be given of the position of Colin Roach's body, or of the fact that a towel was found draped across his chest;

vii) that the inquest rules made it impossible for these and other matters to be properly investigated; in particular the police officers statements, and other records from the police station, could not be examined by the family's lawyers;

viii) finally, that the jury themselves complained that the case "could have been investigated more professionally and more extensively".

15. When this memorandum is presented to the Home Secretary he will be obliged to consider the request for a public inquiry afresh. He will no doubt have access to the inquest evidence, and can verify that the points made about the evidence are factually correct. If they are, a very strong case will have been made that this grave and tragic matter has not been fully explained, and that a local inquiry is necessary. In my view this is certainly a case where an inquiry under section 32 could and should be established.

16 If the Home Secretary maintains his refusal, I will be ready to examine his reasons to see whether, in the light of the principles set out above, any grounds for a legal challenge can be established.

Tony Gifford, Q.C.

Appendix 4a
Correspondence

Rev D. Moore,
c/o P.O. Box 8,
136/138 Kingsland High Street,
London E8 2NS

METROPOLITAN POLICE
No. 3 AREA HEADQUARTERS
CITY ROAD POLICE STATION
4/6 SHEPHERDESS WALK, N1 7LF
Telephone 01—488 5161

Your ref.:

Our ref.:

28th August, 1985

Dear Sir,

    Commander Taylor, currently serving with 'C' Department at New Scotland Yard, has referred to me your letter concerning the inquiry into the death of Colin Roach which you are to chair.

    I should advise you that no member of this force may submit evidence to any inquiry however constituted without the permission of the Commissioner.

    It is right that you should know that the Commissioner will not give permission in relation to any inquiry which is not judicially constituted, and whose proceedings and impartiality are not subject to regulation and scrutiny according to the established constitutional machinery.

    While police cannot participate in your inquiry it is a matter of some concern that you have felt the need to formulate one. The events surrounding the death of Colin Roach were fully aired in the established procedures which must be followed after a death in such unusual circumstances, and in which police took their full part.

    I accept that your inquiry is intended to deal with wider issues than those which directly surround the tragic suicide of Mr Roach, and you have indicated that you will also be examining the role of Stoke Newington Police Station and the black/police relationships in the area. I feel I must point out that many of the issues which you will need to address are just the sort of matters which should be dealt with by a Police/Community Consultative Group under the provisions of Section 106 of the Police and Criminal Evidence Act. Were such a Group in existence in Hackney in conformity with Home Office guidelines, then police would not only be willing but would be bound to attend and consult with the concerned groups. It is for that reason, among others, that it is my continuing wish that such a group is formed in the Borough in the near future.

Yours faithfully,

M.D. RICHARDS
Deputy Assistant Commissioner

Appendix 4b
Correspondence

The Reverend David Moore
C/o PO Box 8
136/138 Kingsland High Street
London
E8 2NS

Form 7110

METROPOLITAN POLICE OFFICE

Community Relations Branch
NEW SCOTLAND YARD
BROADWAY LONDON SW1H 0BG
Telephone 01-230 1212 Ext.

Your ref.:

Our ref.:
GN 91/83/10

9th September 1985

Dear Sir

I refer to your letter dated 15 August 1985, concerning the Committee of Inquiry into Policing in Hackney, of which you are the Chairman.

It is to my knowledge that Mr M D Richards, Deputy Assistant Commissioner for the police area which includes the London Borough of Hackney has already written to you concerning the attendance of police officers before your Committee.

The principles which were stressed in that letter continue to apply. I feel I must also point out, as I know Mr Richards did, that the questions which are likely to arise during the course of your deliberations, could be dealt with most adequately in the police/community consultative group for Hackney when it is formed. I hope this will take place in the near future.

Yours faithfully

L T Roach
Commander
Community Relations Branch

Appendix 5
The Trials of Those Arrested During the Campaign for a Public Inquiry

The following account represents an edited extract from the evidence to the Inquiry of the Community Alliance for Police Accountability (CAPA), a group based in Tower Hamlets, which provided volunteers to observe the demonstrations and the trials, as well as providing legal assistance to people who had been arrested. The figures and descriptions reproduced here also appeared in CAPA's annual report for the year 1983 – 1984.

1. **The Demonstration of 14 January 1983**

    (a) **Charges and Convictions**
    Numbers arrested: (8)
    Original charges: (13)
    Findings of guilt: (5)
    Conviction rate: 38%

    Breakdown of Original Charges
    Threatening behaviour (7)
    Assault on Police (2)
    Obstruction of police (1)
    S.18 Assault on Police
    (wounding with intent) (1)
    S.20 Assault on Police
    (malicious wounding) (1)
    Offensive weapon (1)

Apart from the s.18 and s.20 assaults, which were tried at Snaresbrook Crown Court, the trials took place at Highbury Corner Magistrates' Court in front of a variety of magistrates, both stipendiary and justices (lay bench).

Of the original 13 charges, there were 5 findings of guilt:
  Obstruction of police   (1)
  Assault on police   (1)
  Threatening behaviour   (2)

and at Snaresbrook, a conviction of the lesser charge of s.20 assault on the police. The defendant was acquitted of the more serious s.18 assault.

Of the remaining charges, 6 were dismissed at Magistrates Court, and one was dropped. At the end of A's trial, when he was convicted of obstructing the police, the magistrate said that the officer was effecting a quite proper arrest (of B) and that A had obstructed this arrest. In fact, B had not yet been brought to trial, so the legality of his arrest had not been established. When B was tried, the case against him was dismissed, thus throwing into question the basis of A's conviction.

(b) **Police Evidence**

Quite glaring inconsistencies appeared in police evidence, and some quite ludicrous assertions. For instance, officers described scenes of enormous public disorder (to justify their numbers and actions) — hundreds of youths scuffling and fighting, missiles being thrown, passers-by dodging out of the way, etc., and yet at the same time managed to have a clear, unobstructed and continuous view from 30 yards away, in the dark from within a police vehicle, of their one target. Officers described an inspector standing in a clearing of several yards in the middle of the road, apparently isolated amongst this mayhem. The inspector himself said he was on the steps of Stoke Newington Police Station! In the dark, from 30 yards away, across a wide main road, with traffic, demonstrators, etc., an officer clearly saw a red and white coke can having its ring-pull pulled, and then thrown in the dark.

Officers, when confronted with photographs clearly showing themselves and others involved with a target (in direct contradictiion often to the evidence they had given, about the positions or numbers of officers involved) would blatantly deny that they were looking at photographs of themselves and their arrests. It was clear to observers in the court that from a senior level downwards, the police had either mismanaged the handling of the demonstration quite appallingly or, more sinister, had deliberately acted in a manner which would provoke and escalate a situation of extreme sensitivity which had a potential for disorder, into something which they would then 'control' by force, arrests and dispersal, rather than by tact, diplomacy or common sense. Once trapped by their own stupidity or culpability, they were forced to carry through the whole sorry process in the courts with fabricated evidence.

Magistrate Johnstone of Highbury Magistrates' Court and a lay bench tried some defendants and ensured a higher conviction rate than might otherwise have occurred. Johnstone sentenced a Black youth to 7 days imprisonment for threatening behaviour, and throughout the trials revealed his attitude to demonstrations by remarks such as "Hadn't you heard there would be an Inquest?" — suggesting that an Inquest was a Public Inquiry, and implying that people therefore had no legitimate reason to be demonstrating.

2. The Demonstration of 17 January 1983

(a) Charges and Convictions

There were 20 charges in all, and one person, originally charged with actual bodily harm on police (which would have entitled him to a jury trial) had the charge changed to the lesser one of assault on the police, which is summarily triable only.

Number arrested: (18)
Original charges: (20)
Findings of guilt: (9)
Conviction rate: 45%
Breakdown of Original Charges

Threatening words and/or behaviour (6)
Assault on police (2)
Obstruction of police (2 including 1 juvenile)

The findings (contested trials):
Assault on police   (1) a juvenile
Highway obstruction   (6)
Threatening words and/or behaviour   (2)

Apart from the juvenile, all the trials occurred at Highbury Corner Magistrates' Court, in front of a variety of magistrates. There were 9 findings of guilt and one person pleaded guilty to an assault on the police.

The findings (contested trials):
Assault on police   (1) a juvenile
Highway obstruction   (6)
Threatening words and/or behaviour   (2)

(b) Police Evidence

Photographic evidence which contradicted that of the police cut no ice with Magistrate Johnstone. We heard the ridiculous assertion that 40–50 demonstrators (shown on photographs to be strung out along the footway, alongside the station, and along the kerb, leaving room for pedestrians to gain easy access) all suddenly bunched themselves up to form a dense, impenetrable mass, which would have meant that on that extremely wide pavement (at least 10 feet,) they would have been about 8 deep, all of whom equally suddenly disappeared and melted according to the photographs, which showed 9 police officers, one prisoner and no other demonstrators. One police officer claimed 200 youths were running along the street, being chased by police, dodging in and out of the traffic. But because he also had to claim that he had a clear, unobstructed and uninterrupted view of his one target, was forced to say under cross examination that there was no traffic.

One person was convicted by Magistrate Johnstone, not on the basis of the evidence presented in the charge against him, but because in his own defence, he acknowledged that he had been on the *demonstration* outside the station some 10 to 15 minutes *before* he was told to move.

There were accounts given by senior police officers of banners, excessive drinking and litter — none of which were apparent from the relevant photographs. We had a non existent WPC, or rather a WPC who claimed to have been a party to an arrest, who was nowhere to be seen in the photographs of the arrest, who had altered her notebook to include the exact words of an officer, who had different types of handwriting in her book due "to a shoulder injury", who admitted reading another officer's notebook to refresh her memory outside the court. We heard lies about not only the number of demonstrators involved, but also the numbers of police. Several other officers had been called from the rest of the division, and there was at least one District Support Unit ("DSU" — formerly known as Instant Response Unit) from another area. We heard one officer say he was never out of sight of his partner, whereas his partner could not agree that this was true. We heard that officers were told to arrest people who were running, to arrest people if they saw a particular senior officer arrest anyone (by pre-arranged order). Demonstrators gave clear evidence of racist abuse, "Black bastard", etc., and in the case of one of the white defendants "We've got a white nigger here". People were assaulted and injured.

3. **The Demonstration of 22 January 1983**

(a) **Charges and Convictions**

Six trials were at Old Street Magistrates' Court, one at Highbury Juvenile/Seymour Place, one at Snaresbrook Crown Court, and the remainder (14) at Highbury Magistrates' Court.

> Number arrested: (22)
> Original charges: (33)
> Findings of guilt: (20)
> Conviction rate: 60.6%
>
> **Breakdown of Original Charges**
> Threatening behaviour and/or words (14)

resulted in 2 people being arrested because they wore brown jackets. The original person was cleared of assault on police, the other had the misfortune to appear before Magistrate Johnstone, and was given 6 weeks imprisonment.

Police lies were constantly refuted by photographic evidence. Officers gave sworn testimony that large groups of youths had surrounded them, kicking and punching, etc. None of this could be seen in the photographs showing them and their targets. There were direct contradictions by police officers of each others evidence about which officers were where, when and involved with whom. Photographs also demonstrated the level of police brutality, and the fear and distress of those in the clutches of the police. Officers substantially changed their evidence under cross examination by defence lawyers, usually after having been confronted by photographs, over quite crucial matters, such as the type or number of blows alleged to have been received, or the numbers of people and the police said to be in the relevant area.

Throughout the trials, one got the impression that it wasn't just a question of 'Grab first, ask questions later', but rather 'Grab first and make up the charges later'.

4. The Demonstration of 12 February 1983

(a) **Charges and Convictions**
Number arrested (9)
Original charges (19)
Findings of guilt (11)
Conviction rate 57.8%

Breakdown of Original Charges
Threatening behaviour and/or words (8)
Assault on police (4)
S.47 assault on police (ABH) (1)
(the juvenile)

S.47 assault on police
(actual bodily harm)   (1)
S.51 assault on police (including one which was originally ABH, but changed to the
summary offence)   (8)
Obstruction of police   (5)
Obstruction of highway   (1)
Obstruction (not known whether it was of the highway or of the police)   (2)
Criminal damage   (1)
Possession of drugs   (1)

At the summary trials, one defendant pleaded guilty to assault on the police and threatening behaviour, in exchange for the dropping of a second charge of assault on the police. One person pleaded guilty to criminal damage. F, charged with assault on the police, threatening behaviour, and possession of drugs (as well as ABH) had the former charges adjourned 'sine die', after being acquitted of ABH at Snaresbrook Crown Court. The jury was hardly out at all, and obviously did not believe a single word of the entire police evidence.

Of the original 33 charges, there were 20 final convictions:

Assault on police   (2) (out of 8, and 1 pleaded guilty as mentioned above)
Obstruction of police   (5)
Obstruction of highway   (1)
Obstruction unknown   (2)
Threatening behaviour and/or words   (9) (1 had pleaded guilty)

(b) **Police Evidence**

It was clear from the trials that there was enormous over-reaction by the police, many from DSUs, and that anyone in the area was at risk of being assaulted or arrested, no matter whether they had committed an offence or not. A cry from the police of "Get the one in the brown jacket" (who was trying to draw photographers' attention to the blood on F)

Obstruction of police   (4)
Obstruction of highway   (1)
Breach of bail   (1)

Of the original 19 charges, there were 10 convictions. One person, charged with 5 offences, pleaded guilty to obstruction of the police and of the highway, in an unsuccessful attempt to effect in exchange the dropping of other charges.

S.47 assault on police (ABH)   (1) a juvenile
Assault on police   (2)
Obstruction of police   (3) 1 pleaded guilty
Threatening behaviour and/or words   (3)
Breach of bail   (1)

(b)   **Police Evidence**

Police evidence revealed that DSUs and police transport were present in some concentration, and were waiting in side roads ahead of the march. They had, it seems, no briefing or clear orders given, and would emerge from their vans with no specific instructions as to why they were de-bussing or what they were supposed to do. Arbitrary arrests followed. It seemed that one quite unjustified arrest led to all the others (. . . .)

5.   **The Demonstration of 12 March 1983**

(a)   **Charges and Convictions**

Numbers arrested   (24)
Original charges   (39)
Findings of guilt   (21)
Conviction rate   (54%)

Breakdown of Original Charges

Threatening behaviour and/or words (12)
   one was added on day of trial.
Assault on police   (7)
(one of these were originally s.47 ABH, dropped to assault and therefore only triable at Magistrates' Court).
Obstruction of police   (12)
Obstruction of the highway   (2)
S.20 assault on police   (1)

Offensive weapon (3) (this charge, almost always preferred under the Prevention of Crime Act 1953, s.1, is triable either way. Those electing trial by jury were denied this, as police withdrew that charge and then recharged the person with possessing an offensive weapon under the Public Order Act, which can only be tried at Magistrates' Court).

    Dangerous driving   (1)
    Undue care and attention   (1)

(b) Police Evidence

CAPA's note-taking did not manage to cover all the trials, due to staff sickness, but those that were covered showed up some extraordinary examples of fabricated evidence. What was striking, though, was the extreme stupidity of the police in expecting the charges to stick. For instance, one young man, M, was charged with possessing an offensive weapon — a banner measuring 8ft 3 inches on poles over 6ft long. It was alleged that he, holding one end of the banner by one pole, repeatedly brought the top banner end of the pole down on several different police officers' heads — officers who were struggling in a dense crowd of people. The pole with which he was supposed to be hitting the heads, was not produced in court. The banner, however, was produced. One glance was enough to show the magistrate that the police story was a complete fabrication. Photographs were also produced, which showed the banner at its full height, and which demonstrated the sheer impossibility of a person maneouvring one end down to strike selected heads and shoulders out of a thronging mass. It clearly could not have been maneouvred down at all, never mind onto 'blue' heads, rather than ordinary heads.

Another trial had 3 officers giving different stories about where they were, where they had come from, why they went into the crowd to arrest D, and where they were in relation to each other in the crowd. In fact, it was clear that the 2 'arresting' officers were not the officers who had arrested D. It was alleged that he used a variety of threatening words, meticulously detailed by police in identical statements. Long sentences of what he was supposed to have said were repeated. From the dense middle of the throng, officers apparently heard passers-by on the pavement say: "Listen to that language!" and "Do you mind?" amid all the noise, confusion and shouting which they had acknowledged was also occurring. One officer claimed he and his partner had gone into the crowd to escort out mothers and children! His partner had no such recollection. However, the best is yet to come. D has an extremely thick Scottish accent. Sassenachs find it very difficult to understand what he is saying. Under defence questioning as to (sic) any special features of D's voice when he was shouting his threatening words, the 2 'arresting officers' could recall nothing of any significance at all. The third, the only one who had had any genuine involvement with D at all, did remember that he had a Scottish accent. The magistrate said: "I have heard conflicting evidence from 3 police officers, only one of whom seems to have noticed your very distinctive Scottish accent" The case was dismissed.

James Roach's trial had perhaps the most blatant examples of perjury. It was alleged he had obstructed in the arrest of S. The officer who had arrested S, claimed that Mr. Roach had intervened, and that he also arrested him. There were 12 photographs in court (from 2 different photographers) showing no signs of his arresting officer, no signs of S in Mr. Roach's photographs, no signs of Mr. Roach in S's photographs, and no sign of Mr. Roach's 'arresting officer' amongst the 12 policemen placing him in the van. Even the lay bench trying him had to concede defeat here, and the case against him was dismissed.

People tried before Magistrates Johnstone, predictably, were convicted. One, F, was just out shopping. After the march had passed, several shoppers, including him, decided it would be safe and convenient to cross the road to get to the shops on the left hand side of the road. Unfortunately, their crossing coincided with the police moving in on the back of the crowd and F, the only Black person amongst the crossers, was grabbed, dragged backwards to a waiting transit, clutching his shopping, and protesting his non-involvement. He was assaulted in the van. He too was held in custody until his appearance at Old Street Magistrates' Court on the Monday. At his trial, officers alleged he had assaulted an officer, by kicking him in the back, thereby obstructing an arrest, and had used threatening words. Photographs corroborated F's version of events. The police had no corroborative evidence. It was simply obvious from his demeanour in court that he *was* out shopping, extremely cost-conscious, and had had no knowledge that there would be a demonstration, and had not been involved in it. He was a young man of good character, working full-time. Johnstone gave him 30 days imprisonment for the 'assault', 14 days to run concurrently for the 'threatening behaviour' and a £25 fine or days imprisonment for the 'obstruction'. In passing sentence, he said: "The police have a duty to keep the streets clear for ordinary shoppers!" F was too shattered, distressed and terrified to appeal against his conviction.

A steward, who had been trying to get the name of an arrested person, to help provide the emergency service with his name so that legal assistance could be provided, was arrested. At his trial, Johnstone made it clear that he thought such action ill-advised. "Didn't it occur to you that he might have done something wrong, and that he deserved to get arrested?" he asked, entirely missing the point that one's right to legal assistance is not dependent upon whether one is innocent or guilty. This remark also suggested to some observing the trials, his attitude towards police evidence — it was per se to be believed, and so there was no earthly point in him hearing the defence.

In one of the cases, the magistrate was so incensed by the police denial of a jury trial for possession of an offenssive weapon — and they were extra-ordinarily blatant about this saying "if he elects trial by jury, we withdraw the charge", took him outside the court and charged him with the same offence under the Public Order Act — that he dismissed the case as much out of annoyance as becauseof the silly nature of the charge. Police evidence was similar to that in the banner trial. C was alleged to have been picking out of a dense throng of police heads to hit with a very large pole, NOT the pole produced in court, which was much smaller, but which, nevertheless, was impossible to wield in the manner described.

6. The Demonstration of 14 May 1983

Only two arrests were made. Both were charged with threatening words and behaviour. One was found guilty, fined £5 and bound over for a year; the other failed to appear and at the time of writing, nothing further is known.

Additional Points and Conclusions

Some additional points need to be made. It was obviously decided it would be in the "public interest" that all defendants be granted legal aid. Normally, highway obstruction and minor public order offences were not legally aidable. At least 13 people were ordered to pay towards their legal costs (one person who was receiving supplementary benefit of £23 per week was ordered by magistrate Johnstone to pay £50 at £10 per fortnight) and several had to pay prosecution costs. One was ordered to pay £300 costs.

At the time of the trials, the recently set up 'pilot scheme', whereby police make prosecution statements available to the defence in summary trials, was not in operation. (The provision for this in s.48 of the Criminal Law Act, 1977 has never been implemented). This meant defence lawyers only had the barest outline of the police's case against their client, often gleaned via a hurried telephone call with the police, or a 30 second glance allowed by police at their papers outside court. Despite repeated requests and representations to the magistrates (who are powerless to order the police, but who pressed them in increasingly strong terms), papers were not forthcoming. The job of the defence lawyers was thus rendered almost impossible. How can a defence be properly prepared and allegations efficiently rebutted, if the details are 'sprung' on the defendant and lawyer once the trial has commenced? So frequently, the police's version of events bore so little resemblance to the actual situation in which the defendant had been, that the account came as a complete surprise. For this reason alone, it was vital to have on hand any photographs which might conceivably have a bearing on the case due to be heard.

Only two of the 84 arrested were able to have a Crown Court trial, where prosecution evidence is made available. One was the case of F, arrested on 22 January 1983. The papers relating to his case were of great value in preparing the defence of others alleged to have been involved in the incident concerning him. The only other way of being able to glean some idea of the likely case against someone was if details in one trial appeared to have a possible bearing on one yet to come. Detective work, inspired guess-work and committed note-taking in the trials were therefore also crucial. By and large, police presented evidence as if each case were somehow a completely isolated little pocket and people who had been present during the trials were able to 'brief' the barristers with a much more coherent picture, which they, in turn, were able to present to the court. Towards the end of the 12 March trials, the impression was gained that Magistrate Barr, in particular, was beginning to form a much truer picture of how things actually were, as opposed to the police presentation, and his increased dismissing of cases bears this out.

Mention has already been made of the practice of the prosecution to withdraw charges when a defendant elected trial by jury and to substitute an identical, or lesser charge, which could only be tried infront of a magistrate.

Nationally, conviction rates in magistrates' courts are much much higher than in jury trials — 82% of all summary trials, and 85% for Public Order and Highway Obstruction offences, in 1982. Therefore, the overall conviction rates of these trials — 52.7%, as opposed to 82/85% — are particularly impressive and significant both for what they demonstrate about the police and the legitimacy of their actions, and the value of co-ordinated defence work.

The police seemed to form a collective view that any white people involved were either 'political agitators' or 'white niggers', or else they found it politically expedient to present the former view. The idea that white people may have been friends of Colin and his family, or that white people should have a legitimate concern about the death of a Black person seemed inconceivable. "What are white people doing on a Black march?" was heard, revealing much about their attitude to the marches, and their subsequent behaviour on them. Only the 14 May march perhaps did not 'look so black' — perhaps that is why it was policed differently.

Apart from the immense tragedy of Colin's death (upon which we make no other comment), and the almost insupportable aftermath for his bereaved family, there is an added tragedy of all those trials and 68 convictions — NONE of which need have occurred.

There are those whose analysis of the police behaviour will be based on the assumption that it is an essential part of the deliberately oppressive racist nature of a highly political police force; others will take a more charitable view, and adduce appalling management and insensitivity, fear and sheer incompetence. Which way it is viewed, the inescapable conclusion is that we are policed by a force which is totally out of touch and totally out of control.

Appendix 6

1. Black People, Misdiagnosis and Mental Health

1.1 As we saw in Chapter 3 the initial police statement which followed the death of Colin Roach suggested that Colin had had a history of mental illness and from this point on the question of Colin's mental state was a crucial one, figuring prominently in police evidence to the inquest. We have given our views on this issue in the relevant chapters of the report. Here, however, by way of background to this issue we will set out the basic details of some other cases involving Black people who have been detained by the authorities or at worse have died in police or some other form of custody, where the 'diagnosis' has been made on the basis of poor or absent medical evidence. We term this conjunction of issues "Misdiagnosis 1". It is in relation to this category that Colin Roach's mental state must be understood. We also consider those cases and issues which give rise to "Misdiagnosis 2" which occur when Black people actually are at risk.

1.2 It is necesaary to set these case-histories in their wider social context. This context is one in which Black people have become increasingly suspicious and questioning of practices and assumptions common to the field of mental health. For example, research has shown that Black people are much more likely than white people to reach a mental hospital through the involvement of the police; in addition, Black patients are twice as likely as white patients to have been sent to their hospital from prison. Research also shows extensive evidence of misdiagnosis of Black people, (especially as schizophrenic, particularly in the case of Rastafarians). Once diagnosed Black mental patients are more likely to be referred to less prestigious hospitals, to be seen by junior doctors and more likely too to be given electroconvulsive therapy.

1.3   A report on mental health prepared for the Greater London Council's health panel during the GLC's 'anti-racist year' 1984 concluded:

> Hence why a number of Black people believe the solutions to the problem of Race and Mental Health cannot be sought or found within the confines of current medical (psychiatric) theory or practice as exists in Britain for they (the psychiatrists) begin their diagnosis with a strong belief that there is something fundamentally wrong with the *culture* of Black people — so when they do admit to misdiagnosis and treatment, this will be justified by the rejoinder that there is an essential mis-understanding of the *culture*. Hence more and more research . . . It fails to address the wider issues, which are in essence political and the specific issue of race and racism.

2.   Misdiagnosis 1: Creating the Victim

2.1   The highly disproportionate numbers of Black people being 'sectioned' into mental hospitals, focusses attention on the role of an initial 'diagnosis' of mental ill health. In countless experiences documented by various Black pressure groups and others, this 'initial diagnosis' is made by someone other than a psychiatrist and yet goes on to influence events, out of all proportion to its validity. This could be the 'layperson' opinion of another 'professional': a prison officer, a judge or a police officer. This phenomenon is not unrelated to the emergence in the psychiatric field of a category of illnesses, reserved for the diagnosis of Black people; they include *West Indian Psychoses* and *Cannabis Psychoses,* which add to the variety of ways in which Black people can be misdiagnosed.

2.2   We relate here just a few examples of 'misdiagnosis', which in the opinion of many is becoming increasingly widespread; Buddy Larrier is one such person who holds this view. Buddy Larrier informed the Inquiry of his experience in the early part of 1977.

He was 'diagnosed' as mentally ill and treated under the powers of section 25 of the 1959 Mental Health Act, (section 2 of the 1983 Act). He did not accept the diagnosis: 'This was mental torture — much worse, by far than physical torture'.

2.3 Following a minor operation, *Buddy Larrier* had to attend the outpatients unit of Lewisham District Hospital. Whilst he was there, he had a disagreement with his sister who had accompanied him and "within 2 hours of the police being called, I was arrested, injected, sedated, transferred to and sectioned into Bexley Mental Hospital".

2.4 "In 1979, *Mrs B* applied for an injunction to stop the racial harassment from her neighbours on the estate where she lived. Later in the year there was a fire at her home. She was accused of starting the fire and because she reacted to this accusation, she was forced to spend one month at Cane Hill Hospital, although it was suspected that she was the victim of racist arson attack.". *(Black people in Lewisham: Which way forward? p. 13).*

2.5 "Something clearly went wrong in the case of Steve Thompson who was transferred from Gartree to Rampton in December 1980, just five days before the end of his sentence. One of the two doctors who sanctioned his transfer under section 72 of the Mental Health Act 1959, on the ground that he was *schizophrenic,* later stated that he had been misled by Home Office allegations, denied by Thompson, of violent behaviour. two of Rampton's own consultant psychiatrists reported that Thompson was neither mentally ill nor dangerous and he was discharged by the Home Secretary after a public and parliamentary campaign". *(Social Services Committee: Inquiry into Prison Medical Service, 12 February 1986 p. 136).*

2.6 The above experiences are only a fraction of the number of innocent Black people who are frequently being 'picked up', diagnosed and 'sectioned' into secure and mental institutions. The case of Richard 'Cartoon' Campbell, however, is even more serious; his plight terminated in his death.

Richard 'Cartoon' Campbell

2.7 Richard 'Cartoon' Campbell, a young Black man, died at Ashford Remand Centre on 31 April 1980, aged 19. A preliminary inquest had found that Richard had died of dehydration due to schizophrenia. The verdict of the later and 'full' inquest was 'death by *self-neglect*' with a rider by the jury criticising the lack of adequate medical staff and facilities at Ashford Remand Centre.

2.8 The death of Richard Campbell was investigated and well documented in the 'Report of the Public Inquiry' into his death, led by Tom Cox M.P. As the Report says, it looked at:

> ... some of the factors that came together to turn a simple remand for reports into a death sentence.

Campbell was just an ordinary, happy-go-lucky young man; very popular and with much to live for. However, on Saturday, 1 March 1980, (the last day his mother was to see him alive), he was picked up by the police who were looking for someone who appeared to fit his description, in connection with an attempted burglary.

2.9 He spent the week (3-10 March) at Lewes Remand Centre, having appeared at Camberwell Magistrates Court. Campbell was in 'good spirits' about this, considering the circumstances, and remained in 'good spirits' while at Lewes. On the day of his expected release, however, Campbell was made to appear at Camberwell Magistrates Court again, albeit before a different bench. He alleged this time that he had been framed by the police:

> This, and his use of Rastafarian language, created doubts as to his *mental state* and the magistrate remands him to Ashford Remand Centre for medical and psychiatric reports.

2.10 Campbell had no solicitor and his probation officer was not called. Soon after his arrival at Ashford he refused both food and drink; he was obviously very unhappy about the situation he had found himself in. One fellow-prisoner remarked that at night he could often hear Campbell crying out at night: 'Give me a chance'.

2.11 On 21 March an independent psychiatrist, Mr. Booth from Queen Mary's Roehampton, was called in to confirm the Remand Centre psychiatrist's diagnosis of *schizophrenia*. This he did, giving as some of his reasons Campbell's "socially inappropriate" behaviour (*lounging on the chair and looking out of the window, while Booth spoke to him*); his *continued insistence that he wants to do something to help the poor and starving in Africa; and his many references to 'Jah' the Rastafarian name for God*.

2.12 From 26-30 March, Campbell was force-fed and though his weight loss was halted, his dehydration continued. On 31 March, he was found dead in his prison cell:

> ... He had died of choking at some time during the night, unheard and unnoticed by any of the duty medical officers.

2.13 Disturbing features of his death include: the racist stereotyping (his identification with Rastafarianism equalled mental instability, the routine diagnosis of schizophrenia) the almost contemptuous disregard for established procedure on the part of the prison and medical service; and an inquest verdict which made the victim uniquely responsible for his death, despite evidence of sloppy practice.

Misdiagnosis 2: Punishing the Victim

3.1 There is a second category of cases, involving Black people, their detainment and the issue of their mental health, where 'misdiagnosis' takes a particular form. It concerns the treatment of Black mentally ill people who, for whatever reason, have been drawn to the attention of the police. In this second category, the victim's obvious mental illness should *not* have been in dispute and yet in the following casehistories, the subsequent death in 'custody' turned on this misdiagnosis; in the sense that the 'misunderstanding' generated factors leading ultimately to death. This was so in the case of Winston Rose (1981), Paul Worrell (1982), James Ruddock (1983), Nicholas Owusu (1983), Clive Tapper (1983) and Michael Martin (1984).

3.2 *Winston Rose*, a boxer who had a history of mental illness but no history of violence, was taken into custody under the Mental Health Act in July 1981. Despite the fact that he had no history of violence, 12 police officers were involved in his apprehension, some apparently having gone to the scene believing they were looking for an escaped criminal, others thinking that Rose was known to be violent.

3.4 Rose died from asphyxiation, having choked on his own vomit after being held in a strangle-hold by police. Police stopped a passing ambulance to try and revive him, but the ambulance staff were unable to release Rose's hands from the handcuffs as one of the officers had driven off with the keys.

3.5 The inquest jury returned a verdict of unlawful killing, but the Director of Public Prosecutions declined to prosecute any of the officers involved on the ground that there was 'insufficient evidence'.

3.6 *Paul Worrell* died in Brixton Prison on 12 January 1982, exactly one year before the death of Colin Roach. According to the prison authorities, Paul Worrell hung himself with a shirt and towel which he had *twisted* together, attached to something and strangled and suffocated himself within five minutes of the prison warder's last check on him. In a publicity leaflet put out on the case, INQUEST asked: If this was so: 'Why . . . was an admitted suicide risk allowed a *spare* shirt, allowed the means and the opportunity for self-destruction? When asked this question, one warder could only respond by laughing . . .'

3.7 Prison doctors failed to diagnose mental illness in Paul Worrell even though his behaviour prior to and including the offence of which he was convicted showed clear signs of mental illness. His family were not consulted and it was initially reported that there was nothing wrong with him until he was remanded a second time and diagnosed as schizophrenic by a consultant psychiatrist. At this point an offer of a hospital bed was made, but was later withdrawn. Worrell had spent four months in prison before he was found hanged in his cell. The inquest returned an open verdict.

3.8 *James Ruddock,* 44, had been living rough for a number of years, had a *history of mental illness* and also suffered from diabetes and sickle-cell trait. He was found lying in Kensington High Street by a concerned passer-by, who saw that Ruddock was poorly clad against the bitter cold of the night of 13 February 1983. The passer-by alerted the police who subsequently arrested Ruddock for drunkenness.

3.9 He was placed in a cell with two other prisoners, and as police Standing Orders require, he was roused and spoken to every half-hour. When roused he was said to have grunted and opened his eyes. After he had been in custody for about three hours, the station Sergeant decided that he was fit to be charged . . . This was an important decision, since police regulations require that a doctor be called if a prisoner is not fit to be charged within four hours . . . It was only when Ruddock could not be roused to go to court in the morning that the police surgeon was summoned. He found that Ruddock was suffering from hypothermia and was 'in urgent need of hospital treatment'. Mr. Ruddock died in hospital the following day. *(INQUEST: Annual Report 1982/83).*

The inquest verdict was 'natural causes attributed by self-neglect'.

3.10 The three worrying features of the James Ruddock case are: the assumption on the part of the police that his behaviour was due to drunkenness; their intent on 'charging' Mr. Ruddock and lack of concern for his welfare; and the finding of an inquest verdict which completely exonerated the conduct of the police.

3.11 *Nicholas Owusu* was arrested in London at 9.10pm on Saturday, 14 May 1983 after neighbours called the police following a dispute between Owusu and his 19 year old niece. Owusu was taken to Rotherhithe police station where he became unconscious. He was then taken to Guy's Hospital where he was pronounced dead at 10.30pm. A post-mortem found that Owusu had drowned in his own vomit. The three officers who arrested Owusu denied using excessive force or doing anything that might have caused him to vomit.

3.12 The family's solicitor established that there had been at least two other courses of action open to the police, other than arresting Owusu and taking him into custody.

> They could have taken Mr. Owusu directly to hospital, as had been done a few days previously... Alternatively, they could have kept Mr. Owusu in the flat while doctors and social workers were summoned... The police witnesses explained that they did not adopt either of these options because they did not regard Mr. Owusu as being mentally ill, despite references to their notebooks to *a man having gone berserk* and to the prisoner acting *like a man who has taken leave of his senses*. The implication behind much of the police evidence was that psychological disturbance was not 'real' illness and therefore could not constitute a medical emergency. *(INQUEST: Annual report 1982/83).*

3.13 The inquest verdict was 'misadventure' after the Coroner had failed to include 'lack of care' among the possible list of verdicts the jury could find.

3.14 In the same year as the death of Colin Roach, on 15 July 1983, *Clive Tapper* was found hanging in his cell in Pentonville Prison. The circumstances surrounding his death are not deemed to be suspicious but they do highlight the lack of care and neglect which many Black mentally patients are subjected to.

3.15 There were two incontestable points about the case. Tapper suffered from depression and could with amazing rapidity switch from a histrionic display of disturbance to a calm state in which he gave every impression of normality.

But clearly the police who arrested him on 23 June 1983, for breaking windows, regarded him as having a history of mental disturbance and as potentially suicidal because, when put on remand to Brixton Prison, he was accompanied by Form 618, which denoted the prisoner as a suicide risk.

3.16 On 15 July 1983, Clive Tapper appeared before a different bench of South Western Magistrate Court and was sentenced for criminal damage. A *photocopy* of the original Form 618 went with Tapper to Pentonville. Being a photocopy, it lacked the distinctive red border which is meant to direct attention to the importance of the warnings it contained. Tapper's file was not marked with the large 'F' that denotes a potential suicide.

Despite the fact that Tapper had had three previous incarcerations and that his suicidal tendencies, possible reliance on drugs and history of disturbance were known, he was placed in a single cell. On the night of his death, it appears that Tapper was not visited for about four hours (the night-duty officer was following the pegging system, established at Pentonville). When light was noticed in the cell at about 1.30am, the duty-officer could not gain immediate access, for it was necessary to summon the official keyholders and any chance of resuscitating the prisoner was thus diminished. *(INQUEST Annual Report 1982/83 and INQUEST Paper B/PR2 T).*

3.17 *Michael Martin,* who came from Lewisham, south London, died in Broadmoor Special Hospital on 6 July 1984. Martin had been receiving treatment at Bexley Hospital where the staff regarded him as sufficiently stable to be allowed home at weekends, but his standing as a 'management problem' seemed sufficient reason for his transfer to Broadmoor. At the inquest into the death it emerged that the events leading up to the death began when another patient continually taunted Martin with racist abuse. Martin asked staff to intervene but when none did, he hit out in desperation at a nurse. Several staff then overwhelmed him and took him to a side room where he was stripped naked. He was then taken to a seclusion room where he was injected with the maximum dose of two major tranquilisers. Within 90 minutes he had choked on his own vomit and was dead.

3.18 The inquest into the death of Michael Martin which was held in October 1984 heard evidence of routine, heavy medication by staff at the hospital and how no special training was given to staff on how to restrain agitated patients without doing them fatal harm. One patient said that beatings and assaults were common and that he himself had been a victim of such assault. The jury returned a verdict of accidental death aggravated by lack of care, the same verdict returned in the case of Richard 'Cartoon' Campbell.